Alchemies of Blood and Afro-Diasporic Fiction

Alchemies of Blood and Afro-Diasporic Fiction

Race, Kinship, and the Passion for Ontology

Nicole Simek

BLOOMSBURY ACADEMIC
NEW YORK • LONDON • OXFORD • NEW DELHI • SYDNEY

BLOOMSBURY ACADEMIC
Bloomsbury Publishing Inc, 1385 Broadway, New York, NY 10018, USA
Bloomsbury Publishing Plc, 50 Bedford Square, London, WC1B 3DP, UK
Bloomsbury Publishing Ireland, 29 Earlsfort Terrace, Dublin 2, D02 AY28, Ireland

BLOOMSBURY, BLOOMSBURY ACADEMIC and the Diana logo are trademarks of
Bloomsbury Publishing Plc

First published in the United States of America 2024
Paperback edition published 2025

Copyright © Nicole Simek, 2024

For legal purposes the Acknowledgments on p. viii constitute an extension of this copyright page.

Cover design: Eleanor Rose
Cover image © Alamy

All rights reserved. No part of this publication may be: i) reproduced or transmitted in any form, electronic or mechanical, including photocopying, recording or by means of any information storage or retrieval system without prior permission in writing from the publishers; or ii) used or reproduced in any way for the training, development or operation of artificial intelligence (AI) technologies, including generative AI technologies. The rights holders expressly reserve this publication from the text and data mining exception as per Article 4(3) of the Digital Single Market Directive (EU) 2019/790.

Bloomsbury Publishing Inc does not have any control over, or responsibility for, any third-party websites referred to or in this book. All internet addresses given in this book were correct at the time of going to press. The author and publisher regret any inconvenience caused if addresses have changed or sites have ceased to exist, but can accept no responsibility for any such changes.

A catalog record for this book is available from the Library of Congress

Library of Congress Cataloging-in-Publication Data

Names: Simek, Nicole Jenette, 1976- author.
Title: Alchemies of blood and Afro-diasporic fiction : race, kinship, and the passion for ontology / Nicole Simek.
Description: New York : Bloomsbury Academic, 2023. | Includes bibliographical references and index. | Summary: "Alchemies of Blood and Afro-Diasporic Fiction focuses on the resurgence of biological racism in 21st-century public discourse, the ontological and material turns in the academy that have occurred over the same time period, and the ways in which Afro-diasporic fiction has responded to both with alternative visions of bloodlines, kinship, and community"– Provided by publisher.
Identifiers: LCCN 2023019766 (print) | LCCN 2023019767 (ebook) | ISBN 9781501377655 (hardback) | ISBN 9781501377686 (paperback) | ISBN 9781501377662 (epub) | ISBN 9781501377679 (pdf) | ISBN 9781501377693 (ebook other)
Subjects: LCSH: Caribbean Fiction (French)–History and criticism. | American fiction–African American authors–History and criticism. | Kinship in literature. | Identity (Philosophical concept) in literature. | Racism in literature. | LCGFT: Literary criticism.
Classification: LCC PQ3944 .S56 2023 (print) | LCC PQ3944 (ebook) | DDC 809/.896073–dc23/eng/20230815
LC record available at https://lccn.loc.gov/2023019766
LC ebook record available at https://lccn.loc.gov/2023019767

ISBN: HB: 978-1-5013-7765-5
PB: 978-1-5013-7768-6
ePDF: 978-1-5013-7767-9
eBook: 978-1-5013-7766-2

Typeset by Deanta Global Publishing Services, Chennai, India

For product safety related questions contact productsafety@bloomsbury.com.

To find out more about our authors and books visit www.bloomsbury.com and sign up for our newsletters.

For Lauren Theisen

CONTENTS

Acknowledgments viii

Introduction: Race and the Passion for the Real 1

1 Genealogies That Matter 31

2 Amnesiac Meditations, or Kinship in the Breach 61

3 Future Ancestors 83

4 Fugitive Belongings 127

Conclusion: Alchemy's Reason 151

Notes 155
Works Cited 188
Index 200

ACKNOWLEDGMENTS

This book owes so much to attentive friends and colleagues who shared their thoughts and offered community throughout the writing process. I would first like to thank Haaris Naqvi and the Bloomsbury team for their support of this project and care in bringing it to fruition. I am also indebted to the anonymous reviewers for their generous recommendations and insights. Conversations at the Society for Critical Exchange theory institutes and the Society for Comparative Literature and the Arts have continually shaped my ideas, and I am particularly grateful to Jeffrey Di Leo, Paul Allen Miller, Brian O'Keeffe, Jacob Blevins, Christian Moraru, Peter Hitchcock, and Sophia McClennen for their energizing acumen, wit, and good cheer. Much of this project took shape in the thick of the coronavirus pandemic. It has served as both a welcome outlet and a stumbling block, and I still sometimes find myself surprised that it managed to emerge. That it did is a testament to all those who provided sustaining support in so many ways, big and small. Deep thanks go especially to Shampa Biswas, Gaurav Majumdar, Chetna Chopra, Susanne Beechey, Matt Bost, Kaitlyn Patia, Lydia McDermott, Lauren Osborne, Peter Shultz, Xiaobo Yuan, Daniel Schultz, Suzanne Morrissey, Lisa Uddin, Jason Pribilsky, and Tarik Elseewi. To my mother, Rhonda, to my grandmother, Margaret, to Mounir Zalloua, and to Lauren, Jim, Evan, Lizzy, and Annie Theisen, who are a constant source of encouragement and inspiration, I am so lucky to have you and owe you more than words can say! Thoughts of my father and my grandfather inhabit all of my writing still. And to Zahi, my partner in critical alchemy and in life, thank you for making the impossible possible, every day.

This project benefited from travel funding and sabbatical support from Whitman College. I am also grateful to the outlets that provided me with the opportunity to articulate my emerging ideas and that have granted permission to reprint these revised materials here: "Troubling the Human, Worlding Gender in Maryse Condé's *The Wondrous and Tragic Life of Ivan and Ivana*," in *Feminism as World Literature*. ed. Robin Truth Goodman. Bloomsbury, 2022. 209–21; "Wakanda and the Politics of Reparation," *symplokē* 29, no. 1–2 (2021): 267–80; "Speculative Futures: Race in Watchmen's Worlds," *symplokē* 28, no. 1–2 (2020): 385–404; "Worlding Interpretation, or Fanon and the Poetics of Disalienation," in *Philosophy as World Literature*. ed. Jeffrey R. Di Leo. Bloomsbury, 2020. 59–70;

"Literature's Purchase: Remaking World Economic Relations in Crusoe's Footsteps," in *Francophone Literatures as World Literature*, ed. Christian Moraru, Nicole Simek, and Bertrand Westphal. Bloomsbury, 2020. 227–38; "Materiality in a Disenchanted Age," in *Biotheory: Life and Death Under Capitalism*. ed. Jeffrey R. Di Leo and Peter Hitchcock. Routledge, 2020. 136–50; "The Inhuman at the Limits of Literary Imagination," *Intertexts* 23, no. 1–2 (2019): 30–43; "Alchemies of Theory," *symplokē* 27, no. 1–2 (2019): 271–9.

Introduction

Race and the Passion for the Real

The Human Genome Project (1990–2003), an international collaborative effort to sequence the complete set of DNA base pairs making up the *Homo sapiens* genome, is frequently portrayed as a valiant and groundbreaking mapping endeavor. "Rather than an outward exploration of the planet or the cosmos," states the project's website, "the HGP was an inward voyage of discovery," one that "gave us the ability, for the first time, to read nature's complete genetic blueprint for building a human being."[1] To characterize the advances in genomic research that both produced the HGP and followed from its success as a cartographic accomplishment ("one of the great feats of exploration in history"[2]) is to highlight, first, not only the human genome's vast expanse (roughly three billion DNA base pairs) but also the structures devised to hold such a massive data set, as well as the techniques required to "read" the finished "blueprint," to turn the collected data into a legible guide for future travelers.

But while genomic research does indeed involve discovery, its projects are also, and importantly, world-making. Genomics participates in shaping and reshaping epistemological, ethical, and political horizons, in shifting understandings of the past and the future, of what constitutes a planet or a cosmos and how we should live in the world. Increasingly, the world, in the genomic era, is conceived as springing from DNA, whose analysis both reveals history and points the way to the future. "The body," Keith Wailoo, Alondra Nelson, and Catherine Lee point out, has come to be seen as "a microcosm of the past," a window or "portal" onto knowledge that can be marshaled "to investigate and adjudicate issues of social membership and kinship; rewrite history and collective memory; arbitrate legal claims and human rights controversies; and open new thinking about health and wellbeing."[3] To take the body as a window onto knowledge of the universe that it contains in miniature is to mistake it as furnishing at once a map of the world and the key to that map. Such a vision of the body evidences a hunger for legibility we might describe as a "passion for the real," a desire to experience reality without mediation, to walk the arc of time as a smooth pathway from past to future.

Alchemies of Blood and Afro-Diasporic Fiction: Race, Kinship, and the Passion for Ontology focuses on this very passion and the role it plays in the resurgence of biological racism in twenty-first-century public discourse, the ontological and material turns in the academy that have occurred over the same period, and the ways in which Afro-diasporic fiction has responded to both with alternative visions of bloodlines, kinship, and community. I explore the relationship between these through the protean figure of alchemy, the semi-scientific, semi-mystical search for gold and the elixir of long life that captures well the drive to find, in biology and blood, the magical stones that will generate and legitimize the knowledge we need, as individuals and communities, to tell us our future.

Hovering between the calculable and the incalculable, between the reproducible and formulaic on the one hand, and the magical and unpredictable on the other, alchemy helps us conceptualize the appeal and transformative force of neoliberalism, the intensified commodification of education and knowledge, that concerns scholars across the university today. Alchemy has long served as a figure for quantification and commodification in critiques of capitalism. In *Capital*, Karl Marx used the metaphor to describe the process by which "everything becomes saleable and purchaseable," by which even the "bones of saints" become transformed into gold, that is, into money, the "radical leveller" through which "every qualitative distinction between commodities is extinguished."[4] Pierre Bourdieu similarly deploys the metaphor to describe the conversion of economic capital into symbolic capital, highlighting the "social alchemy" involved in "the transformation of arbitrary relations into legitimate relations, *de facto* differences into officially recognized distinctions."[5] Stephanie Smallwood points up the perverse process by which humans themselves are converted into commodities in the slave trade through this alchemy of devaluation and revaluation, as slaves' human pricelessness is denied and their social worth converted into economic worth, into currency, a number, a price tag.[6] According to Achille Mbembe, this alchemical feat was without precedent in Western modernity: "The Black Man, despised and profoundly dishonored, is the only human in the modern world whose flesh has been transformed into the form and spirit of merchandise—the living crypt of capital."[7] Alchemy in these uses figures the material transformation of social value and social property into private property; the ideological determinations of equivalence and value at work in that transformation; and the arbitrary or reversible character of a process dependent on belief rather than essential, immutable properties.

Yet this picture of alchemy does not exhaust its potential or its politics. If alchemy's social magic requires mutability, a susceptibility to change, it is also in this sense that critics have deployed the concept conversely to name resistance to commodification, resistance to calculation, and resistance to the constriction or deadening of human experience. Recent developments and dispositions within humanistic disciplines—in particular the turns to ontology, realism, new materialisms, and (re)enchantment that have emerged in response to the neoliberal erosion of the university and the life-threatening socio-ecological crises produced under a racialized capitalist order—can also helpfully be described as alchemical in their dual yearning to touch the real and re-enchant the work of knowledge production. Alchemy highlights surprise and delight in transformation, as well as the opacity of poetic or cultural creation, the mystic, mystifying, or incalculable dimension of creolization, of the recuperation or recreation of lost pasts, or of the process of subject formation. But alchemy appeals as well for its emphasis on matter itself—the materiality of bodies and of the world in which they are entangled. In Afro-diasporic writing from the Americas, alchemy serves as a recurring metaphor for struggles against static essentialism and the inertia of history, for the process by which absence is transmuted into presence, by which something is made out of nothing, racial categories transformed, effaced pasts given new flesh, or denigrated life, negated life, brought into the bounds of the human. These transformations—such as the transmutation of slaves into subjects and rightlessness into rights, as Patricia J. Williams argues in her generative work, *The Alchemy of Race and Rights*—require extraordinary energy and a persistent collective effort in favor of dynamism over stasis. "The making of something out of nothing took immense alchemical fire—the fusion of a whole nation and the kindling of several generations," Williams asserts. She specifies further, "And this was not the dry process of reification, from which life is drained and reality fades as the cement of conceptual determinism hardens round—but its opposite. This was the resurrection of life from ashes four hundred years old."[8]

To speak of alchemy is to insist on the material processes at work in changing life and the intense effort, the high heat of the fire it takes to break through inertia or active resistance to the revaluations sought. Thus, while alchemy's conceptual appeal lies in part in its very capaciousness as a metaphor, its ability to evoke a host of symbolic metamorphoses, I use it in this study to examine more specifically those passionate engagements with material life that seek to know and harness its reality as foundation or, alternately, that strive, often against all hope, to transmute the immutable, through modes of cultural production that take seriously both the weight and inertia of ontology, and the material, transformational capacity of the symbolic.

To think through conceptions of race, ethnicity, and materiality circulating within both humanities research and popular culture, I ask in this book how the figure of alchemy can help scholars, first, to address the epistemological and affective investments in the "real" marking both academic and mainstream discourses. What drives the surging passion for ontology—for matter, bloodlines, and genetics—today? Second, I explore how developing an eye for alchemy might reshape our understanding of the intersections and divergences between scholarship trends and a broader *Zeitgeist*. To do so, I take a comparative approach to cultural production, examining speculative fiction and film, neo-plantation narrative, counterfactual history novels, and museums and public memory projects in the French Caribbean and the United States.

Ontological Touchstones

The first decades of the twenty-first century have witnessed a growing commitment in the humanities to investigating matter and the "real" itself. New materialism, speculative realism, object-oriented ontology (OOO), ecocriticism, posthumanism, affect theory, and actor-network theory are but a few of the critical orientations shaping an interpretive horizon centered on ontological concerns. If these movements diverge in their understanding of being and their methodological approach to its study, they share an urge to move beyond the preoccupations of the previous "linguistic" era: the construction of the subject and knowledge in language and the epistemological critique of this mediation and its effects, including, often, the uneven and inequitable production of gendered, racialized subject positions. For speculative realists and object-oriented ontologists, prioritizing discursivity traps philosophy in a "correlationist cage," to use Quentin Meillassoux's influential term, cutting thought off from reality and condemning it instead to circle endlessly around its own relation to the real. Correlationism, speculative realists hold, is the position that "we only ever have access to the correlation between thinking and being, and never to either term considered apart from the other."[9] In other words, as Meillassoux explains, "the thesis of the correlationist [. . .] is that I can't know what reality would be *without me*."[10] To break through this impasse and rectify "the failures of philosophy to claim the real,"[11] we must cease centering our analyses on the subject and the limits of its knowledge, asking not *how* our experience of the world mediates our understanding of it but rather *what* reality is, what we can indeed know of the world, beyond our perceptual horizon. In this sense, the turn to ontology expresses a "passion for the real," a craving to experience the world unmediated, free of the "deceptive layers of reality," as Slavoj Žižek describes it, following Alain Badiou.[12] If for Badiou, the passion for the real was embodied in the twentieth century by the violent modernist impulse to destroy the world of appearance in order to get at the concrete thing, to what is "immediately practicable, here and now,"[13] in the age of ontology this passion takes the form of a more generalized allergy to mediation, to any undo separation from being, from reality itself; this attitude pervades popular culture and academia alike.[14]

In the humanities, Meillassoux has championed the cause of reclaiming a materialism worthy of its name particularly forcefully. His characterization of twentieth-century materialist thought as suffering from a correlationist illness (under the influence of Marxism, psychoanalysis, and especially Derridean deconstruction) hints at the stakes of this debate and the affective investments involved in the search for new touchstones for our time:

> Ever since Derrida in particular, materialism seems to have taken the form of a "sickened correlationism": it refuses both the return to a naïve pre-critical stage of thought and any investigation of what prevents the "circle of the subject" from harmoniously closing in on itself. Whether it be the Freudian unconscious, Marxist ideology, Derridean dissemination, the undecidability of the event, the Lacanian Real considered as the impossible, etc., these are all supposed to detect the trace of an impossible coincidence of the subject with itself, and thus of an extracorrelational residue in which one could localize a "materialist moment" of thought. But in fact, such misfires are only further correlations among others: it is always for a subject that there is an undecidable event or a failure of signification.[15]

The subject in this metaphor becomes a kind of addictive substance inducing an unhealthy dependency in need of a cure. Philosophy finds a remedy for this sickness in speculative realism's mathematics (Meillassoux), in the relational ontology of Karen Barad, and in the flat ontology of object-oriented ontology (represented most famously by Graham Harman) or actor-network theory (Bruno Latour), all of which reject human exceptionalism and affirm instead immanent, monist theories of being that reject subject-object dualisms.

Meillassoux's metaphor also works as a mirror, however, which, when turned back on the new ontologists, reflects a hunger for authenticity, an insatiable drive for the "real thing" transforming philosophers into "junkies of Being," as François Laruelle has quipped.[16] What drives this drive? The thirst for the real and true stems to some extent from a "fashion-conscious" concern for the next new thing, as Bruce Robbins notes,[17] but it is also indicative of a larger intellectual and cultural shift away from the habits of the humanities—of the humanities under the sway of "Theory." This passion for the real springs from a sense of failure and fatigue as academics take stock of the decline of stable employment opportunities in the humanistic professions, hostility toward public education in general and the university in particular on the political right, resurgent fascist movements across the globe, and the catastrophic warming of the planet. Evaluating the lessons of the George W. Bush presidency, for example, Sharon Best and Stephen Marcus observe that the "demystifying protocols" of a hermeneutics of suspicion seem outdated and "superfluous" in an era where violence is hypervisible, information is instantly circulated over the internet, and lies are flagrant.[18] The advent of the Trump regime and the exacerbation of post-truth politics would seem on this view only to confirm the need for new analytical strategies.[19]

Furthermore, authoritarianism and information wars have been abetted, critics like Bruno Latour have argued, by the Theory era's investment in an epistemological skepticism too easily co-opted by climate change deniers and purveyors of alternative facts. "Entire Ph.D. programs are still running," Latour famously wrote in 2004, "to make sure that good American kids are learning the hard way that facts are made up, that there is no such thing as natural, unmediated, unbiased access to truth, . . . and so on, while dangerous extremists are using the very same argument of social construction to destroy hard-won evidence that could save our lives."[20] For Latour, these threats urgently require a change of course, one that begins by acknowledging our own past errors: "The mistake we made, the mistake I made, was to believe that there was no efficient way to criticize matters of fact except by moving away from them and directing one's attention toward the conditions that made them possible."[21] The skeptical energy of critique has won the day, but Latour finds the consequences devastating: "the Zeus of Critique rules absolutely, to be sure, but over a desert."[22] Critique's "*critical barbarity*"[23] only "subtract[s]" from reality, neglecting to "add" to it, dwelling in negative deconstruction rather than the positive reconstruction of social reality.[24] Ontology serves as a weapon against epistemological skepticism's corrosive effects.

Following Latour, Karen Barad believes that theory's critical modes of engagement—demystification, demythification, deconstruction—have lost their edge: "I am not interested in critique. In my opinion, critique is over-rated, over-emphasized, and over-utilized."[25] Like many critics distancing themselves from the linguistic turn, Barad couches her objections to existing doxa in posthumanist terms as a move away from the hegemony of the Human and toward a materiality transmuted into something more vital: "feeling, desiring and experiencing are not singular characteristics or capacities of human consciousness. Matter feels, converses, suffers, desires, yearns and remembers."[26] Similarly, Jane Bennett takes issue with anthropocentric inquiries fetishizing the human subject and questions about "what is commonly taken as distinctive or even unique about humans."[27] Bennett argues in favor instead of trading human subjectivity for "thing-power," and exchanging suspicion and negativity for "positive, even utopian alternatives"[28]—in short, for an inclusive model that speaks to all matters, human and nonhuman. Such a new materialism seeks to re-enchant the life of objects, enabling us to see the vibrancy of matter and disabusing us, following Adorno, of our "hubris of conceptualization" in order to foster a "utopian imagination" in its place.[29] This is the new task for thinking:

to no longer think exclusively about human beings. To do so, Bennett acknowledges the paradoxical need to turn to "anthropomorphism" as "an attempt to counter the narcissistic reflex of human language and thought."[30] In fact, human beings "need to cultivate a bit of anthropomorphism—the idea that human agency has some echoes in nonhuman nature" and that even simple organisms possess a "certain 'freedom of choice.'"[31]

Bennett is cognizant of the impossibility of her alchemical task (to "give voice to a vitality intrinsic to materiality"[32]), but she believes we must persist in the attempt nevertheless. This "enchanted materialism"[33] is necessary, on this view, if we are to shake off the subject-object dualism of Western thought. Like Latour and Barad, Bennett seeks to enlarge our understanding of agency to include the nonhuman:

> I believe in one matter-energy, the maker of things seen and unseen, I believe that this pluriverse is traversed by heterogeneities that are continually doing things. I believe it is wrong to deny vitality to nonhuman bodies, forces, and forms, and that a careful course of anthropomorphization can help reveal that vitality, even though it resists full translation and exceeds my comprehensive grasp.[34]

Dynamism is not only on the human side (the active subject); the nonhuman material world (the allegedly passive or dead matter of objects) possesses a vibrancy of its own (irrespective of human existence) that demands deep appreciation and careful attention: "By 'vitality' I mean the capacity of things—edibles, commodities, storms, metals—not only to impede or block the will and designs of humans but also to act as quasi-agents or forces with trajectories, propensities, or tendencies of their own."[35] Indeed, Bennett insists, "everything is, in a sense, alive."[36]

Bennett's alchemy is informed by a "desire to cultivate theoretical modesty"[37]; we might say she makes use of *strategic* anthropomorphism (the attempt to speak for nonhumans, to vocalize their agential reality) to avoid repeating modernity's arrogant anthropocentrism. Transmuting theory into a post-critical mode of enchantment means shifting from "human hubris"[38] to a care for the absolute reality of things-in-themselves, from a human-centered model of value to a reconfiguration of the "demos"[39] that would include the nonhuman as well. This form of post-critique is not apolitical but is better described as a posthumanist politics: "How would political responses to public problems change were we to take seriously the vitality of (nonhuman) bodies?"[40]

This question, like Latour's before it, speaks directly to the relationship, or lack thereof, between the ontological and the political, or ontology and history more broadly, in the work of ontology's new exponents. Far too often, the turn toward ontology becomes in effect a flight away from racism as an analytical and political problem. What becomes of beings, their specificity and their historically situated lives, when we orient analysis toward being itself under the heading of flat ontology? While some scholars neglect such questions altogether in their flight from anthropocentrism, those that do take up politics as an explicit concern for posthumanism still risk glossing over the specific problems facing those humans persistently treated as nonhuman objects. In spite of Black radical thought's long engagement with animalization as a facet of racialization, for example, "critiques of 'human exceptionalism' and anthropocentrism in critical animal studies," writes Che Gossett, "often presume that the human in the human/animal divide is a universally inhabited and privileged category, rather than a contested and fractured one."[41] Critical Black Studies foregrounds, by contrast, this very contestation over the bounds of the human and the struggle to reshape a racial matrix that elevates whiteness to the level of humanity while animalizing and demonizing Blackness. As Zakiyyah Iman Jackson shows, "the history of blackness's bestialization and thingification" involves "the process of imagining black people as an empty vessel, a nonbeing, a nothing, an ontological zero, coupled with the violent imposition of colonial myths and racial hierarchy."[42] The persistence of anti-Blackness in its various forms attests not only to this ongoing ontological negation but also to the persistence of the category of the human itself, the form of being in opposition to which Blackness is defined.

Like new materialism, object-oriented ontology risks smoothing over the fractures produced by racism by universalizing division, treating it as a feature of all objects, which withdraw some part of themselves from relation and thus escape our full grasp. Harman aims through such an approach, for example, to democratize the field of beings; his "flat ontology [. . .] *initially* treats all objects in the same way, rather than assuming in advance that different types of objects require completely different ontologies."[43] But as Jeffrey Jerome Cohen notes, "important human differences (especially race and gender) tend to vanish from attention" when we turn to ontology as a "flattening device" bringing all objects onto the same plane:

> When things are examined as they exist for themselves, they can seem to exist beyond feminism, critical race studies, environmental justice, history. No man is an island, but after the ontological turn every object might be. Perhaps such isolation is the necessary consequence of movement beyond critical anthropocentrism. Yet withdrawal into mystery extracts objects from the urgent human stories in which they participate as props and actors.[44]

OOO treats race as a cosmetic difference, not as an ontological problem, covering over the divisions within the figure of the human and eliding what Alexander Weheliye describes as the "sociopolitical processes that discipline humanity into full humans, not-quite-humans, and nonhumans."[45]

Posthumanists who espouse flat ontology fail to acknowledge that, in the words of Nahum Chandler, the Black subject is "an exorbitance for thought," standing "outside of all forms of being that truly matter."[46] The "metaphysical infrastructure"[47] of such posthumanist thought is marked by anti-Blackness. Indeed, as Zakiyyah Iman Jackson argues, "the resounding silence in the posthumanist, object-oriented, and new materialist literatures with respect to race is remarkable, persisting even despite the reach of antiblackness into the nonhuman—*as blackness conditions and constitutes the very nonhuman disruption and/or displacement they invite.*"[48]

The posthuman passion for the nonhuman frequently obfuscates questions of race and racism. Exiting the orbit of the subject is premature when the racialized history of the human is ignored or covered over. As a counter to this neglect, Critical Black Studies has foregrounded the role of anti-Blackness in the making of the human subject. Afropessimist Frank B. Wilderson III traces anti-Blackness to the twin birth of modern humanism and slavery, exposing the political ontology at work in fashioning the humanist subject as profoundly anti-Black. The modern human emerged and defined itself by its non-slave status. Its ontology was forged in opposition to the slave as Black. Under chattel slavery specifically, in contrast to other forms of servitude, the bodies of slaves were reduced to Black flesh, with "flesh" denoting "that zero degree of social conceptualization," as Hortense Spillers writes.[49] The transatlantic slave trade subjected the enslaved to alchemical terror, "ungendering" these stolen lives and depriving them of their corporeal desires:

> First of all, their New-World, diasporic plight marked a *theft* of the *body*—a willful and violent (and unimaginable from this distance) severing of the captive body from its motive will, its active desire. Under these conditions, we lose at least *gender* difference *in the outcome*, and the female body and the male body become a territory of cultural and political maneuver, not at all gender-related, gender-specific.[50]

This is an ontological transmutation without precedent. For Wilderson, the ontological devastation done to African lives by the Middle Passage was even more pronounced than the Shoah to which it is sometimes compared. "Jews went into Auschwitz and came out as Jews, Africans went into the ships and came out as Blacks," he argues. "The former is a Human holocaust; the latter is a Human *and* a metaphysical holocaust."[51]

To use the term "metaphysical holocaust" is to emphasize that racial slavery was unlike all prior forms of slavery. It did not arise as a form of punishment contingent on reversible political dynamics, as witnessed, for example, in the practice of enslaving the defeated after a military conquest. Racial slavery ontologized Africans as slaves. It transformed "the African body into Black flesh."[52] This instrumentalization of Black flesh had widespread impacts: it was "the burning fossil that fueled capitalism during its primitive era,"[53] and it helped frame the parameters of bourgeois labor, clarifying what separates the human worker from the slave.[54] If European humans possess their labor power as a commodity to sell, the slave is itself being as commodity. Work is ontologically impossible for the slave; it is the privilege of the human, a category from which Black people are excluded.[55] The worker's alienation under capitalism is contingent (on socioeconomic conditions that can change), but the Black person's alienation is permanent under white civil society.

For Afropessimists, there is no hope of redressing anti-Blackness so long as this ontological wrong goes unacknowledged. While slavery legally ended, the constitutive exclusion of Black people from the privileges of human subjectivity has not; it lingers in what Saidiya Hartman calls the "afterlife of slavery."[56] Juridical reform is not the solution insofar as it misconstrues anti-Blackness as a problem of inclusion, as a problem, in principle, resolvable from within the existing socio-symbolic order:

> Legal liberalism, as well as critical race theory, has examined issues of race, racism, and equality by focusing on the exclusion and marginalization of those subjects and bodies marked as different and/or inferior. The disadvantage of this approach is that the proposed remedies and correctives to the problem—inclusion, protection, and greater access to opportunity—do not ultimately challenge the economy of racial production or its truth claims or interrogate the exclusion constitutive of the norm but instead seek to gain equality, liberation, and redress within its confines.[57]

In other words, Alchemy at the level of legal rights stops short of unravelling civil society's "metaphysical infrastructure."

Spillers similarly argues that Black captivity persists in a society that designates Black people as "emancipated":

> Even though the captive flesh/body has been "liberated," and no one need pretend that even the quotation marks do not *matter*, dominant symbolic activity, the ruling episteme that releases the dynamics of naming and valuation, remains grounded in the originating metaphors of captivity and mutilation so that it is as if neither time nor history, nor historiography and its topics, shows movement, as the human subject is "murdered" over and over again by the passions of a bloodless and anonymous archaism, showing itself in endless disguise.[58]

Slavery's "systematic reincarnations in the contemporary world" pose an intractable, haunting challenge to post-slavery societies.[59] The violence of institutional maltreatment, incarceration, extrajudicial persecution, and police brutality and murder continues to circumscribe and obliterate the lives of "free" Black folks, who are targeted not for what they do but for who they are—for the fact of being Black itself. The very presence of Blackness, write Jared Sexton and Huey Copeland, is "a scandal to ontology" and "an outrage to every marker of the human."[60]

This fear of nonbeing sparks racial anxiety. Blackness haunts white folks. As a result, anti-Blackness proliferates and lives on in the collective unconscious, circulating in the libidinal economy "of desire and identification, of energies, concerns, points of attention, anxieties, pleasures, appetites, revulsions, and phobias," or in other words, "the whole structure of psychic and emotional life"; though "unconscious and invisible," this libidinal economy has "a visible effect on the world, including the money economy."[61] Skimming over the foundational role of anti-Blackness in the modern capitalist order—by declaring the subject-object divide false and the human an illusory concept that must be expanded to include nonhuman animals and objects—condemns us on an Afropessimist view to reproducing the systems sustaining and sustained by anti-Black racism. This move is dangerously misguided because responding to the violence of humanism by simply jettisoning the category of the subject and urging a paradigm shift fails to take into consideration the libidinal economy of anti-Blackness, the psychic or affective dimensions of an anti-Black racism that pervades civil society. What is required, from an Afropessimist perspective, is nothing short of the destruction of this economy and the social order it supports.[62] Without acknowledging anti-Blackness, proponents of posthumanism ironically prolong the devastating legacy of the very human subject they seek to dethrone.

Genomic Hopes

Creating a new world from the ashes of modernity's holocaust of being requires change of alchemical proportions, a massive psychic, economic, social, and political transformation exceeding the confines of current conceptualization. For Afropessimists, this alchemy must take an apocalyptic form, the demolition of white civil society, or "the end of the world," which is the "only thing ... worth the effort of starting," as Wilderson reminds us, echoing the call passed down to us from Aimé Césaire and Frantz Fanon.[63] This alchemic upheaval involves shaking the ontological foundations of what it means to be a human subject. As Wilderson argues, "you [non-Blacks] have to attempt to undo your touchstones of cohesions, both filial (the family or other community into which one was born) and affilial (forms of association that are voluntary)—that which makes you present as a human subject in the world."[64] Others, however, have turned to more moderate, reparative approaches in response to the ontological wound of racial slavery, including, notably, genetic genealogy. If Afropessimism's passion for the real frequently takes the form of a desire to unmask the ideological fantasy of postraciality and disclose the reality of the anti-Blackness that subtends the symbolic order, those invested in genomics look to the flesh, and the science that decodes it, for the means to heal the wounds inflicted on the flesh itself. Genomics holds out the hope of remedying "natal alienation," the violent enslavement and uprooting of Africans from their communities, which for Afropessimists condemns Blacks to "social death."[65] Genetic genealogy—the reconstruction of family trees and population migrations through DNA analysis, alongside archival sources—offers diasporic Black folks the promise of identity and community, of forming new kinships founded on evidentiary procedures that enjoy broad public respect in the United States, Britain, and the West broadly.[66]

The passion for the real expressed in the turn to genomics stems in part from dissatisfaction with the now commonplace assertion that race is a social construct, insofar as this statement has come to function as the beginning and the end of conversations about racism. Of course, the constructivist thesis concerning the origins of race holds true. For antiracist thinkers there can be no return to a pre-critical racial realism that assumes race to be a coherent category, tied to phenotype or blood, across time and place. "Race is the child of racism, not the father," as Ta-Nehisi Coates poetically notes.[67] Even as he has championed genetic testing through his PBS series *Finding Your Roots*, Henry Louis Gates, Jr., also continues to align himself with this tradition, reaffirming that "we're all admixed. You know, no matter how different we appear phenotypically, under the skin we're 99.99 percent the same."[68] This passion for the genomic real reflects instead a hunger to locate and narrativize identity, to give it a genealogy and foundation. *Natal alienation is not destiny*. Rediscovering one's own lost roots now appears as a genuine possibility, with the help of genetics' alchemical force. And this by itself holds out the promise of alleviating the suffering and abandonment of the African diaspora.[69]

The appeal of genetic genealogy can be described as alchemical because it brings together techne and social magic, seemingly furnishing, as Nadia Abu El-Haj puts it, "evidentiary grounds on which [. . .] certain practices of self-recognition become possible, legible, desirable, and truthful."[70] DNA ancestry testing is widely experienced as a paradigm shift capable of repairing incomplete and mistaken histories, stripping away the layers of fog and misrepresentation surrounding Black and Indigenous peoples' pasts, filling in holes in the documentary record, and grounding new futures on solid knowledge. As Alondra Nelson observes, for many in the African diaspora in particular, whose communal memories and kinship relations were sundered by slavery, the arrival of genomic roots testing represented "a cutting-edge answer [. . .] to a central enigma of African America—a remedy that seemed ripped from the pages of a sci-fi novel."[71] Science, because DNA analysis relies on the systematic study of the natural world and constantly evolves as empirical evidence is gathered, tested, and debated; fiction, because genomic analysis makes the previously impossible possible, smelting solid gold out of ethereal dreams.

Genetic ancestry testing's troubling similarities to the racial sciences of the nineteenth and twentieth centuries have given many scholars pause, however. Indeed, genetic genealogy emerges from within long narrative and epistemic traditions supporting the perception that kinship ties and racial or ethnic identity are located in the body, in flesh and blood. Even as it reshapes such traditions, it also newly authorizes them in particularly convincing ways. While based on a finer-grained understanding of the genetics of organic life, the genomic paradigm invests DNA with the qualities so long attributed to blood, a substance cast as the locus of irremediable purity or distinction. Rather than merely working to discredit earlier popular understandings of blood as the carrier of racial identity, nobility, and personality traits, genomic thinking re-enchants biological determinism by redirecting the effort to "read" race through the broader category of blood toward DNA, the alphabet or building block that makes of blood a revelatory text. Constituting a "practical marker of difference," as Gil Anidjar discerns in his critical genealogy of early Christianity,[72] blood, functioning as a master signifier, came to fashion and determine "the channels and motions that carry the family, the class, the race, the nation, and the economy too"[73] in the modern period. Anidjar unearths, among other continuities between Christianity and secular modernity, a Christian passion for blood purity that underlies both the anti-Blackness of the one-drop rule and the biological anti-Semitism of Nazi ideology. Blood represents "one in an economy of symbols—natural or not—that have appealed to the collective imagination" and that "we have yet to denaturalize";[74] genomic thinking, as manifested both in amateur enthusiasm for genetic genealogy and in the expert work that supports it, often tacitly recycles the racial understanding of blood as an ontological marker of identity, belonging, and exclusion. As Achille Mbembe observes, "race has once again re-entered the domain of biological truth, viewed now through a molecular gaze. A new molecular deployment of race has emerged out of genomic thinking."[75] The implications of this shift, he notes, are mixed. "Genomics, for instance, has produced new complexity into the figure of humanity," revealing "multiple affinities between humans and other creatures or species," thereby shaking up human exceptionalism and prompting us to reconsider how we relate to our nonhuman kin.[76] "And yet," he continues, "the core racial typology of the 19th century still provides a dominant mould through which this new genetic knowledge of human difference is taking shape and entering medical and lay conceptions of human variation."[77]

A host of anthropologists, historians, and journalists, along with a number of geneticists, have similarly warned that genetics and genomics (or the study of genetic material with a focus on individual genes and heritable traits in the first case and an emphasis on whole genomes and the interrelation between their parts in the second) are being understood by laypersons—but also some researchers—to confirm the existence of biologically distinct human "bloodlines" or "races" corresponding to socially defined racial categories. Such conceptions potentially reauthorize old beliefs not just in racial diversity but in individual- and population-scale genetic determinism, racial hierarchies, and the various supremacist projects designed to accrue power to those (still typically white people) who think themselves to be situated at the top of a health and intelligence ladder. The complex re-visioning of intrahuman and interspecies kinships that genomics offers gives way, under the persistent racial capitalist paradigms that structure our lives and research, to preoccupations with identifying and hierarchizing biological differences in order to then manipulate genetic material and "optimize" organisms.[78] The move from this digital financial newspeak to the eugenics of old is not such a leap. When "race politics" takes a "genomic turn," Mbembe cautions, racial stratification and injustice almost inevitably follow.[79]

Genomics readily serves as a new bottle for old wine for several reasons, including methodological weaknesses in genomics research itself; popular media translations of select results for laypersons (which sometimes leave out complex caveats about study design and limitations); lack of scientific literacy in the general public; and the prioritization of consumer preferences and preconceptions—along with the loss of transparency and capacity of the community at large to question and reproduce analyses independently—that comes with the privatization and commodification of genetic ancestry testing services. As Abram Gabriel notes, "Americans both revere and mistrust scientists, and this ambivalence leads to unrealistic beliefs about the scientific process"; these dueling attitudes, combined with corporate interests in delivering pharmaceutical therapies or individualized ancestry results developed from repurposed methodologies ill-suited to this task, contribute to the circulation of overblown claims about the genetic foundation for racial differences.[80] Medical researchers invested in preventing and curing disease, for example, must disentangle sociogenic factors (disparities in exposure to stress and environmental risks or in access to health care, for instance) from genetic predispositions in order to correctly identify etiologies and develop treatments, yet pharmacology and molecular biology studies frequently use social, phenotype-based racial identifications as proxies for genetic populations.[81] Given that there is greater genetic variation within geographic population groups than between them; that risk of disease in many cases correlates more closely with environmental and behavioral factors (along with age) than with genetic predisposition; that genetic predisposition itself frequently involves multiple genes and complex gene interactions rather than single gene mutations; and, finally, that perceived phenotypical similarities mask genetic differences, using social categories to make inferences about genetic leads to unvalidated and potentially dangerous conclusions.[82]

As a site for investigating popular conceptions of racial identity and attitudes toward science, as well as the intersections between academic institutions, private corporations, and government, direct-to-consumer (DTC) genomic testing companies are ripe for analysis of genomic thinking's contours and influence. DTC genomic testing companies take part in what Abu El-Haj has described as the "phylogenetic turn"[83] in both mainstream science and popular culture: the "increasingly pervasive and powerful field of scientific research and social practice" by which "genomic knowledge is being harnessed in efforts to reconstruct histories both individual and collective."[84] "Testing companies," Abu El-Haj argues, "constitute the most concrete and direct 'network' (Latour 1987) through which genetic history's epistemic things and truth-economy circulate in the public domain."[85]

Some DTC testing companies take more liberties in their presentation of DNA evidence's significance than others, burying explanations of methods and implications deep in their websites and giving correlations more causal weight in their sales rhetoric than is warranted. Orig3n Inc., a company founded in 2014, provided some startling examples of such tactics on their now-defunct consumer website, Orig3n.com. Subpages on the site did lead readers to an explanation that their DNA tests reveal *probabilities* that can influence risk assessment—for example, a test, as the company put it, can "hint at what might lie ahead," but it cannot "tell you what to do next."[86] Yet Orig3n.com's home page and test kit advertisements played up the tests' ability to reveal our uniqueness and inform our behavior, in a language reinforcing deterministic notions of our genome's influence over our physical and emotional traits. We are invited to "find out" whether our genes "have the qualities" that San Francisco 49ers general manager John Lynch is looking for in his draft picks, or to "discover what [we] should be eating," recasting the problem of evaluation—of assessing risks and making value judgments—as a problem of merely accessing information, of accessing a key that will unlock predictive data.[87] Language that reminds us that we are dealing with probabilities—with risk or likelihood—alternates with offers to tell us who we "are" and how our genes "determine" our traits. "Are" we worriers or warriors? There's a gene for that.[88] Caveats notwithstanding, worrying specters of social control and eugenics hover behind these offers to enhance well-being through access to genomic information. Orig3n's products displayed this perhaps most visibly in a "Child Development" package purporting to give us information about our child's "potential," presumably so that we can orient their behavior toward fulfilling activities—toward sports that are "a good match"—or take remedial action to make up for genomic deficiencies.[89] In addition to the ethical questions we might raise about the commodification of genetic material and the child's rights to privacy and control over that material, what is fascinating and disturbing about the ways genomic knowledge is represented in marketing such as this is the ambiguous relationship between determinism and agency, between being and becoming, that such knowledge implies: on the one hand, our genes appear to steer us toward certain paths, making us better suited for some modes of being than others, while, on the other, offering DNA tests for sale presumes that the ability to know these determinations, to know what we "are," allows us to act upon them in some way in order to become something else or to mold those under our care or control—our children—into something else.

The social dimension and implications of the question "What am I?" are foregrounded more explicitly in the services offered by Ancestry—a company focused on genealogy that offers DNA ancestry testing as well as subscription access to vital records and social networking tools. Ancestry offers tests that provide information about "your origins from over 1000 regions"[90] and that match you with potential biological relatives in their databases. Ancestry's conceptualizations of ethnicity rework a number of older tropes—perhaps most strikingly in its pie-chart representations of ethnicity as a percentage. On the one hand, Ancestry celebrates admixture; the American client base is assumed to be of mixed ethnicity, and mixing—the stories of migration and intermarriage that ethnicity tests reveal—is embraced as that which makes us unique, that makes us "what" we are. Yet there is no admixture without the assumption of pure stocks available to be mixed together in the first place, and Ancestry's neat, separable, and bounded slices of pie appear in these advertisements as a kind of happy flip side of the same logic underpinning the one-drop rule: the notion that ethnicity, like race, is located in the body, in the flesh and blood, and that it is measurable.

"Ethnicity" is the term of choice used by Ancestry, but we might wonder whether genetic ethnicity is anything other than race. The term is not explicitly defined in promotional materials but is linked to origins and regions; digging deeper into the site leads to more precise explanations of the methods and results obtained by genetic ethnicity tests, which implicitly locate ethnicity in a period of human history occurring after the migration of humans out of Africa and across the globe, but before 1492 and modern mass migrations spawned by European imperialism. This is a period in which humans have formed regional groups across the planet whose putative internal coherence and genetic distinction from other groups are deemed significant enough to constitute ethnicity. What clients actually receive from Ancestry is an "ethnicity estimate," along with a map showing probable regions in which their ancestors lived during this period. Beyond the initial pie-chart number, customers receive a numerical range representing variations in the amount of ethnic similarities found at each of the multiple portions of their DNA that are tested and compared with Ancestry's reference panel: a database, they explain, "of over 68,714 DNA samples from people with deep regional roots and documented family trees."[91] Ancestry's reliance on the terms "deep," "ancient," and "distant" in describing ethnicity reflects, I believe, popular white American conceptions of ethnicity as a biological and cultural identity grounded somewhere other than contemporary America.[92] But it also reflects the ways customer demand, in privatized research, shapes the priorities of population genetics. "Genetic ethnicity" is first defined in the 2013 "Ethnicity Estimate White Paper" issued by Ancestry's team of population geneticists, computer scientists, statisticians, and computational biologists as "an estimate of the ancient historical origins of [customers'] DNA"; genetic ethnicity testing, they write candidly, is "of less relevance to genealogical research relating to the last five or ten generations," but "it may reveal intriguing clues about the distant history of one's ancestors. Our customers," they add, "have overwhelmingly expressed interest in receiving the results of this analysis."[93]

It seems to be popular conceptions of "ancientness" that prevail here over physical anthropology's uses of the term, because "ancient" in this paper does not mean the time period in which early *Homo sapiens* was first evolving, but rather sometime after the fall of the Roman Empire. "Under perfect circumstances," the authors explain:

> we would construct our reference panel using ancient DNA samples of the true ancestors of each person likely to be an AncestryDNA customer. For example, since many of our customers have ancestors from the United Kingdom, we would prefer to have samples in our reference panel from the Angles and Saxons, who represent the historical populations present in Northwestern Europe.[94]

Defining Anglo-Saxon as a non-admixed ethnicity involves establishing a start date for history and determining what counts as population migration and admixture and what doesn't: history—and ethnicity—begins with Angle and Saxon settlement in Britain. In specifying that they understand migration across "large distances" to produce ethnic admixture,[95] the authors make clear that only certain sorts of migrations are deemed ethnically significant. Ethnic significance itself may unwittingly serve as the measure by which migration sizes are classified as large or small, rather than the reverse. Developing a reference panel of living individuals judged representative of Anglo-Saxon ancestors or other groupings can involve merely reproducing predefined notions of significance or giving preference to genetic data that demonstrate the difference one sets out to find. As Troy Duster notes, even between arbitrary population groupings, such as Los Angeles residents and Chicago residents,

> it is possible to find statistically significant differences in allele frequency at *some* loci [on the genome]. Of course, at many loci, even at most loci, we would not find statistically significant differences. When researchers claim to be able to assign people to groups based on allele frequency at

a certain number of loci, they have chosen loci that show differences between the groups they are trying to distinguish.[96]

This is not to say that there are no statistically significant genetic differences between human populations, but rather that the crux of the problem lies in defining and interpreting significance. Ethnicity testing relies heavily on consumers' conceptions of sameness and difference, purity and hybridity, and the point at which human history has some bearing on present identity.

The stakes of debates over ethnicity testing's role in reinvigorating old beliefs in racial purity are high, for as Paul Gilroy warns, essentialist, ethnonationalist conceptions of race have come to impinge dangerously on all aspects of political life, on the way we live together—or reject contact with others—in community:

> The widespread appeal of racialised group identity and racism, often conveyed obliquely with a knowing wink, has been instrumental in delivering us to a situation in which our conceptions of truth, law and government have been placed in jeopardy. In many places, pathological hunger for national rebirth and the restoration of an earlier political time, have combined with resentful, authoritarian and belligerent responses to alterity and the expectation of hospitality. [. . .] I want to insist that this notable deterioration in our political culture and institutions cannot be understood without paying careful attention to the specific dynamics both of race as a matter of political ontology, and of racism as a variety of political speech. Race and nation are now primary sources of groupness and absolute ethnicity. They are supposedly endowed with a special power to restore certainty and find stability amidst the flux of precarious life in increasingly dangerous conditions.[97]

Discourse about race and its doppelganger ethnicity matter—to our social arrangements, to our practices of coexistence, and to our use of violence. In light of these observations, "it behooves us to be less romantic about what all this DNA swabbing reveals," writes Patricia J. Williams. "I worry," she continues, "about the craving to 'go back to Africa,' to 'connect with our Yiddishness' or to feel like new doors have been opened if we have an Asian ancestor. The craving, the connection, the newness of those doors is in our heads, not in our mitochondria."[98]

Kim TallBear points out the detrimental impact of such genomic thinking on ways of imagining and understanding Indigeneity: "Indigeneity recast as genetics becomes a discourse of scarcity and death, rather than what it is, an indigenous social movement, a discourse of survival."[99] Rather than protecting Indigenous communities by enhancing tribal sovereignty, genetic testing more often restricts modes of defining tribal membership (displacing cultural knowledge and community as important elements of belonging) and risks eroding the legitimacy of Native epistemologies and self-determination, since techniques such as "across-the-membership application of 'parentage' tests can contradict hard-won legal foundations that are the source of contemporary indigenous governmental authorities."[100] At the same time, TallBear notes, the relationship between older racial categories and new understandings of genetics is not unidirectional; both genomic science and Native concepts of blood as more than a biological substance work to refashion colonialist notions of biological essentialism, rendering the embrace of DNA analysis a complex practice whose impacts can vary.[101]

Alondra Nelson raises a similar concern in her study of the role genetic analysis plays in Afro-diasporic reconciliation projects. "Why turn to DNA for leverage in racial politics," she asks, "given the fraught history of scientific racism from Linnaeus to the present?"[102] Her answer to this question hinges on an understanding of DNA "as Janus-faced";[103] genetic analysis in itself is neither emancipatory nor repressive, but rather is subject to multiple interpretations and harnessed today for sometimes contradictory purposes. Thus, "political actors engaging genetics in their political claims-making are not necessarily guilty of self-delusion. Rather, it is precisely because they have a deep appreciation for the complexity of race as a political category that they are mobilizing it as such."[104] If genomic arguments have been twisted for use by white supremacists—who have engaged in public displays of milk-chugging as proof of whiteness, just to take one vivid example of the ways aggregate-level data about lactose tolerance mutation rates in various populations get redeployed as evidence that racial differences exist on a biological level[105]—genomic knowledge has also been put to the service of public memory projects and litigation seeking redress for racialized inequities.[106]

Far from an impartial arbiter capable of clarifying history and identity with certainty and settling political debates about how we should live and relate to one another, DNA analysis is a profoundly social undertaking shaped by varying interpretive commitments. The dangerous ease with which genomic evidence has been seized upon in biological determinist arguments points to the seductive power of genomic hope, the promise of firm grounds on which to found action. But the very pliability and social character of DNA analysis also demonstrate that genomic reason is open to intervention and refashioning. Faced with this opening, the question for antiracist thought becomes how best to struggle with or against the new touchstones occupying the center of social and academic life.

Against Ontology, or Fugitive Alchemies

For Paul Gilroy, the entanglement of academic work with the alarming rise of racist and nationalist separatist movements in many places across the globe should give us pause when considering commitments to ontology. Debates over ontology among scholars never remain strictly intramural; rather, they have impacts on mainstream trends and are shaped by these larger forces in turn. For this reason, he argues that "we should be sceptical about the seductions of the ontological turn recently promoted in the study of race politics" because such a framework "has become disastrously complicated by prospective nostalgia for the easy, essentialist approaches that were dominant when assertive cultural nationalism ruled the roost."[107] To approach racism as primarily an ontological problem is to risk misrepresenting its violence as "eternal," that is, as unassailable. "Du Bois' 'color line' was a contingent, historical arrangement: substantial yes, but never invulnerable," Gilroy asserts. "Such systems are more usefully considered historically than metaphysically. My resolute commitment to their undoing is premised on appreciation of their constitutive power."[108] Fighting racism on the terrain of ontology risks the "absolutization of blackness" decried by Mbembe, a reification that forecloses change, denying the "infinite and reparative horizon" under which being, as becoming, actually unfolds.[109] An effective historical stance, on this view, is one that admits dialectical, interrogative openness, as Mbembe puts it; in Gilroy's terms, such an approach accounts for the "amputation" of being under racialized modernity that Afropessimist ontology rightly highlights (following Fanon's observation) while also acknowledging and opening up possibilities for generating "epochal change," for a being (humanity) understood as a historical, humanist, or planetary project.[110]

Being is not destiny, but if the color line is not eternal, it is also true that color lines, in their shifting manifestations, are long-lived; the term "epochal" points to the magnitude of the task at hand. In order to perform an alchemy radically transforming racist economic, psychic, and political systems, Gilroy argues, "it is imperative to remain less interested in who or what we imagine ourselves to be, than in what we can do for one another both in today's emergency conditions and in the grimmer circumstances that surely await us."[111] This distinction between being and doing—between a metaphysical preoccupation with the whatness distinguishing separate identities from one another and a historical inquiry into dynamic relations among subjects in community—is framed here as one of degree and critical orientation. To take a position against ontology in this sense is not to deny the performative efficiency of racism, to use Žižek's phrase, or the ways in which racism touches the very being of racialized subjects. Rather, it is to foreground a particular understanding of being as relational doing stretching into an as yet undefined future and to dwell on the question of responsibility to others in that doing. What forms of response are we or can we become capable of, and what would it take to make "conviviality and care" a "transformational practice" alchemizing the world in which we live?[112]

Centering antiracist work on responsive doing disrupts not only the absolutizing impulses of ontology but also the static opposition between *res* and *verba*, between thing and word, reality and its representation, that often haunts anti-essentialist critiques of race as a social construction. The struggle against racism cannot limit itself to demystifying ideas. Racist violence is illustrated and enacted through language, but as Fanon showed long ago, racist discourse interpellates, reducing one to "an object among other objects [. . .] locked in this suffocating reification."[113] Racist ideology is not simply a mask that can be lifted to reveal the untouched real below; rather, it is "an interpretation that determines the very being and social existence of the interpreted subjects," for being is not the stuff of abstraction and eternal essences, but rather a matter of historical, socio-symbolic positioning.[114]

But if being is indeed socio-symbolic, this also means that it is subject to radical alteration, to counter-alchemies. Hortense Spillers's pointed observation, "Sticks and bricks *might* break our bones, but words will most certainly *kill* us,"[115] highlights language's very material force. Slavery's ungendering, its conversion of women into captive flesh, points to a gap in the very symbolic order that establishes gender, a breach open to rebellious, "insurgent" rewritings through which new fleshly potentialities, a "radically different text," can be forged.[116] In Fanon's work as well, language, the means of interpellation, is one of the key materials out of which ontological-historical transmutations must be wrought. As an overwhelmingly important medium of relationality in human life, language represents a major concern for Fanon throughout his writing, from its mediating role in the doctor-patient relationship to its alienating function under colonialism to its capacity to spark decolonial imagination and rally collectivities in the form of combat literature. *Black Skin, White Masks* opens with a wrenching study of language, a "phenomenon" Fanon describes as being of "fundamental importance," for it is through language that worlds are opened or foreclosed, that the status of human being in the eyes of others (and in one's own eyes) is achieved or denied; "to speak," Fanon asserts, "is to exist absolutely for the other. [. . .] A man who possesses a language possesses as an indirect consequence the world expressed and implied by this language."[117]

Language serves as a lifeline to others, a means for constructing and maintaining a self. Dispossessing someone of language—be it in the isolating institutional structure of the 1950s psychiatric hospital or in the colonial context of Fanon's native Martinique, where "human" status is tied to speaking French and abandoning Creole—thus has catastrophic consequences. Reconstructing the self in language becomes, then, a key priority for Fanon, in therapy and in activism. "The discovery of writing," states Fanon in the inaugural issue of *Notre Journal (Our Journal)*, the weekly publication he established for the Blida-Joinville Hospital, "is certainly the most beautiful one, since it allows you to recall yourself, to present things that have happened in order and above all to communicate with others, even when they are absent."[118] The reflexive character of writing allows one to sort through memory and construct a self through narration, but most importantly ("above all") it is an act of connection, of hearing and being heard by the other. Reading and writing are acts of analysis, creation, sharing, and revision—in short, acts of relational poiesis.

Poetic discourse serves Fanon's project of disalienation in at least three interconnected ways. It provides a means for taking account of realities that have gone unseen from other vantage points, for better addressing those who would turn away from such realities, and for articulating the precise relationships between the particular and the universal, a task necessary to political change. In his preface to the original edition of *Black Skin, White Masks*, Francis Jeanson captures some of this force that the literary takes on in Fanon's writing when he describes Fanon's demands in the book as "unfitting, improper, ill-adapted, almost unspeakable, *unobjectifiable* [pas 'sortable,' inconvenante, inadaptée, presque indicible, *non objectivable*]."[119] Writing from a colonized position—that place of madness—creates a double bind: how to communicate something of this out-of-jointness, which is antithetical to the very narrative and epistemological norms governing intelligibility?

Aimé Césaire's earlier approach to this question taps a passion for the real—for oppositional truths found in blood—in the attempt to find an outside location from which to forge such a poetics. As Donna V. Jones notes, this fusion reinscribes colonial racial thinking at the same time as it aims, in tension with this rootedness, for a Négritude aesthetics that valorizes Blackness as a dynamic, lively materialism:

> Contemporaneously with the early versions of the *Notebook*, Césaire would write in an introduction to Frobenius's writings: "But there flows in our veins a blood which demands of us an original attitude toward life ... we must respond, the poet more than any other, to the special dynamic of our complex biological reality." Yet even this affirmation of what we know as pseudobiology speaks of a "passion for the real"; Césaire is attempting to awaken his readers from the dreamscapes, ideologies, and imaginaries of the colonial world and to affirm black life and the cosmos just as they are—perfect.[120]

Though Fanon parted ways with Négritude on the question of rooted identities, he recognized in this movement a wellspring for those who move through the world in bodies constantly suffering scrutiny and denigration; "consciousness needs to get lost in the night of the absolute, the only condition for attaining self-consciousness," he argues, and Négritude was the effort to actively grasp Black being, to express that paradoxical experience of nonexistence.[121]

As Fanon makes clear in his critique of Jean-Paul Sartre's analysis of the Négritude movement as a stage to be subsumed in the dialectic, poiesis begins when expression comes alive, moving in a dynamic relation of address and exchange that remains unpredictable, undetermined by any inexorable ontological or historical order. When Sartre "located Negritude in a dialectical history that has white racism for its first term," Robert Bernasconi explains, his mistake in Fanon's eyes was not that he was wrong to grasp Négritude as a movement that shores up an essentialist conception of identity (a critique Fanon shared), but rather that his statement, written from the position of a white subject, "keep[s] intact the structure that serves to produce the problem," the structure within which "he, a white man, asks Blacks unilaterally to renounce the pride of their colour."[122] In pronouncing this, Fanon argues, Sartre "forgets" the specificity of Black experience, the fact that "the black man suffers in his body quite differently from the white man," and that his needs—specifically, the way he lives consciousness's need to "get lost in the night of the absolute"—are different from those of whites.[123] In using the verb "forget," Bernasconi points out, Fanon suggests that Sartre "knows but does not know," that his knowledge of racism is limited by his standpoint, which allows him to forget an experience of suffering that can only and always be painfully present to Black people.[124]

A crucial problem then, for Fanon, is to develop a mode of expression that "obliges white readers," as Bernasconi puts it, "to consider what we prefer to ignore and what we too easily dismiss as beyond our understanding."[125] The challenge, then, lies not just in bringing to light, on a cognitive level, the contours and limits of situated knowledge[126] but in pushing readers to engage in the construction of new worlds from the place where they find themselves.

Fanon remained all too aware that cries of pain do not necessarily lead to revolution.[127] To shift readers, the language of analysis must similarly refuse to remain in its place. The result, perhaps in *Black Skin, White Masks* most prominently, is a language that Jeanson characterizes as "quasi poetic."[128] Hovering between poetry and essay, between autobiography, sociology, and psychoanalysis, Fanon's style pushes against accepted categories and terms of debate, bringing affect into realms where it is excluded while insisting on the value of clinical study and argument.[129] If Jeanson's characterization points to the unsettling effects of this juxtaposition, it also reminds us that "poetic" is, in Fanon's work, a relational term, not one that can be defined once and for all through clearly identifiable formal characteristics. What matters is that expression break through inertia, that it find a way to sustain unsettlement—epistemological and affective—and that it give support to an inventive, alchemical reworlding.

In this antiracist intervention, then, language, or poetics, plays a crucial role in sabotaging existing ontologies. It does so by serving as a medium through which to spirit thought and affect away from their current place, in a move that might be described, with Fred Moten, as paraontological. For Moten, the term "paraontology," which he adopts and adapts from Nahum Chandler, frames negativity as a kind of fugitive againstness, a resistant movement of disruption that differs from nonbeing, or the negation of being, as an ontological predicate. Paraontology points to the inadequacy of "given ontologies," which fail to account for existence, and more specifically for Blackness, understood not as a property of Black people but as "a constant demand for an ontology of disorder, an ontology of dehiscence"[130] or "a desire for and a spirit of escape and transgression of the proper and the proposed."[131] Paraontology, Blackness, queers the "proper" (being and its humanist grammar); it disturbs and unsettles, working against—alongside or apposite to—ontology's form-giving, meaning-making schemas. In this it is a kind of *marronage*, a marooning alchemy, or what Patrick Chamoiseau calls "an alchemy of roundabout resistance [*résistance détournée*],"[132] an oblique mode of transformation that works on and through the given, negatively but not ex nihilo.

In insisting, contrary to Afropessimists, on the "paraontological distinction" between "blackness or the thinking of blackness" on the one hand and "black people" on the other, Moten stresses that Blackness is irreducible to bare life, to the pathologizing effects of political ontology.[133] Blackness as such reminds us that freedom and slavery were never mutually exclusive. "The history of blackness," writes Moten, "is testament to the fact that objects can and do resist."[134] Moten refuses to align freedom exclusively with the marks of sovereignty; such an alignment only leads to what Neil Roberts describes as the "disavowal of slave agency"[135] (and, we might add, the disavowal of Black agency in the afterlife of slavery). Moreover, Blackness, or the fugitive mode of the Black op, Moten claims, is "the condition of possibility of politics" and thereby also of what he calls Black optimism.[136] This opening for change does not depend on a reassertion of the subject's sovereign agency, but rather on the constitutive otherness or outside created alongside the imposition of constraint, on the multiplicity and movement of being that cannot be contained by ontology even as it is constrained. In this Moten takes inspiration from Édouard Glissant, likening this fugitive resistance to the Glissantian *détour*, a constrained but also escaping glide, to the assertion and practice of opacity in the face of demands for clear and comprehensible categories,[137] and to what Moten describes as "a rhizomatic voluntarity" or "involuntary consent of the volunteer," a giving over of ourselves to improvised, unforeseeable multiplicities—in short, he notes, quoting Glissant, a "consent not to be a single being."[138]

A fugitive alchemy begins with this paradoxical decision, this queer or inventive undoing. The moment "one consents not to be a single being and attempts to be many beings at the same time," the moment one consents to "lose" oneself to change, to accept change as a source of creativity and liberation rather than a loss of sovereign identity, is often occasioned by departure or diaspora.[139] Diaspora—both chosen and unchosen—moves one away from rootedness; "for me," Glissant explains, "every diaspora is a passage from unity to multiplicity."[140] More than a historical shift, though it does also reflect historical realities, this passage is a realization of the world's "true self"—a self that is multiple, in a state of ceaseless, dynamic creolization.[141] This true state—in which the goals of unity have been abandoned and multiplicity embraced—does not yet fully exist in the world but must be brought into being, which also means it must be sustained as movement. For Glissant, as for Moten and for Fanon before them both, poetics plays a key role in this effort specifically because of poetry's attentiveness to differences, the "fabric" or "weave of the living":

> Until now, it was believed that like merged with like, and that the self opposed that which was different from itself. *A could not be A and not-A.* That's what they told us in philosophy, in mathematics, etc. You cannot be, and be something else. So the different was the contrary of being; it was nonbeing. And that assumed that there was a world of being, a world of likes, and that there was a world of nonbeing that was a nonworld and that either didn't exist at all or only existed with reference to being. Being exists, nonbeing does not [...]. I conceive reality as made up not of likenesses but of differences. There's no likeness and differences; there's only differences. And the rhizome of these differences forms the weave of the living and the canvas of cultures. [...] Poets are best equipped to grasp differences, the infinity of differences existing between sound and silence. I think that this is the best approach to take toward the different. Differences are the living stuff of life.[142]

Glissant's insistence on liveliness does not reflect a posthumanist vitalism invested in objects, but rather a rejection of the static antagonisms characterizing contacts with reified otherness in so much of the world today in favor of an open-ended, horizontal exchange of Relation that allows the world's multiplicity to come forth. "Well before Hegel," Glissant explains,

> it was known that being and nonbeing combined, I didn't invent that notion—it's the dialectic. But I want us to bring that dialectic back into the real, not just into philosophical thought or theoretical reflection. [...] Whether in the Francophone, Anglophone, Arab, Chinese, Japanese world, what's specific in the definition of the other is that this other is not just considered different. The other is considered as contrary. Now, in the world, there is no contrary. The dialectic of differences is something I agree with, but not the dialectic of contraries, because the dialectic of contraries assumes that there's a truth of here, and its contrary over there. [...] Everything is alive; everything is a Relation of differences—not contraries,

but differences. Accordingly, the dialectic is not a linear approach toward that which is contrary. The dialectic is a total rhizome of what's different.[143]

Glissant's passage points to two different paths that alchemies of blood can take. Alchemy can traffic in contraries, lead and gold, driven by a passion for the authentic and immediate, by a thirst for a new touchstone. Genomic thinking, with its passion for blood as key to the truth of history, ethnoracial identity, and kinship, often takes this route, as does the ostensibly countervailing belief in postraciality, which blithely asserts that racism is dead and that the best way to keep it so is to banish race from thought and law. "The postracial," observes David Theo Goldberg, "is a mode of social magic: the alchemy of racism into nonracialism, into deracination. It sacralizes the negation in the name of desacralizing anti-racist struggle. It etherealizes racisms in the spirit of *its* overcoming."[144] Genomic thinking, with its peculiar investment in blood, is not incompatible with postracialism, in that each depoliticizes blood—the first by approaching it as an object of a supposedly disinterested science whose job is merely to uncover existing truths, and the second by denying its existence and thereby its relevance to political struggles. For postracial-genomic enthusiasts, blood, transmuted into DNA, is at once excised from a racist biological framework and put to the service of grounding and personalizing identity. In this light, the postracial alchemy of blood celebrates both the negation of race and the rediscovery of blood's revelatory powers. This alchemy purports to deliver blood from racist ideology while remaining identitarian in its orientation.

By contrast, an insurgent alchemy of blood militates against normative appeals to transparent, rooted identity, embracing the expansiveness and elusiveness of difference while refusing "resignation to the world as it appears."[145] On this view freedom and poiesis depend on one another and must be continually reinvented. Expressive form is intimately tied to thought, feeling, and embodied particularity; in dialectical relation these can certainly regress into unfreedom or congeal through inertia, hence the necessity but also viability of a poetics of fugitivity. This is a counter-alchemy that understands an antiracist life to be a life "relationally unrestricted"[146] that gives *consent not to be a single community, consent not to be beings that determine their kin in advance*. Such an alchemy accepts the absence of guarantees and fixed, irreversible states of being—and yet it is this very open-endedness and unpredictability that provides the conditions for new imaginings and modes of relation to arise.

Alchemy, as an analytical lens and social practice, muddles the line between literal and figurative meaning, drawing attention to the connections between matter and interpretation, possibility and constraint, at the center of debates over race, blood, kin, and community today. Evocative of ancient magic and wonder, but also of hope beyond hope for radically different futures, alchemy beckons us to take seriously the enchantments offered both by ontologies promising keys to sure knowledge and also by fugitive efforts to unsettle these sedimented modes of relation and reshape desire itself. I use the term in descriptive and prescriptive senses alternately, to highlight at once the entanglement of alchemy and counter-alchemy—both of which share an investment in ontology and in the affective, social, and political stakes of their objects—and the difficult but nonetheless real reversibility of their differing transformations. The desire to naturalize, ontologize, and fetishize realities, identities, kinships, and bloodlines arrests becoming's movement; it drives alchemies of being that obfuscate their trace, covering over their originary or founding violence. Yet alchemies of becoming—counter-alchemies that harness the insurgent force of being otherwise—hold the emancipatory potential to set that becoming in motion once again.

The chapters that follow trace alchemical movements in varied genres of antiracist cultural production—literature, film, television, museums and museum catalogues, citizen genealogy and storytelling—in order to draw out the entangled relationships between form, media, and audience in the construction of community and the contestation of its meanings. This book focuses on two sites grappling with the afterlives of slavery, the United States and the French Caribbean *départements* of Guadeloupe and Martinique. The histories of these different post-plantation Americas are of course deeply entwined, and antiracist writers and theorists from the United States and France, as we have already seen, have long been in close conversation with one another, across the borders of language and national political ideologies whose differences—France's color-blind republican universalism versus the United States' decentralized identity politics—are often played up in discussions surrounding racism. This study seeks to foreground some of these conversational ties while also exploring how some apparently convergent French Caribbean and US practices of alchemy speak differently to different audiences and what might be gained from putting these works into closer relation with one another. If these societies arguably still function for their racialized members as "occupied territories," to echo James Baldwin's searing indictment of the US police apparatus's relationship to the country's most vulnerable Black citizens,[147] these occupations are enacted and lived differently and have thus been met with a range of inventive challenges to the status quo.

Chapter 1, "Genealogies That Matter," focuses on antiracist efforts to counter ethno-supremacist movements through alternative modes of civic engagement with genetics, genealogy, and material culture. I turn first to Henry Louis Gates, Jr.'s promotion of genetic genealogy as a tool for community building in his PBS television series and educational initiatives, and consider this case study alongside similar engagements with genealogy and material artifacts in the Mémorial ACTe museum of slavery and the slave trade in Guadeloupe, France, and the National Museum of African American History and Culture in Washington, D.C., which opened in

2015 and 2016 respectively. Together, these forays in material culture shed light on the multiple ways in which alchemical invention and resistance are framed and practiced in genealogical memory work. As a response to what Ruha Benjamin has termed "institutionalized kinlessness,"[148] or the entrenched social, political, and economic structures through which kinship bonds are persistently disrupted in post-slavery societies, genetic genealogy and artifact-rich museums hold out the alluring promise of rectifying historical erasures with the aid of compelling, "hard" facts. Yet in appealing to the body or the object as the source of such knowledge, such practices also lend themselves to an ontology of being that informs a range of countervailing, deterministic claims about the body's or the past's fixed identity and capacities. For this reason, the projects studied in this chapter show, the struggle to foreground becoming and its creative possibilities cannot rely on appeals to materiality alone, but rather must aim to reshape communities' dispositions toward material objects and the interpretive habits through which they encounter them.

Chapter 2, "Amnesiac Meditations, or Kinship in the Breach," turns to the resources that fiction provides for engaging and reshaping a passion for the real. Here I put in dialogue two novels that stage amnesia as a metaphor for historical trauma and a symptom of yearning for unmediated authenticity, a longing for secure knowledge of the self's most foundational structures. *L'empreinte à Crusoé* (Crusoe's Print, 2012), Patrick Chamoiseau's radical rewriting of Daniel Defoe's famous castaway story, and Octavia Butler's queer vampire novel, *Fledgling* (2005), offer thematically resonant but aesthetically diverging inquiries into the complex relationships between nature and culture, instinct and memory, freedom and dependence, corporeal plasticity and bodily constraints, bloodlines found and bloodlines forged. This chapter probes the models of symbiosis, autoimmune solidarity, and openness to relation these novels put forward to contest what Chamoiseau describes as modernity's "diseased" modes of individuation binding subjects to hollowed out modes of subsistence, with an eye for the particular ways in which fiction works to rekindle creative energies and transform their ends.

Chapter 3, "Future Ancestors," extends Chapter 2's inquiry into fiction's alchemy by turning to recent works that tap the prophetic force of speculation: Damon Lindelof's HBO series *Watchmen* (a 2019 adaptation of Alan Moore and Dave Gibbons's groundbreaking 1986 comic of the same name), Ryan Coogler's film *Black Panther* (2018), and Fabienne Kanor's novel *Humus* (2006). Speculative fiction foregrounds the explicitly counterfactual—alternative worlds, pasts, and futures that recognizably depart from our own reality as we see it. Its capacity to remake worlds hinges on its very status as invention, its staging of the otherworldly, the impossible, and the unimagined. In this, it opposes the passion for what is, orienting us instead toward what might be, along with what we might be reluctant to recognize as part of our current reality. Taking up these three works' efforts to prophetically reenvision the past in order to create new futures in the afterlife of slavery, this chapter explores the contrasting visions of lineage and inheritance that they forge through their varying investments in being and becoming.

Building on this understanding of alchemy as a form of memory or history-telling aimed not at recovering a confining literalness but rather at what Glissant terms a "prophetic vision of the past,"[149] Chapter 4, "Fugitive Belongings," explores alchemy as a rebel tactic and disquieting paraontological force in the struggle to bring new modes of living out of the "zone of nonbeing" to which Black life has been relegated, as Frantz Fanon described it.[150] Colson Whitehead's *The Underground Railroad* (2016) and Maryse Condé's *The Wondrous and Tragic Life of Ivan and Ivana* (2017) revolve around the weight and horror of history's inertia, the despairing persistence of whiteness as the marker and exclusionary boundary of the human, a category that continues to give coherence to the nation-state, its rights and property-based legal and commercial systems, and its anti-Black libidinal economy. Yet against an inertia so obdurate as to pass for being, these novels insist on the alchemical force of fugitivity, the insurgent power of an inventive undoing that gives the lie to being's stasis. Centering maroon acts of evasion and sabotage, *The Underground Railroad* and *The Wondrous and Tragic Life of Ivan and Ivana* adamantly reclaim the disorder at the heart of becoming, the fugitivity that sets poesis in motion. In this, they join the other works studied in this book in foregrounding at once the serious constraints of material configurations and their unexpected malleability, the deadening persistence of ontologies of being and the magical liveliness of an alchemy of becoming.

1

Genealogies That Matter

As we saw in the introduction, DNA analysis is an eminently malleable, social practice, and the alchemy of genomics can take contradictory forms. Marshaling genomic evidence can serve to reinforce older notions of race as a biological reality, but it can also work to upend the status quo and enact new modes of living and relating in the wake of social death. This chapter considers the importance of genetic and genomic testing to Afro-diasporic genealogical memory work, as well as the status of DNA among other objects of concern for kin-keeping practices. What does materiality signify and mean to such projects? How, in other words, does matter come to matter as an anchor for kinship's recovery or invention? In the following pages, I turn first to Henry Louis Gates, Jr.'s promotion of genetic genealogy as a tool for community-building in his Public Broadcasting Service (PBS) television series and educational initiatives. I then consider two contemporaneous and similarly motivated endeavors that engage material culture as a force for communal healing: the National Museum of African American History and Culture in Washington, D.C. (inaugurated in 2016) and the Mémorial ACTe museum of slavery and the slave trade in Guadeloupe, France (which opened in 2015). These projects share a commitment to illuminating the mechanisms and impacts on the Black diaspora of what Ruha Benjamin has described as "institutionalized kinlessness,"[1] an entrenched form of violence that strips one of family, community, and identity. All three give significant though varying weight to genealogical research; genealogy is central to Gates's initiatives, while both the NMAAHC and the MACTe include centers for Afro-diasporic genealogical research as one component of their architectural, educational, and community-building designs. At the same time, each puts its faith in a different touchstone—and thereby in differing understandings of agency and reparation—in the effort to counter anti-Black violence and nurture a more "*kinful* existence."[2] What is at stake in these counter-alchemical practices is not simply the ability to shape the present and future contours of a governing episteme but also the right to live and to keep kin. These are political, affective, and ethical struggles over whose lives and families matter, and whose are insubstantial. How, I ask in this chapter, do these varying approaches to genealogy intervene in this struggle and to what consequence?

Reclaiming Roots

One of systemic kin-killing's most devastating features—from slavery's annihilation of kinship ties in the conversion of humans to chattel to the ruinous destruction of Black lives and family ties today through police violence, environmental racism, maternal mortality, and hyperincarceration, among other forces—is its tendency to obliterate the very traces of its own violence. The destruction not only of family bonds but also of their remembrance, as Saidiya Hartman shows in *Lose Your Mother: A Journey Along the Atlantic Slave Route*, was a crucial weapon of subjugation deployed against slaves. "In every slave society," Hartman observes, "slave owners attempted to eradicate the slave's memory, that is, to erase all the evidence of an existence before slavery," for "a slave without a past had no life to avenge. [. . .] The absentminded posed no menace."[3] Though a highly effective strategy of control, such violence, Hartman notes, also requires enormous alchemical force, both physical and symbolic: "More than guns, shackles, and whips were required to obliterate the past. Lordship and bondage required sorcery, too."[4] Among the "herbs, baths, talismans, and incantations" used to induce amnesia in the captives before their journey—and whose memory outlives the names of the enslaved in the "twice-told tales" Hartman hears during her travels in West Africa—was the plant known in Hausa as *manta uwa*, meaning "forget mother":

> *Manta uwa* made you forget your kin, lose sight of your country, and cease to think of freedom. It expunged all memories of a natal land, and it robbed the slave of spiritual protection. Ignorant of her lineage, to whom could the slave appeal? No longer able to recall the shrines or sacred groves or water deities or ancestor spirits or fetishes that could exact revenge on her behalf, she was defenseless. No longer anyone's child, the slave had no choice but to bear the visible marks of servitude and accept a new identity in the household of the owner.[5]

These medicinal rituals performed before the captive's departure launch the destruction of memory that continued in different forms across subsequent generations, as families were continually sundered, and their lives reduced to anonymous or pseudonymous entries in written property records accounting for them as possessions.

Yet the fact that this destruction, devastating as it is, remains incomplete speaks to the resistance put up by the enslaved and their descendants, who were never fully and irreversibly transformed into the "blank and passive automatons" the majority society so desired.[6] And for those who have been repeatedly deprived of their kin past and present, through violent separation, death, and the historical erasure of ancestors' names and origins, tools like genetic testing and genetic genealogy, which have also been embraced by the majority society, hold a significant promise for resistance, reparation, and redress. The excitement they generate reflects first what Nadia Abu El-Haj has described as "the epistemological power of genetic facts," or "the ways in which their very facticity makes certain choices and certain kinds of affiliations available and truthful, and others less so."[7] Genetic analysis provides a form of knowledge privileged today as most reliable—a means of identifying individuals and their biological kin that is produced by a disinterested third party through methods that can be repeated and confirmed by others. But the appeal of DNA also lies in its seeming resistance to historical erasure. This quality stems from its physical durability over time as well as its popular status as a foundational "blueprint" encoding every human's unique individuality in every fragment of the body—a singularity preserved in all the minute traces we leave in our wake and that gives to DNA evidence a powerful aura of incontestability. As Henry Louis Gates, Jr., puts it forcefully, if American slavery was an "alchemical institution that strove mightily to transform human beings into things," its power was neither invincible nor irrevocable, for "our ancestors brought something with them that not even the slave trade could take away: their own distinctive strands of DNA."[8] If the surname stripped from the enslaved served, Gates argues, as the tincture or "Philosopher's Stone" catalyzing this monstrous metamorphosis, DNA now takes its place as a formidable, counteracting elixir of life, a tangible, inalienable magic of renaming that breaks through the historical paper trail's previously impenetrable dead end, transforming effaced ancestors and their estranged descendants into kin.[9] It allows us "to resurrect and preserve our ancestors," who "are not meant to languish in perpetuity in an archive, the all-too-fragile written records of their lives gathering dust and mildew, decaying daily."[10] DNA holds the promise of countering what Orlando Patterson first dubbed "natal alienation," the seemingly permanent condition of ontological uprootedness marking the Black diasporic experience.[11]

Can this recourse to the body serve to refashion the very horizons that produced this uprooting and that continue to constrain the forms of agency and resistance available to the uprooted? In other words, can the flesh itself remedy the ontological reduction of Blackness to flesh? The deployment of DNA as a weapon of recovery raises questions echoing those that

Saidiya Hartman poses of the depiction of the enslaved's suffering body in abolitionist literature: "Does this not reinforce the 'thingly' quality of the captive by reducing the body to evidence in the very effort to establish the humanity of the enslaved? Does it not reproduce the hyperembodiness of the powerless?"[12] By centering the body, rather than the resistant agency of the enslaved and their descendants, genetic ancestry testing takes the ontological ravishment of slavery seriously as its inescapable ground. Slavery effectively did produce thingliness, severely constraining agency not only under captivity but also after abolition, when the "constricted humanity of the enslaved," as Hartman demonstrates, was reshaped into the "abased and encumbered individuality of the emancipated," the liberal, self-possessed subject, site of responsibility and blame, held to be not only solely accountable for his own future success but also already in debt to society for his liberation.[13] In this sense, to seek remedy through genetics is not, then, to opt for the master's tools from among a panoply of choices, but rather to work from within the absence of choice, from within the historically imposed constraints of embodiment in order to contest the ways in which the body has been made to speak—to give, in short, the body a different voice. To call the success of such recourse alchemical is to acknowledge the magic required to transform flesh into narrative, thingliness into subjectivity, against the social and political grain.

To call this effort magical is also, however, to acknowledge its fragility, potential failure, or impossibility. If the recovery of ancestral genealogies and ethnic roots does serve to empower individuals by responding to a passion for being, a hunger for knowledge, grounding, and a life purpose portrayed as unavailable without such an understanding of one's ancestors, its success as a conduit to community-building relies heavily on the specific notions of individuality, autonomy, interdependence, and biological determinism deployed in the analysis and interpretation of its results. The narrative woven around DNA is foremost and most often a narrative of identity and origins—origin as the source of identity and identity as the source of agency, political solidarity, and change. What becomes of relationality and shared projects when the body, the molecule, form their ground?

Henry Louis Gates, Jr.'s efforts to put genomic testing to the service of civic engagement and antiracist struggles serve as a revealing case study bringing these questions into sharper focus. Gates's work in this field has become well known and appreciated in the United States through his long-running PBS series *Finding Your Roots*, which has been on the air since 2012 and draws an audience of close to seventeen million.[14] The show emerged from two earlier series hosted by Gates that centered on genealogy and genetics: *African American Lives* (2008–9)—concentrating specifically on the impact of slavery on African Americans and the exclusion of African American struggles from dominant historical narratives—and *Faces of America* (2010), which shifted focus to a multiracial cast and solidified the format later adopted by *Finding Your Roots*. These series aim to paint a portrait of American diversity that brings the country's citizens together in community while addressing power dynamics and violence in American history. To approach this goal, *Finding Your Roots* uses the particular—the genealogical histories of individual celebrities, two or three of whom are brought together in each episode under a broad theme—as a window onto the general, creating a composite picture of the nation's past and its present identity. As Gates puts it in the book companion to Season 1, "The history that we share makes us who we are and connects us all as Americans, from the big events that shaped history to the smallest details of our ancestors' lives. As Congressman [John] Lewis reminded me of Dr. King's old saying, while our ancestors came to this land in different ships, we're all in the same boat now."[15] Through this format, the show stresses a mosaic model of national belonging—or "gumbo" or "jazz," to use the driving metaphors from Season 1, Episode 1's focus on New Orleans[16]—one in which individuality is preserved, yet the sum of the parts adds up to a coherent whole. The common format used in each episode—beginning with each guest's initial knowledge of their history through family stories, then presenting the "book of life" the research team has prepared as a visual aid and narrative anchor for the family trees, photographs, written records, captivating stories, and DNA test results revealed to them and the audience—reinforces the message that all guests belong within the same national-historical and personal psychological frame, and, moreover, that their interests converge. Such a framework casts Black and Brown histories as relevant and worthwhile to other audiences to the extent that they function as a mirror or solicit audience identification and empathy. Your story is important to me because it illuminates something about myself; my story deserves your attention because it tells you something useful about you. We may live in peace without fear of "losing" ourselves in the exchange.

Commentary offered by Gates and echoed by his guests frequently figures DNA itself in similar terms; humans' genetic similarity (the over 99.9 percent of our genetic code that is identical in all human beings) is invoked as reason to believe in our connectedness and capacity to live well together, while varying haplogroups, along with unique DNA sequences that descendants share with their forebearers, serve as carriers of distinct histories and distinguishing family traits. In this sense, the show reinforces yet also reshapes slightly the ideological ideal of the American melting pot. Admixture is celebrated but no single contribution to American hybridity is ever fully melted down; rather, individual ingredients retain something of their unique character even as they fuse and recombine with others, raising questions about the role of genetics and culture in (over)determining one's present life and future. This preference for an emergent hybridity, rather than a completed national fusion, allows the program to shift emphasis back and forth from human ingenuity and agency—the capacity to transcend one's origins and constraints—to unchanging facticity—that which one cannot change or overcome. Genealogy and genetics are conscripted first to free subjects from forms of domination—racism, sexism—that operate through a reduction of selfhood to the flesh by pointing to histories of ancestors who beat the odds and escaped (or paved the way for their children's escape) from captivity, sexual violence, discrimination, and deadening labor. DNA is also put to the service, however, of recalling to attention the embodiment of those whose social positioning—whose whiteness and masculinity—allows them to forget it, unearthing, for example, unwanted knowledge of slaveholders in the white family tree or demystifying claims to Native American ancestry. The same evidence—genetic kinship—is advanced to support visions of untethered individual possibility and ethical or civic obligations and constraints tying one to others.

How the celebrities at the center of these stories respond to these differing conclusions helps bring into view the consequences of turning to DNA as a touchstone for cultural change. Gates frequently prompts guests to share their thoughts on the relationship between nature and nurture in shaping communal connection and individual action, and offers commentaries that keep the inquiry open and alive. While Season 1 guest Kevin Bacon (commenting on the six degrees of separation social theory with which his name became associated in a famous 1990s game) muses that "it's a beautiful concept, that we are connected; that we all essentially climbed out of the same swab,"[17] others wonder whether specific character traits like ambition or professional interests are shaped by our genes. "I asked Maggie [Gyllenhaal] where she thought the Silbowitz women got their incredible drive," writes Gates. "'I feel like it must have had something to do with their parents,' she answered. 'But I don't know. Maybe it's in their blood.'" Gates echoes her, reflecting, "Perhaps Maggie's middle name, Ruth, wasn't the only thing she inherited from her grandmother, who had died before she was born."[18] As guests try to make sense of the research team's genealogical discoveries and genetic testing results, they often reactivate older interpretive frameworks and terms, invoking blood and bloodlines as material and social channels through which personality traits, athletic or musical ability, or a passion for farming or crafting are passed down either biologically or culturally, through the examples forebearers set with their own lives and actions or through the values and oral family histories relayed from generation to generation. Rooting celebrity success in a tree and narrating history as a story of hardship and overcoming can reinforce dueling conclusions: I/we would not be where we are without the humble and often overlooked ancestors in our past, or exceptional people spring from exceptional stock. In allowing ambiguities regarding the role of genetics in this transmission to persist (i.e., in refusing to answer the question of the extent to which particular traits are influenced or determined by genetics or environmental factors), the show refrains from making claims about genetic causality that have yet to be tested and proven, but it also de-emphasizes explanations of the distinctions between causality and correlation, as well as the assumptions, methods, and current unknowns in genomic science. Playing up the nature-nurture mystery allows speculation and fascination to flourish, providing guests (and viewers) with the opportunity to interpret the findings to their liking.

Given its goal of bringing Americans together through knowledge of the past, the series emphasizes above all the transmission of positive traits and stories of hardships overcome that serve as inspirational examples for the present. Though it flirts at times with the regressive language of biological determinism—and thus risks reaffirming the notion that "blood" is the carrier of distinct sets of ethnic or racial traits, be they phenotypical, cognitive, or moral, lending to the concept the aura of legitimacy genetic science enjoys without bringing greater precision and caution to the audience's understanding of descent—the series firmly embraces genealogy and genetic ancestry tracing as social goods with the power to uncover proof of human and American resilience and to motivate viewers to work toward the goals of the American project: freedom, inclusion, and well-being for all. The show displays a strong commitment to historical education as a lever for progressive social transformation, even as its focus on recovering roots risks countering this move by highlighting continuity over mobility. If *Finding Your Roots* seeks to unearth hidden actors in personal and national pasts, and thereby rewrite historical myths, history still belongs to the victors—no longer the majority elites alone but rather those who have achieved victory in evolutionary terms, that is, those who have produced successful, surviving offspring. Centering historical narratives on genetic relations writes some neglected ancestors back into the story, while excluding other kin: those branches of the family tree that bear no leaves and those whose ties are forged through something other than genes.

How guests and viewers respond to the findings presented depends as much on their personal experiences and social situation as knowers as it does on the findings themselves. Season 1 guest Geoffrey Canada, educator and president of the Harlem Children's Zone, grew up knowing very little of his family history and concludes that knowledge of one's roots nourishes one's capacity to imagine and bring about alternate futures. "I know so many young people who think they're part of the Bloods. That's what they really think, that that's who they really are," Canada explains to Gates. "And if you ask them, 'Well, what else do you belong to?' they couldn't tell you anything, because as far as they know, their life began right here in Harlem, and that's what they know, and these are the connections." Genealogy, he continues, can infuse people with a sense of purpose by grounding their identity in that of a people with a history of accomplishments: "And if you were to go to them and say, "Let me tell you a little bit about your people and what your people have done," it would give them a place to see themselves in a larger context."[19] Reflecting on the meaning of the research presented to her and the role of DNA in shaping the person she is, actor Tina Fey, who was raised in contrast with a strong sense of her family's Greek heritage, comments, "DNA is part of it, certainly," but adds, "The thing I take away from this is that your choices contribute to who you are."[20] Responding to a similar question posed by Gates, humorist and essayist David Sedaris emphasizes personal kinship relations over lines of descent, suggesting as well that chance contingencies shape who we come into contact with in our lives: "It was my family, my immediate family, not even going any farther. [. . .] I would include my parents in that. They created an environment, the perfect environment, the perfect little petri dish for me by having exactly the brothers and sisters that I had. If you had removed one of them, I wouldn't be the person I am now."[21] Finally, some guests reject lineage as a major factor in one's life choices. Commenting on his ancestor Bird Griffin, a slaveholder, Pastor Rick Warren argues, "I am responsible for my decisions. I am not responsible for my parents' decisions. Now responsibility means we are response-able. We are able to respond. [. . .] I have no responsibility for Bird Griffin. But I do have a responsibility as an American to say that enslaving three and a half million people was evil. [. . .] I don't honor blood. I honor character."[22] Exploring the results of genealogical and genetic ancestry research can thus be a deeply moving and reorienting experience or a glimpse of history that leaves little trace on one's sense of identity and present responsibilities.

In a more direct educational context, the potential and limitations of genomic testing as a kind of hook or Trojan horse for non-racist or antiracist historiography come into view even more clearly. One curricular initiative that I would like to examine here for its more complex engagement with scientific methods and its modeling of community is *Finding Your Roots: The Seedlings*, a PBS web series documenting a summer STEM camp for ten to thirteen-year-old students and its companion curriculum package, developed by Henry Louis Gates, Jr., and a multidisciplinary team of researchers. In addition to distribution through PBS, the series is available, along with accompanying pedagogical aids for instructors, on a dedicated website hosted by Penn State (http://www.fyrclassroom.org/). Child participants in the Finding Your Roots Genetics and Genealogy camps submitted DNA samples in advance, then participated on site in training activities with professors, learning principles of evolution, scientific reasoning, and genomic science. After their ethnic ancestry results (as analyzed by 23andMe) were revealed, they then studied population migration and learned to conduct genealogical research, using databases, libraries, and oral history interviews.

In the opening episode of the web series, Gates and fellow team members Dr. Nina Jablonski and Dr. Brandon Ogbunu explain that the project uses students' fascination with themselves—what they are and how they "fit" in the universe—as a way to get them excited about science and history

("Episode 1"). The model of selfhood fostered by the camp and the curriculum available for educators to download in many ways pushes back against the reduction of knowledge to information by stressing active, collaborative inquiry and data interpretation rather than assimilation. Daily worksheets emphasize hypothesis formation, empirical observation, and inductive, data-based reasoning. They also include a reflective, four-part journaling component called "Putting It All Together"—"What was the *best* part of your day? How did you help someone today (including yourself!)? I really wish you/we/I would have. . . . Today I learned . . ."[23]—designed to develop in students the habits of synthesizing their experiences and thinking of themselves as scientists and community members who are self-reliant, collaborative, and attentive to others all at once. Bringing together students from the United States and Canada, the camps also situate this work in a transnational context emphasizing research community and partnership over cohesion through national identity.

The educators use genetics to approach colorism and histories of racial violence in two main ways. The first plank of the program, genetic ethnicity testing, serves as a springboard for conversations about forced migration, slavery, and to some extent, sexual violence under slavery. The second examines skin color as an evolutionary adaptation to varying levels of UV radiation exposure across the globe (exposure to sunlight breaks down folate, a necessary nutrient for successful reproduction, while increasing the production of vitamin D required for calcium absorption; differing local solar conditions led to the selection of differing genes regulating the amounts and types of melanin in various populations' skin). A third activity inviting students to compare genotype and phenotype—genetic composition versus observable traits—also helps nuance an understanding of DNA and its relation to phenotype by showing that, as Dr. Ogbunu puts it, DNA "doesn't tell the whole story."[24]

By using genetic ethnicity as the key unlocking children's curiosity and excitement at the start of the curriculum, the project relies to some extent on the same problematic metaphors that we saw in the introduction: ethnicity as a calculable percentage and a focus on "what" you are that risks emphasizing individual affiliations with the past and eclipsing the questions of who one might or should become, or how one might go about constructing and cultivating kinship relationships well. Throughout the series, the children are asked not only "Who are you?" but also, repeatedly, "What are you?" Because the focus is on the details of descent and its genetics, this can produce results that are counterintuitive to a layperson: for example, the case of fraternal twins who learn that they have each inherited different "amounts" of British and Irish genes due to randomness in the process of DNA transmission from parent to child. In other cases, children's predictions are verified, as with one young woman who had calculated based on family history that she would be 99 percent European and who learns she is 100 percent European ("I knew it, I knew it!" she exclaims in delight at seeing her working hypothesis confirmed).[25] Some children must grapple more directly with a history of slavery than others; one young woman, when asked what she thinks she is, explains that she thinks she'll be 20 percent European, 60 percent Native American, and 20 percent North African because she knows something about Native American and North African cultures and really likes them. The professor gently corrects her by asking again, "But what do you think you *are?*" He then explains how the slave trade caused forced migration from Sub-Saharan Africa to the Americas, and the student revises her hypothesis ("I think I am 60% Sub-Saharan African, 20% Native American, 20% European").[26]

On the one hand, the lesson that we cannot will facticity to be different is valuable for drawing attention both to the roles of power and violence in shaping the being of community and to the need to care for the given. But the burden of learning this history—or of bringing precision to what one already knows, through family stories and personal experiences of racism and colorism—can fall in the classroom primarily on children already socially identified as Black. The web series' use of one-on-one vignettes reinforces the impression that private explorations of past violence are the primary points of entry into the topic (though concerns for the child participants' privacy and their ability to have open, frank conversations together may have led the producers to omit some group discussions or more sensitive content from the final film). An approach that foregrounds class participants' individual genealogical and genetic ancestry stories has the benefits of engaging scientific methods in concrete and appealing ways, countering misconceptions about the biology and significance of skin color, and modeling for students of color in particular the importance of their family histories and experiences, which become valued objects of research in a culture that routinely denigrates or dismisses them. At the same time, an approach that depends on the diversity of a given set of individuals to drive conversations about race and violence has limitations as an antiracist tool in classrooms marked by sharp power differentials, as well as in segregated, predominantly white districts, where testing results may reinforce the false impression that the classroom is a representative microcosm of the nation and that America's origins and identity are more homogenous than they are.

If the investment in the body as the locus of identity and of a crucial but previously inaccessible supplement to the historical record of human descent and migration plays an important role in the impact of these series and educational initiatives on popular conceptions of race and kinship, so too do their portrayals of these diverse interpretations of genealogy and genetic ancestry, and ultimately, their takes on the mechanisms through which familiarity with genealogy is converted into political, antiracist action. Just as they approach DNA as encoding both individual uniqueness and collective identity, *Finding Your Roots* and *Finding Your Roots: The*

Seedlings also conceive of the capacity to act on historical knowledge as at once a matter of personal agency and communal solidarity. In this, and in their funding structure (which includes support from government and private sources, both for-profit and non-profit[27]), they reflect values similar to those that structure numerous public-private partnerships in the United States, particularly the belief that public goods (such as education or health care) are most efficiently produced by private specialists and organizational structures, and that the public itself can best be conceived as a collection of individual actors who deserve and benefit from public goods as individuals. In such a cultural and political environment, the study of genealogy serves as a curious, "Janus-faced" hinge and hook, to take up Alondra Nelson's vivid figure again.[28] While the personal psychological fulfillment and commitment to individual action that studying one's family tree can foster is certainly not incompatible with broader political struggles, the particularization of genealogy does risk rooting political solidarity in identities rather than shared projects, if not depoliticizing racism altogether by framing it as a matter of individual conscience and personal responsibility rather than systemic and institutionalized violence.

Objects of Meaning

Genetic genealogy's enchantment lies in its seeming ability to repair broken family and communal ties, and to restore honor to the dead, by extracting from the body those kernels of unbroken code that eluded slavery's annihilating force and that link descendants and ancestors together in a tangible, indestructible chain stretching across both time and space. It is heavily invested in the material body as a decryptable map to the past, and in the retrieval and dissemination of genealogical knowledge as a catalyst for social change. These genealogical projects emerge from and sustain a passion for the real—a hunger for purpose and direction grounded in "hard" evidence—yet they prove to be unruly generators of meaning, for their transformative energies can be channeled into varying or even opposed ethico-political visions of community and responsibility. The enthusiastic production of ever more precise genetic knowledge prompts not only the question of how best to interpret this information—how to make sense of it, how to arrange our lives and act in light of the evidence at hand—but also, and just as importantly, what other ways of knowing, what other bodies of evidence are neglected, crowded out, or disqualified when genomics, the contemporary incarnation of bloodline, comes to dominate an epistemic horizon, an economy of truth.

Lonnie G. Bunch III, founding director of the Smithsonian's National Museum of African American History and Culture (NMAAHC), foregrounds this question in advancing his vision of the museum's mission in a conversation with Voice of America. "In many ways, we're comfortable as Americans that we're shaped by our genetic DNA, but we forget we're shaped by our historic DNA as well," he states, using a revealing metaphor. "So, I wanted people to understand how issues of race go back hundreds of years, and how if we don't understand that history, we can't address them and make the changes we need."[29] History is like DNA in that it constitutes a foundation structuring the present-day body politic and its ills. Yet while the field of genetics currently holds great social, political, and economic capital, historiography, by comparison, does not; genetics becomes the central referent and "language" into which other ways of knowing are translated and made legible, while historical causality and its complexities begin to slide into oblivion.

The phrase "historic DNA" reflects the gravitational pull of genetics as an explanatory framework, yet it also counteracts this force by transforming DNA into a metaphor and thus multiplying its signifying possibilities. "Historic DNA" inscribes DNA research in a dynamic field of power characterized by a contested struggle for meaning. In short, the idea of "historic DNA" works to historicize our relation to and investment in the materiality of blood and its present-day avatar. And if DNA is popularly conceived as a finite (though extremely long) code to be deciphered methodically in order to unlock its knowledge (genomic scientists' cautions against such a reduction notwithstanding), "historic DNA," Bunch argues, should be seen instead as an ever-growing palimpsest whose interpretation and meaning will always be tied to the needs of the present and the contemporary questions we ask the past to answer. "This museum," as he puts it in a discussion with Anthony Bogues, "is about layering in, building stories of complexities, of trying to change the major narratives. It is curatorially about how to be a change agent."[30] Embracing this vision of curation as a transformative response to social death entails, to a certain extent, letting go of the desire for completion, for a fully achievable decryption, in favor of the frictions and fulfillments of communal debate and open-ended projects for the future. At the same time, the power of material artifacts to testify to history—to impress on viewers a sense of the past's reality and prompt an engaging affective response to it—beckons strongly as an antidote to a range of obstacles in the path of antiracist work, from indifference to the history of race and racism, to the denial of facticity, to outright hostility toward interpretive disagreement and debate, as displayed particularly visibly in recent US state legislative efforts to ban public educators from defining racism as anything but "the product of prejudice" or "American history" itself as "something other than the creation of a new nation based largely on universal principles stated in the Declaration of Independence."[31] As Paul Williams notes,

> the association of the museum with all things historically precious and valuable is one that remains largely stable in the public consciousness.

[. . .] Memorial museums, for their part, are acutely aware of the role of primary artifacts, not only because they give displays a powerful appeal, but also because in many cases they exist as tangible proof in the face of a debate about, and even denial of, what transpired.[32]

For these reasons, the NMAAHC roots visitor experience in collections and positions its other initiatives as branches extending from this center that allow visitors to interact with collections in manifold ways. The museum's architectural design taps into the multiple significations of the underground to associate historical artifacts, and historical time, with rootedness, fertility, and foundations, as well as burial, oppression, and furtive opposition. Museumgoers are encouraged to begin their tour by taking a glass elevator down to the lowest of the three object-rich subterranean galleries. Descending dates pass by on the wall outside as visitors sink to the era of slavery and freedom (1400–1877), while a staff member explains where (and when) they are headed. Visitors then wind their way upwards through the era of segregation and the civil rights movement, before emerging into the light-filled concourses above ground, rising three stories high, to explore community, culture, and vistas of the capital city through the latticework of the museum's bronze corona. Located on one of these upper levels is the Robert Frederick Smith Explore Your Family History Center, which provides access to databases and workshops on conducting genealogical research. Genealogy is presented as one integral pathway into African American history and culture, alongside oral history, interactive digital exhibits, artwork, food traditions (in the museum's Sweet Home Café), and the artifacts that form the museum's base. Spaces set aside for reflection—a Contemplative Court on the underground level that filters natural light through a ring-shaped cascade of water, as well as reflection booths where visitors can record their stories and thoughts on the exhibits—invite visitors to dwell physically in the space, rest their bodies, and mull over what they have seen, encouraging both introspective withdrawal and communal sharing.

In their material persistence, in the way they occupy space and give concrete expression to scale, artifacts can "sing" to museum visitors, as Bunch puts it,[33] more intensely than other modes of expression, holding out a promise similar to that of genetic genealogy in that they "speak" an occluded history, tracing lines between past and present that help anchor the adrift and their efforts to make sense of themselves and their rapport with others. Yet, as Bunch also affirms, "artifacts don't speak by themselves"; they do so from within a web of relations to other objects and interpreters.[34] The influence of an object depends on a kind of social magic, a willingness to give weight and respect to the "stuff of history,"[35] to grant it the force of evidence. Collections draw their power to make worlds and forge kinfulness as much, then, from the practice of collecting—of entering into community with objects and others—as from the artifacts collected. Or more precisely, how communities practice collecting shapes the specific forms that worlding and kinship take and the extent to which the artifact, as a touchstone, comes to support communal and kinful creativity or to congeal into an aura and arrest its inventiveness.

One of the most striking and most often commented displays in the NMAAHC is an artifact that speaks directly to institutionalized deathworlds and kinlessness, the struggle against them, and the role of material objects in this work: the coffin of Emmett Till, the fourteen-year-old child whose mother's insistence on holding an open-casket funeral for her son after he was brutally disfigured, murdered, and thrown into the Tallahatchie River while visiting relatives in Mississippi in 1955 is credited for sparking outrage against white supremacist violence and spurring civil rights activism. The story of how the NMAAHC came to collect the casket similarly encapsulates a number of the tensions marking the museum's emergence as at once a product of Black resistance and a testament to the constriction of Black agency under slavery and in its aftermath. In 2005, fifty years after his murder, Emmett Till's body was exhumed and positively identified as his own through forensic dental and mitochondrial DNA examinations performed under the direction of the Cook County Medical Examiner's Office as part of an investigation opened by the US Department of Justice and Federal Bureau of Investigation (FBI) in order to determine whether new criminal charges could be brought in the case. He was then reburied in a new casket in accordance with Illinois state law; Burr Oak Cemetery was to oversee the storage and repair of the original for use in a future memorial. The casket was discovered four years later, however, discarded and decaying in a shed; funds donated for its refurbishment had been stolen.[36] Till's family then offered to donate the casket to the Smithsonian, which restored it and created a memorial to Till in the NMAAHC.

The casket's odyssey echoes in significant ways that of Emmett's body, which was discarded by murderers intent on disappearing him, only to be found, honored, and reinvested with symbolic meaning by caring family and mourners determined to save him from historical erasure. As the casket's near loss to the elements recalls, while Emmett and his mother have become civil rights icons today, this outcome was not guaranteed by any arc of history. The coffin's precarious state of limbo and disintegration recalls the long odds facing Emmett's family in their battle, first, to keep him safe as a Black child vulnerable to harm, and, second, after his death, to hold his killers to account. The DNA identification of Emmett's remains came about through his family's long fight (alongside supporting activists and organizations such as the NAACP and the Southern Poverty Law Center) to achieve some measure of justice for the child. "The State of Mississippi would not reopen the case unless we could prove that the body buried at the cemetery was Emmett's," explained Till's cousin Simeon Wright,[37] who witnessed his kidnapping and also provided a DNA sample for the

2005 analysis.[38] Mississippi district attorney Joyce Chiles similarly described the collection of such evidence during autopsy as a standard element of the homicide investigations today required for indictment, as contrasted with the 1955 trial and acquittal of Roy Bryant and J. W. Milam, at which "there was no scientific forensic evidence."[39] Though a Laflore County grand jury empaneled to review the evidence in 2007 declined to issue any indictments, the investigation succeeded in achieving what FBI spokesperson Frank Bochte described to *The New York Times* as the Bureau's primary goal: "The first and foremost thing we're trying to do is to put to rest any theories that the body inside there is not Emmett Till. We would like to settle that issue once and for all."[40]

What is most striking about this belated process of identification is that DNA testing does not in fact simply fill a void in knowledge about Emmett Till's death. Rather, it transmutes one form of knowing into another, granting legitimacy to all those who testified in 1955 to Emmett's identity, but whose credibility was questioned during the trial: Emmett's great-uncle, Mose Wright, the first family member to view the body and recognize it as his great-nephew's, Emmett's cousins, who confirmed that the ring found on the body, engraved with Emmett's father's initials, was his, and, most vividly, Emmett's mother, Mamie Bradley (Mamie Till Mobley), who gave detailed testimony in court explaining how she knew the body to be her son's, and who pushed for press coverage and public awareness of the murder by allowing a viewing of her son at his funeral and circulating photos of his beaten corpse to confront Americans with the brutality of anti-Black racism.[41] DNA testing confirms what was already known, but in so doing it stamps what was taken to be circumstantial, unverifiable testimony with the seal of solid fact, shoring up its own truth value and the criteria by which evidence is judged substantiated or not. Though little doubt about Emmett's identity existed at the time of the murder (and even less after Bryant and Milam, once acquitted, sold their confession to *Look* magazine under the protection of double jeopardy laws), defense lawyers strategically focused on creating uncertainty about it, repeatedly questioning the prosecution witnesses' motives and reasoning and introducing witnesses of their own who argued that the body was so badly mutilated that it was unidentifiable and so decomposed that death must have occurred several days before Till's disappearance. "Tell me, Mose," asked Defense Attorney C. Sidney Carlton during his cross-examination of Mr. Wright, "if Emmett Till had not disappeared, would you have identified the body in the boat as Emmett Till?"[42] This remarkable question not only reflects the defense's attempt to question Wright's state of mind or catch him in an inconsistency, but it also tries to recast Wright's very knowledge as a disqualification. What he knows—that Emmett was perceived to have whistled at a white woman or spoken to her disrespectfully; that this put the child at risk of severe beating or lynching; that his great-nephew was abducted from his home at gunpoint before his very eyes; that Bryant and Milam had threatened to kill Mose if he ever told anyone they were at his house that night; that the boy had never returned; that the body pulled from the Tallahatchie River looked like Emmett's and that his own sons had reliably identified the child's ring—is construed in this line of questioning as undermining his ability to "know" who the body truly was. True knowledge, on this reading, is—and in fact must be—abstracted from circumstance. To know that Emmett is missing is already to know too much; in this maddening loop, the identification of the body can only properly proceed independently of the facts that led the sheriff's office to ask Wright to accompany them to the river to identify the body in the first place.

What ways of knowing and feeling does Till's casket, now empty, restored to its original condition and displayed in a secluded room of its own, elicit or foster? Because it indexes so viscerally both absence and presence, death and survival, both the murderous physical and symbolic violence of anti-Blackness and the countervailing resistance to that violence manifested in Black communities' practices of kin-keeping, political protest, and public acts of memory, the casket has come first to exemplify the tensions between agency and constraint that the NMAAHC seeks to present to visitors. As a material object, the casket's very form—that of a box—visually echoes, Radiclani Clytus has argued, that of the museum and the National Mall itself, recalling and signifying on a powerful figure of containment in African American history stretching back to the hold of the slave ship. It is a shape that also evokes the creative forms of resistance practiced by those who have been repeatedly boxed in—a "subversive ingenuity that African Americans were forced to cultivate" and whose modes of expression remained "ironically bound to those delimiting practices that sought to curtail black livelihood."[43] For Bunch, the NMAAHC must engage these ironies and tensions directly in order to accomplish its mission. "There are many people who have said to me that this has to be a place that inspires a new generation and that you inspire more by telling positive stories than by exploring difficult issues. But I would argue that this museum has to give people some sense of 'tension,'" Bunch explains to Anthony Bogues.[44] To embrace tension is first to acknowledge and give space to the horror of stories like Till's, despite the risk, on the one hand of distressing and immobilizing viewers, or, conversely, of playing into the voyeuristic tradition of displaying Black pain for the entertainment and consumption of non-Black people. To embrace tension is also, however, to raise agency and historical causality as questions for the public to contemplate, while grappling with the force of dominant historical narratives—stories of triumph through individual perseverance and heroism as well as through progressive legislative reform and due protection under the law—in and against which visitors inevitably situate their experience of the exhibits. "People will certainly be able to come and get those positive images and those thrilling stories about 'the famous firsts'; but I think those images of a positive nature are only powerful when they're contextualized by the difficulties," Bunch elaborates. "For example, let's think about Madam C.J. Walker [1867–1919]. How does a black woman create that kind of entrepreneurial enterprise at a time when white supremacists are burning down black businesses simply because they think black people shouldn't be in business? It's *that* tension that I want."[45]

The Emmett Till Memorial also highlights the conflicted status of artifacts as at once springboards for interpretive debate, enchantingly "hard" pieces of evidence displayed with the aim of closing gaps and settling questions of fact once and for all, and objects of reverence eliciting particular rituals and affects bound up with their inscrutability. For a museum like the NMAAHC, whose mission is precisely to bring public legitimacy to a history and culture so often degraded or depicted as nonexistent in majority narratives, artifacts take on an important and complex status as persuasive authorities. They are charged not only with evoking and confirming the reality of past events but also, in their survival, with recalling, synecdochally, the absent dead they once touched, while restoring, through their contrasting objecthood, the subject status stripped away from African Americans treated as things. In this they take on a living-dead quality: lively in their obdurate survival and ability to revive memories of the ancestors, to bring the past into the present, inert in their role as instruments of others' agency, be they tools of torture wielded against African Americans or products of their own creative labor.

As Bunch recalls in his memoir detailing the process of bringing the museum into being from nothing but an unfunded congressional mandate, the gravity commonly ascribed to artifacts weighed heavily on design and funding decisions:

> Was the challenge of acquiring and the cost of maintaining collections necessary? Should NMAAHC be driven by technology rather than artifacts? While I believed NMAAHC had to master and use technology in ways I would have never imagined earlier in my career, I thought the acquisition of collections was even more important, especially for a museum that was part of the Smithsonian galaxy. When visitors come to the Smithsonian, they appreciate the technology, but they come to see the Wright Flyer, the Ruby Slippers, the giant dinosaurs, or James Whistler's painting of the Peacock Room. [...] To be credible, I felt that NMAAHC needed to have collections that rivaled the traditional holdings of the Institution.[46]

Moreover, what Bunch has described as the "one axiom that shaped the museum careers of curators of color," which was "the belief in the paucity of objects that illustrate African American history and culture," gave particular urgency to this question of credibility and the desirability and impact of collections in relation to other forms of representation.[47] As Paul Williams has noted, "compared to conventional history museums (dedicated to the stories of, say, an immigrant group, a form of labour, or a region or nation) there is a basic difficulty with the object base of memorial museums: orchestrated violence aims to destroy, and typically does so efficiently. The injured, dispossessed, and expelled are left object-poor."[48] Yet as Williams's language suggests, object poverty is relative rather than absolute, and specific forms of violence—domination, extermination, cultural genocide—produce different kinds of loss. The process of collecting over 35,000 artifacts in the span of ten years demonstrated to Bunch that "the prevailing wisdom" about African American object poverty needed to be revised; "what we discovered," he argues, "was a paucity of effort and creativity rather than a scarcity of collections."[49] Like Till's casket—which came to have particular historical weight not only because it served as a cradle for Emmett's remains but also because of its role in the highly publicized funeral and the glass top that was specially crafted for it to shield the body while allowing viewing—the overwhelming majority of these objects began their public lives as heirlooms or "objects of meaning" for individual families[50] and owe their safeguarding to families' determination, against destructive social forces, to maintain kinship connections and pass down a material heritage intertwined with oral history. That these pieces (and, ultimately, 70 percent of the NMAAHC's collections) came from family homes and their private worlds scattered across the country—and literally from "basements, garages, and attics"[51]—speaks to the creative tactics that kin deploy to maintain their bonds, as well as to the systemic atomization of families and communities that necessitates such moves in the first place.

The NMAAHC's collections strategy, carried out in large part through the traveling Save Our African American Treasures program,[52] foregrounded world-building and kin-keeping by prioritizing community artifact preservation and consciousness-raising over the secondary goal of acquisitions, and by positioning the museum as a neighbor providing services to the community rather than simply extracting donations from them. Inviting families to bring photographs, documents, heirlooms, keepsakes, and other objects related to African American life to a local venue where they could consult with historians and archivists and receive guidance and resources for preserving their materials, the Save Our African American Treasures program aimed to validate the public's sense of personal and historical value, but also to expand that understanding of value and encourage preservation of ephemera that community members might otherwise discard. In so doing, the initiative connected individuals, family members, local community organizations, and Smithsonian staff, forging a public space of dialogue and care in which participants were encouraged to view themselves as active and significant keepers of history. Built on this model, the NMAAHC continues to emphasize the expansion and maintenance of participatory kinship-community networks, a dialogical model of engagement with artifacts and community members, but also a culture of object care and community interaction that borders on sacred ritual.

The importance of the sacred to the NMAAHC is perhaps strongest and most visible in the Emmett Till Memorial, and in museum staff's understanding of the casket as one of the institution's "most sacred objects."[53] To call an artifact sacred is to stake an ontological claim, to performatively reshape the very being of that object, the encounters one has with it, and the ways we interact with one another in its presence. It is not merely to describe a relationship of honor between visitors and artifacts but to bring one about, to perform a social alchemy investing the object with sacred meaning and the public with a sense of responsibility or purpose in relation to it. In a public American institution unaffiliated with any specific religion, the sacred can take on a civil religious sense, and in highlighting Mamie Till Mobley's struggle to wrench meaning from Emmett's murder, to transform his death into a mobilizing event advancing the fight for civil rights, the museum's presentation reinforces the belief that American history is a story of progress achieved through legislative and cultural efforts. The NMAAHC itself came into being (after a century-long struggle) through an act of Congress; its successful fight to be located on the National Mall and its architectural emplotment of African American history as a story of elevation similarly emphasize the importance of uplift through inclusion in the state over more oppositional or antinationalist aims. But the notion of the sacred invoked in the Emmett Till Memorial also encompasses traditions of belief and practice developed alongside civic values—life, liberty, the pursuit of happiness, representation through democratically elected government, justice for all—whose self-evidence is anything but for Black folks to whom these rights have been denied. Visitors to Emmett's memorial encounter a series of frames shaping their experience of the exhibit as one of pilgrimage, enjoining them to move, act, and feel in the space in particular ways. The memorial is located in a secluded room of its own on the concourse devoted to "Defending Freedom, Defining Freedom: The Era of Segregation 1876-1968." An anteroom featuring enlarged photographs of Emmett and his mother in moments of happiness before his death tells Emmett's story through its contemporary coverage in *Jet* magazine (the press outlet that agreed to publish photos of his body) and through the words of Mamie Till Mobley, whose work is also memorialized in this space.[54] The casket room frames the visitor's experience as one of contemplation and remembrance; photography is forbidden, signaling that the casket and other visitors' viewing should remain undisturbed and unreproduced, while a mural of the choir who sang at Emmett's funeral service at Chicago's Roberts Temple Church of God in Christ similarly positions viewers as mourners paying respects. A pew set up before the small casket invites visitors to reflect, grieve, and recuperate, while a staff member's presence both reinforces the solemnity of the memorial and serves as supportive institutional resource for those experiencing distress. This display design stresses the singularity and weightiness of the artifact as a testament to what happened while also turning attention to the authority and practices required to sacralize anew that which has been desecrated: Emmett's life, Emmett's body, and, post-exhumation, Emmett's casket itself, a desecration that touches Emmett's extended family in violating their kin-keeping practices.

The ties between the present memorial and the original church service give Christian overtones to the understanding of the sacred at work in the space, lending to redemptive readings of Till's death as a sacrifice from which some good emerged. Yet by pulling viewers into the performance of ritual honoring, the exhibit also fashions visitors into caring kin, reviving Mamie Till Mobley's practices. In so doing it enacts what Zhaleh Boyd, and Ruha Benjamin after her, has called "ancestral co-presence," or an invocation that aims to "make present the slain and call upon recent ancestors—Tamir Rice, Sandra Bland, Michael Brown, Ayana Jones, and so many others—as spiritual kin who can animate social movements."[55] To call on forebears this way is to participate in an Afro-diasporic tradition that stretches back to resistance figures such as Queen Nanny, Boukman, and Gullah Jack, and that "troubles the line between the biological living and dead by calling forth spiritual practices of ancestral communication."[56] It is also, Benjamin argues, to participate in a tradition of making kin beyond the biological altogether, of forging "fictive" kinships with community members, living and dead, in response to and in defiance of slavery's disruption of blood networks and those ethics of care that center the biological family.

As a memorial the Emmett Till exhibit stands out as unique among the NMAAHC's collections in that it urges visitors not simply to learn about Emmett's murder but to practice commemoration and honor. At the same time, the memorial can be understood as the epitome of the museum as a whole, which many visitors consider to be a site of pilgrimage, as they do the grounds of the Mall, on which it sits. "For African Americans," Lonnie Bunch stresses, "the Mall is sacred ground."[57] It is so, he explains, because it was formerly plantation land worked by the enslaved and because it has long served as a political and cultural gathering place where African Americans have mobilized. It is thus a site that calls for differing responses at the same time: introspective remembrance of the dead and communal protest, the acceptance and practice of honoring the past, and a dialogical contestation over its meaning and the future actions history spurs us to. In such a space, the museum comes to serve at once as a reliquary and a living body, a monument to the absent dead and a presence that calls for active engagement. The sacred heart it contains—Emmett Till's casket—drifts between legibility and inscrutability; it becomes a mobilizer for renewed political action in the footsteps of previous civil rights activists, an index of the unspeakable that points to the irreducible singularity of Emmett himself and the unredeemable horror of his death, and, finally, a cherished, living extension of Emmett's body that calls out for respect and response without enjoining visitors to adopt any one specific course of action. As an entity of its own rooted in the land, its skin of bronze serving as "a visual antidote" to the "historical amnesia" through which African Americans' "dark presence" is repeatedly "overlooked or undervalued," the NMAAHC acts not merely as a container but as an active participant in the landscape, a body pointing to the now invisible ancestors who tread the grounds before.

In this push and pull between unquestioning honor and incitement to communal debate and action, the NMAAHC operates above all an alchemy of disposition. Through the medium of the object and its sacralization, the NMAAHC shapes visitors' availability to community and political action but leaves the content of that action undefined; it beckons visitors to act as kin-keepers—and excludes any form of action that would kill kinship—yet leaves open to interpretation and debate how kinship and care should best be lived.

Rhizomes and Refusals

In a 2007 essay written in response to French president Jacques Chirac's request two years earlier that he spearhead the development of a national center devoted to memorializing slavery, the slave trade, and abolition, Édouard Glissant takes up a diverging position, expressing wariness of filiation as a source of identity or ground for one's life purpose:

> This national Center will be what the descendants of slaves and the descendants of slavery's supporters make of it together. Consequently they will cease to be descendants of anything at all; they will become lucid actors in their present life for the reason, or the common-place, that they are joining the world, our world, together.

> Ce Centre national sera ce que les descendants des esclaves et les descendants des esclavagistes en feront ensemble, ils cessent dès lors d'être des descendants de quoi que ce soit, ils deviennent des acteurs lucides de leur présent, pour la raison, ou le lieu-commun, qu'ils entrent ensemble dans le monde, notre monde.[58]

If such a center achieves its mission—to break the public silence surrounding the history of slavery, to fill this gap in memory that eats away at individuals and their community, and to instantiate a new mode of remembering and relating to one another—it will help free citizens, and the collectivity they form, from bondage to the past, from bondage to fixity itself. Elaborating on the role memory plays in bringing about this ontological transformation from static rootedness to mobile, relational multiplicity—and the consequences of this role for public French debates over the nation's *devoir de mémoire*, or duty to remember—Glissant draws on Frantz Fanon's impassioned conclusion to *Black Skin, White Masks*:

> You don't repair memory like a fuse box. Our duty here is rather a duty to know, to be cognizant, and in the case of slavery, a duty to re-cognize. And it is knowledge alone that will revive memory. But knowledge also prepares the way for the encounter with the other, on a terrain cleared of tangled parahistorical troubles. This is what Frantz Fanon meant when he declared he did not intend to be the slave of slavery. To not blindly put down stakes in the mass suffering of slaves past, even if they are his ancestors. He also wanted to look elsewhere, to other peoples who suffer, to other thinking that shares.

> On ne répare pas la mémoire, comme une boîte à fusibles. Nous avons plutôt là un devoir de connaissance et, dans le cas des esclavages, de re-connaissance : et c'est la connaissance, et elle seule, qui ravivera la mémoire. Mais la connaissance prépare aussi la rencontre avec l'autre, sur un terrain enfin dégagé des embrouilles parahistoriques. C'est ce que Frantz Fanon voulait dire quand il déclarait ne pas entendre être l'esclave de l'esclavage. Ne pas camper à l'aveugle sur la souffrance de la masse des esclaves passés, même si ce sont ses ancêtres. Il veut aussi regarder ailleurs, vers d'autres peuples qui souffrent, vers d'autres pensées qui partagent.[59]

For Fanon, the attachment to ancestors, to biological lineage, is inextricable from the racial identities in which his contemporaries find themselves "locked"—"The white man is locked [*enfermé*] in his whiteness. The black man in his blackness."[60] For Black folks, to conceive of oneself as defined by one's ancestors and of one's life as devoted to reliving their deeds is to mistake essence for existence, to confine oneself to the facticity of Blackness and thereby also to accept to dwell in the "zone of nonbeing" to which Black folks have been consigned.[61] Fanon insists on this point in his concluding declarations, arranged as a poem of "two or three truths":

> I am not a prisoner of History. I must not look for the meaning of my destiny in that direction.

> [. . .] I am a black man, and tons of chains, squalls of lashes, and rivers of spit stream over my shoulders.

> But I have not the right to put down roots. I have not the right to admit the slightest patch of being into my existence. I have not the right to become mired by the determinations of the past.

> I am not a slave to slavery that dehumanized my ancestors.
>
> [...] The misfortune of the man of color is having been enslaved.
>
> The misfortune and inhumanity of the white man are having killed man somewhere.
>
> And still today they are organizing this dehumanization rationally. But I, a man of color, insofar as I have the possibility of existing absolutely, have not the right to confine myself in a world of retroactive reparations.
>
> [...] The black man is not. No more than the white man.
>
> Both have to move away from the inhuman voices of their respective ancestors so that a genuine communication can be born.[62]

The connection between an affiliation with the ancestors and the perpetuation of racial identity (and thus the reason why one must refuse the confinement of lineage, of any form of blood-based kinship) is historically produced, but no less constraining because of that; one turns to ancestry as a resource and guidepost from within a diseased or "morbid" social universe[63] which has reduced lineage to biology, to a color line marking every aspect of life and constricting one's being. The quest to champion the civilization of one's ancestors and avenge their suffering stems from the desire to achieve whiteness, the measure of all things worthy. This is a desire inculcated by a sick society and can only function as a reinscription of whiteness's terms, as a temporary (and delusional) balm for Black alienation, not its cure.

To refuse ancestral identity is not, however, to deny history's relevance or grip on the present, its influence on the material conditions shaping agency and resistance. "We have not yet done away with racism, nor racist forms of anti-racism," notes Glissant;[64] Fanon's assertion of the subject's existential freedom is matched by his insistence that material struggle is essential to accomplishing disalienation in its psychic and economic forms. What concerns both Fanon and Glissant is rather the misidentification of the present with the past, the misperception of identity as static and fixed. If it is a mistake, Glissant stresses, to believe that the descendants of the enslaved have inherited their ancestors' suffering—a pain that cannot truly be known by those who have not lived "the intolerable Gehenna" of slavery—they have nevertheless received from their forebearers a cultural heritage, a mode of being in the world: "we inherit their accomplishments, their patience and their tenacity, the humbleness with which they kept the memory of the Country from Before, and, once they had lost it, the tenacity with which they maintained their new relationship to the new land, ... and we have inherited their works."[65] Those who live in the shadow of the slave plantation have also inherited memory, or rather disruptive gaps in memory that constrain our ability to enter into relation with others as "actors in our present lives," to enact the solidarities Glissant views as crucial to human flourishing:

> We know that, above all else, racists in every country fear and hate mixing and sharing. This, more than anything, is why the memory of slavery is precious. Like the memory of any massacre or genocide, it matters to world equilibrium. Not because memory is indispensable, nor because morality requires it of us, but because *the absence of memory* leaves in each of us an irreparable weakness. And also because every recovered memory is above all a tool for solidarity between peoples.[66]

As Glissant explains this point in his earlier work, *Caribbean Discourse*, the holes in memory created by the violent dislocation of the enslaved and the continued alienation of their descendants in the Americas have persistent traumatic effects, including the inability to grasp and relate actively to one's social and physical environment, which are experienced instead as imposed and unalterable.[67] Moreover, because the history of slavery is a history of creolization—of "mixing and sharing" blood, languages, cultural practices, modes of being—on a global scale, its remembrance pushes back against what Glissant describes in *Mémoires des esclavages* and elsewhere as root identity, *l'identité racine* or *l'identité racine unique*—a conception of identity as springing from a single root, as fixed, hermetically sealed, incapable of being split or shared ("impartageable"), and, more often than not, to be exalted over others' identities.[68] To maintain the memory of slavery is to keep in view, by contrast, the fundamentally rhizomatic or relational character of identity, whose multiplicity and openness to the other, to creolization, should be cultivated rather than repressed in the name of unicity.

In its architecture, its curatorial vision, and its existence itself, the Mémorial ACTe seeks to embody a Glissantian understanding of memory and that fugitive alchemy Fred Moten calls "rhizomatic voluntarity," or an opening up of the self to impromptu, unpredictable multiplicities. "Neither abbreviation nor acronym for its longer nomination," as Renée Gosson points out, the doubled and opaquely capitalized name of the center itself—Mémorial ACTe, Centre caribéen d'expressions et de mémoire de la traite et de l'esclavage (or Memorial ACTe, Caribbean Center for the Expression and Memory of the Slave Trade and Slavery)—"escapes fixity and defies logic" while also strongly foregrounding a conception of memory as produced by and productive of action.[69] Glissant's work is cited in support of the MACTe's mission in promotional materials explaining the center's genesis and goals, and in particular by Victorin Lurel, president of the Conseil Régional de Guadeloupe who, along with the Comité International des Peuples Noirs (CIPN), launched the development of the project in 2005: "Édouard Glissant asserted that 'Forgetting is an offense, and memory, when it is shared, abolishes this offense. Each of us needs the memory of the other. . . . And if we want to share the beauty of the world, if we want manifest solidarity with its suffering, we must learn to remember together.'"[70] Beyond Glissant's work on collective memory, such Glissantian notions as rhizomatic identity, archipelagic thinking (stressing multiplicity and lateral relations over "continental" preoccupations with rootedness, unicity, and vertical hierarchy), and the resistant power of opacity permeate the physical design of the structure itself as well as the selection and juxtaposition of contemporary art and historical artifacts in the permanent exhibit's six archipelagoes. Conceived by a local Guadeloupean firm who took as their guiding concept the English phrase "silver roots on a black box," the MACTe's building is designed to pay respect to the millions who died enslaved (symbolized by the quartz chips shimmering on the surface of the box), to evoke the opacity as well as the generative capacity of the history contained within the black box, and to represent, through the silver latticework reminiscent of the rhizomatic aerial roots of the *figuier maudit*, or bearded fig-tree, the intertwining and tenacious new forms of life that emerged from that history.[71] In the prominent place it gives to artwork and abstraction, alongside artifact displays, the permanent exhibit adheres to Glissant's declaration in *Mémoires des esclavages* that such a center should eschew "realistic reconstruction" which "captures nothing at all" because it "will never come close to the cruelty of the bowels of the slave hold and the recesses of the Plantation."[72] Artists and artworks, he adds, should avoid mimetic styles and should be selected for their "complementarity" and "attunement to one another," not for their isolated individual merit.[73]

This principle of complementarity creates a dynamic tension between elucidation and opacity, in the goal of fostering the critical, participatory dialogue that Glissant identifies as the center's fundamental task and one that is especially important for its youth outreach: "to invent modes of relation and interaction with each visit."[74] More precisely, the center's exhibits, Glissant argues, must not rely solely on "objective," impartial approaches, which remain detached from any investment in the topic or responsibility toward it; rather, these exhibits must engage visitors through "the *risk* of comprehension," which, "if only through the excesses of an overly subjective partiality [...] forces a confrontation with the obscure and the deferred."[75] Many of the MACTe's curatorial choices suggest such an intention. Whips and chains used under slavery are displayed in conjunction with an enormous, interactive multimedia display of the *Code Noir* (or Black Code) of 1685 (a collection of articles asserting King Louis XIV's power in the colonies, declaring slaves to be "meubles," movable property, and setting out regulations for their treatment), as well as with Abdoulaye Konaté's 2011 *Biometric Generation*, an embroidered and appliqué quilt arranging fabric cut-outs in the form of human bodies in horizontal lines next to a figure of the US' Statue of Liberty to prompt reflection on migration, biopower, and confinement in contemporary times. Objects, engravings, and paintings from the era of slavery are recontextualized by works such as Kara Walker's 2012 *The Palmetto Libretto (Sketch for an American Comic Opera with Fort Sumter)*, a pastel and graphite drawing in four parts that reenvisions Currier & Ives-style depictions of the Confederate attack on Fort Sumter by writing slavery's graphic sexual violence into the frame and foregrounding the entanglement of race, sex, power, and fantasy through visual mirroring and role reversal. Discussion of the Haitian Revolution is similarly coupled with Mario Benjamin's 2012 *Toussaint Louverture – Jean-Jacques Dessalines – Le roi Christophe*, an abstract, gestural triptych of portraits that disallow any straightforward appraisal of these leaders' acts.[76]

This approach to slavery and the slave trade raises several questions about the types of knowledge that art, and opacity more specifically, generates, as well as the emancipatory possibilities of refusal, or what we might describe as acts of *marronage* or marooning. One exhibit at the MACTe in which these lines of inquiry converge in a particularly striking way is Thierry Alet's installation *La voleuse d'enfants* (The Thief of Children). Situated in the Center's first archipelago, "The Americas," on an island (a thematic space) dedicated to "Amérindiens et résistance" (Native Americans and Resistance), *La voleuse d'enfants* consists of three side-by-side groups of evenly spaced wood blocks, each painted a single bright, glossy color, arranged in horizontal lines of different lengths against a black wall, creating an outline reminiscent of poetry stanzas on paper. Slight variations in size and wood grain distinguish the rectangular blocks from one another up close; from a distance their three-dimensional quality and individuality recede, bringing out the shape of each whole and creating an impression of pixelated flatness and conformity between the parts, in which the vivid colors stand out as seemingly random or mysteriously ordered choices whose logic begs explanation. Positioned near exhibits dedicated to Indigenous resistance to European conquest and the surviving Arawak, Carib, Nahuatl, and Tupi-Guarani words in use in Guadeloupe and Martinique today, *La voleuse d'enfants* evokes most immediately the physical and cultural genocide of Indigenous peoples in the Americas. Read in the context of the Atlantic slave trade, the piece's title—which is both specific in its evocation of unjust capture and loss, and metaphorically open in its use of the generic term "thief"—evokes the violent seizure of captives in Africa, the struggle over lawful control of one's own body and children, as well as the separation of families, instrumentalization of human reproduction for profit, and theft of childhood more generally under slavery. The title's gendering of the thief in the feminine (*la voleuse*) draws attention to still other metaphorical possibilities while also signaling that the viewer's interpretive freedom is not unlimited. Like its masculine counterpart (*le voleur*), *la voleuse* can only index a referent of the same grammatical gender, be it a woman who steals or an abstract feminine noun personified as a thief: war (*la guerre*), history (*l'histoire*), writing (*l'écriture*), culture (*la culture*), religion (*la religion*), the Church (*l'Église*), colonization (*la colonisation*), or France (*la France*), to take just a few examples. This title thus encourages viewers to relate the piece's abstraction to the historic events at hand, to refrain from unmooring it from this context, while also disallowing, through its feminization (particularly in a highly gendered language like French in which the masculine still commonly passes for universal in the absence of a neuter option) any singular or definitive identification of the thief, or even of the perspective from which an act is defined as theft, given that any attempt by the enslaved to resist—refusing work, fleeing, killing oneself or one's child—became, under the master's law, an attempt to "steal" property and labor power from their legal owner.

The explanatory placard, catalogue description, curricular guides, and artist statements about the piece frame it more precisely as a "color code" devised as an inventive response to the *Code Noir* of 1685, a document remembered most notoriously for defining slaves as objects of property who can neither own anything themselves, enter into contracts, nor participate in court proceedings (but who must nevertheless receive Catholic baptism and religious instruction); for declaring that children will be slave or free following the status of their mother; and for detailing acceptable punishments for various crimes, including beating, whipping, branding, severing the calf, and death (but not "torture," which is explicitly forbidden). Alet's color code functions similarly to Morse code in replacing each letter of the Latin alphabet with a color; it aims to free people identified as Black from the code governing their social existence while also liberating encoding itself from its historical use as a tool of subjugation. "Against black, associated for centuries with slavery, servitude, miserable poverty, laziness, and dark shadows," writes Alet in a draft manifesto,

> color acts in principle as an emancipator, a liberator. The color code thus symbolically transforms all the pejorative perceptions of Black men and women into a more just, joyous proposition, one that is open to the world, full of promises and incredibly rich in meaning. The code, as a societal instrument, is no longer read as a solely repressive principle, but rather as the catalyst for a law that would apply to both oppressor and oppressed, each forced to dialogue with one another on the same level.[77]

Inspired in part by personal experience, in part by the MACTe's commissioning a piece engaging the Carib language, and in part by the artist's long-standing reflections on language and writing, *La voleuse d'enfants* uses this color code to "translate" into a different sensorial language three versions—French, Creole, and Carib—of a specific text: the Catholic prayer Hail Mary.[78] Read in this light, *La voleuse d'enfants* draws connections not only between past slavery and present-day postcolonial patterns of family disruption but also between the natal alienation of Africans, the near-elimination of the

Indigenous Caribbean peoples and their oral languages, and the principles of cultural assimilation—or cultural genocide—enforced during the colonial period following abolition in 1848. Under conquest, Mary, the mother of God in the Catholic tradition, comes to signify all that the subjugated are enjoined to leave behind—kin, ancestral beliefs, ancestral language, and community in the here and now—and all that they are enjoined to embrace: the new, exemplary mother; the adopted language of her worship; monarchs, priests, and masters, her earthly representatives; resignation to suffering and penance for sin in the here and now; the promise of fatherly love and communion with kin after death.

Can stolen kin be restituted? *La voleuse d'enfants* suggests not; the installation refuses to reconstruct the children ripped away, but instead indicts the thief, indexing a loss that remains, the piece proposes, unrecoverable. At the same time, in foregrounding and transmuting the mechanisms of theft, *La voleuse d'enfants* advances a vision of relation, of kinfulness, grounded in the inventive power of translation and the palimpsest. The color code, Alet argues, will at first be experienced as one does a foreign language one is constrained to learn, as a formidable, even traumatizing, presence that one grasps by relating it back to one's first language word-for-word. The wager he makes in this project is that over time, the color code "will become a fully-fledged alphabet in its own right, with a life of its own." Thus, while it springs from the tools it accuses—the Latin alphabet, the French language, and the *Code Noir* legalizing social death—the color code's naturalization "would in itself constitute a form of emancipation from the Latin alphabet," making way for "other modes of communicating" that grasp the sensorial world differently.[79] Alet's color code can be likened to a Promethean appropriation and transmutation of language or the epiphytic flourishing of the *figuier maudit* that grows in and through the substrates that support it—as does the MACTe itself on the grounds of the Darboussier factory—incorporating and transforming these historical strata and their traces.

Entanglements That Matter

In foregrounding the inventiveness of art in a center devoted to the memory of slavery and the slave trade, the Mémorial ACTe, like Alet, rejects understandings of maroon resistance that frame it as a wholesale break from oppressive systems, and instead adopts a vision of *marronage* akin to what Yarimar Bonilla has termed "strategic entanglement," or "a way of crafting and enacting autonomy within a system from which one is unable to fully disentangle."[80] In this, it is not unlike the project of genetic genealogy, which seeks to harness the fiery enchantment of DNA for social transformation, or the National Museum of African American History and Culture, which bends established institutional power and rituals of sacralization to the needs of Black communities. Yet the MACTe locates its touchstone, its alchemical power, in the spark that flies between art and artifact, between silver root and black box, when the visitor enters their midst.

The lure of genetic genealogy, the imperative of historical DNA, and the appeal to and of opacity are all informed by an unmistakable passion, a yearning to attend to and redefine Black being, to remedy its seemingly permanent state of alienation. As we have seen, however, the turn to the real is a double-edged sword; it can enable connections with prior generations in the service of collective healing, but it can also entrap one, as Fanon warns, in a rigid "tower of the past," hardening being into a fixed form.[81] Bringing about disalienation is not simply a matter of choosing the right touchstone—as if one particular form of DNA (biological or historical) or aesthetic arrangement will produce a failsafe magic. Rather, perhaps we need to recall, with Fanon, "that the real *leap* consists of introducing invention into existence."[82] Alchemy's future—its political efficacy—relies on its capacity to enact change from within an existing horizon, to spark newness in the spectator's orientation. Inventive genealogies kindle metamorphosis; they cast community as a matter of making and the act of making what matters to a kinful life.

2

Amnesiac Meditations, or Kinship in the Breach

Historical memory, to recall Édouard Glissant's assertion, is essential to both individual agency and a thriving communal life. Breaches in memory wound the social body, rupturing relationality itself, our capacity to encounter one another and build worlds together. A deep concern to remedy and stave off historical amnesia thus informs many engagements with slavery and its legacy. The inability or unwillingness to confront the horrors of the past stands as an obstacle to social healing and invention, even as efforts to recover history risk immobilizing memory or reinscribing fixed identity categories. Public cultural projects such as memorial museums, as we saw in Chapter 1, offer competing responses to this dilemma in the ways they negotiate the tensions between witnessing and reinvention, recovery and creation.

In this chapter, I consider the fictional staging of amnesia as a figure not only for historical loss but also for the passion for the real: a hunger for a reality unmediated by the social, freed, even if temporarily, from normativity and its strictures. Fictions revolving around amnesia give expression to this yearning for the real, for the blank slate of truth laid bare, and involve the reader, happily or tensely, in the quest to see and live reality in the raw. Stripping their protagonist of their social knowledge—their normative sense of identity, history, and custom—amnesia plots focus attention on the body's kinetic memory, instincts, and needs. These narratives invite readers to interrogate the "essential" or "proper" nature of the self and consider how such selves can and should go about (re)building community and new ways of being in the world.

If amnesia wounds subjectivity, disabling the ego's workings and bearings, it also enables subjects to reorient themselves to themselves and to the world, including their kin. This chapter explores two narratives that ask what it means to dwell in amnesia, to live with and through a form of alienation that not only wounds but also radically refashions one's vantage on a troubling, even carceral, and deathly social order: Patrick Chamoiseau's *L'empreinte à Crusoé* (Crusoe's Print), a 2012 reimagining of Daniel Defoe's famous tale of survival, and Octavia Butler's final, 2005 novel *Fledgling*, a story of symbiotic solidarity that similarly defies the values of sovereignty and mastery underpinning a rapacious libidinal economy.[1]

Alienation and Rebirth

Deprived of a name, family, and interpretive frameworks through which to make sense of the unfamiliar environment into which they have been thrust, Chamoiseau's Robinson Crusoe and Butler's Shori Matthews both live an experience evocative of natal alienation, that condition of ontological uprootedness marking enslaved Africans and their descendants. Chamoiseau's retelling unfolds under the shadow of slavery, a central frame and driver of the plot, and also pushes the isolation of Defoe's hero to a harrowing extreme, as a thought experiment through which to explore the possibilities for resurrecting life from the barest of circumstances. The narrative begins with a July 22, 1659, entry from a ship captain's diary commenting on the ceaselessly surprising wonders of the "new world": the tranquil beauty of a sea of blue algae marks a magical interlude in what is revealed to be a slave transport headed for Saint-Domingue and Brazil. The story then jumps to the lively voice of Chamoiseau's Robinson, who recounts his tale in a single, long sentence. This man is not only stranded on a tropical island but also an amnesiac who remembers nothing of his past; he does not know who he is, where he is, or how he arrived on this shore carrying only a saber and baldric inscribed with the name Robinson Crusoe. Moreover, though he believes himself to be the sole survivor of a ship whose wreck sits just offshore, in actuality this Robinson has been deliberately marooned. As we learn in the final pages, the man calling himself Crusoe is an erudite African hunter named Ogomtemmêli, who had accompanied Captain Robinson Crusoe on several slave-trading voyages before an accident on board causes him to lose his memory and suddenly revolt against this practice. Fearing the impact of his agitation on their trade, Crusoe and his men assault Ogomtemmêli and abandon him to fend for himself, in keeping with their customary means of dealing with unmanageable disruptions to the ship's order such as "captives who were raving mad, contagious, or possessed by demons" (228). Ogomtemmêli thus begins his exile as a dangerous, phobic object cast away from society in an attempt at quarantine. He is the infectious agent, the germ of revolt that threatens to bring down the edifice of slavery, and the deserted island is understood to be a secure containment zone, a cage cut off from contact by miles of water all around. Butler's Shori, for her part, loses her entire memory in an attack motivated by a similar desire to preserve the social status quo and the notions of racial-species superiority that underpin it. Perceiving Shori's family as a threat to all vampires, or "Ina"—a companion species living in mutualistic symbiosis with humans—the Silk clan attempts to kill them all because they have successfully edited Shori's genes; she carries human DNA in her germ line, darkening her skin and allowing her, and any future children she may bear, to tolerate exposure to sunlight. The novel begins just after this murderous violence, of which she is the sole survivor. Awakening alone in a cave, gravely injured, remembering nothing of the past, unable to cognitively process her surroundings or function beyond the most basic instinctual level, Shori must painstakingly recover language and history, seek out allies to help her fend off future attacks, and build new kinship bonds with symbionts in order to survive not only biologically but also psychologically and socially.

Like the enslaved whose communal transmission of ancestral memories has been deeply disrupted, Chamoiseau's Robinson carries in his body a haunting feeling of suffering, an "immense pain" indexing something unbearable in an "undecipherable past" (26). While Shori's amnesia does anesthetize the pain of losing her cherished relatives and deeply bonded symbionts, the theft of her knowledge is also lived, and perceived by other Ina, as a "scar," to use her Ina father's words (72), a numb wound that cannot fully heal. "All of my life had been erased, and I could not bring it back. Each time I was confronted with the reality of this," Shori muses about her inability to remember her human mother, "it was like turning to go into what should have been a familiar, welcoming place and finding absolutely nothing, emptiness, space" (132). The absence of memory and history—of personal recollections and accumulated social wisdom—puts life out of joint. It is a weighty, present stumbling block that preoccupies Robinson and Shori, impairing their attempts to orient themselves and project a future for themselves, to know where or to whom to turn, as Shori's description suggests.

Yet although these texts both give voice to the experience of memory disruption and its harms, they take as their focus amnesia's afterlife—the forced rebirth that amnesia occasions and the question of what shape that new life can and should take. The first person Shori encounters after her accident calls her Renee, or "reborn," as a placeholder for her missing name, explaining, "That's sort of what happened to you. You've been reborn into a new life" (13). Shori herself echoes this thought when she wracks her mind in search of her past. Recalling "the blindness and pain" that consumed her entirely in the cave, she reflects, "I had emerged from it almost like a child being born" (26). The breach in her memory forces a kind of phenomenological epoché in her process of recognizing her world; beyond merely bracketing her assumptions about her environment, amnesia wipes out Shori's previous understanding of biology, physics, and social order, compelling her to build a sense of self and relation to others anew by closely scrutinizing her sensations, perceptions, kinetic memories, and thought processes. Robinson, too, interprets his stranding, and the suspension of familiarity it brings, as a passage toward a new life. When Captain Crusoe returns years later to see what has become of the man he abandoned, the latter gives a vivid description of his own regenesis, his sense that he is giving birth to himself in communion with the island and with this stranger he is now encountering, as if for the first time:

> my lord, I was born again this year of which I knew nothing, at this equinoctial hour on my forgotten island, probably at the very instant when I felt as if I was slipping through two masses of light; one emanating from the glistening of the ocean, and the other formed by the implacable phosphorescence of the beach; and what I was bringing with me as I made my way forward between them was not only my body, my parasol, my animal-skin clothes, my rattly musket, or even this saber bouncing against my leg in its baldric; no; it was a mental and physical splendor encapsulating these twenty years of solitude during which I managed, despite everything, to tame misfortune [. . .] (19)

Narrated as a flashback, from a position of retrospective wisdom, Robinson's tale teasingly invites the reader to participate in a familiar hermeneutics of recovery, in a quest to regain knowledge lost by following leads and piecing together clues—a plot that often culminates in popular literature and film with the sudden restoration of the protagonist's repressed memories, and the confirmation of what readers and viewers suspected all along. Yet Chamoiseau's narrative refuses this move; his Robinson remains amnesiac to the end, focused instead on the "splendor" his meditations have produced, a new disposition toward what and who is to come. For both Robinson and Shori, the rebirth amnesia offers represents above all an opportunity, and an obligation, to cultivate meaningful relations with others. Shori's amnesia disturbs her most sharply when it throws into question her capacity to act ethically toward others, particularly toward the symbionts who give her blood and feed her emotional needs, and whom, in turn, she intensely wants to protect and comfort. Her attempts to restore her memory, and, failing that, to connect with others like her who can instruct her, are sparked by her fear of hurting Wright, the first person she chances across after her accident and with whom she forms an addictive blood bond before she understands what is happening. Though she feels in her body that taking blood from him, and, eventually, from his neighbors, is right—her hunger is satisfied while the humans enjoy the rush of pleasure and healing powers her venom brings them—her ignorance gnaws at her. She fears not only accidentally harming those who feed her but also the unknown implications for their lives. "It bothered me somehow that it had all been so easy," she reflects after discovering her powers to subdue and delight her humans. "[. . .] It felt wrong to me that I was blundering around, knowing almost nothing, yet involving other people in my life. And yet it seemed I had to involve them" (26). Amnesia points up a double bind that she does not know how to navigate, nor even, in her ignorance, how to articulate precisely: she must eat to live, and yet, she is unsure how to eat well, how to involve others in ways that preserve their self-determination.

As it unfolds in these fictions, then, the amnesia plot takes seriously the renewed, post-genomic fascination with the nature-nurture question today, but raises questions about how this question bears on the ways we organize our relations to others, our social and political life. In staging amnesia as a loss of social knowledge requiring the reconstruction of an ethics of relation, these fictions invite us to reconsider the ontological foundations on which relationality rests. What self, if any, remains in the absence of this knowledge? What does it mean to begin with unfamiliarity, to cast the meditative self as a "fish out of water"? Metaphors used to describe amnesia often suggest that it "strips" the subject, or more precisely the brain, down to its essence, revealing a more fundamental substrate, a blank slate, on which a new self can be written into being; similarly, theories (and critiques) of alienation imply a set of basic needs that must be met for human subjects to flourish, an alignment of self and world that must be set right to rectify estrangement. In staging, through the figure of amnesia, a kind of ontological reset, what role, these texts prompt us to ask, does fiction have to play in illuminating these conditions and opening up new ways of being?

Solitude as Opening

L'empreinte à Crusoé is one of hundreds of Robinsonades and rewritings inspired by Daniel Defoe's 1719 novel, *The Life and Strange Surprising Adventures of Robinson Crusoe*. Following on so many earlier engagements with the tale, including Michel Tournier's *Vendredi ou les limbes du Pacifique* and Saint-John Perse's writing on the subject, Chamoiseau himself admits that he struggled to find a path into this rich material that would open it up in new ways.[2] Yet in the very impasse that *Robinson Crusoe* presents lies what Chamoiseau has identified as literature's most important task today: to confront that which is static, fixed, or unyielding until it begins to open up. Beyond advancing our understanding of the world as it currently exists, what Chamoiseau seeks in rewriting *Robinson Crusoe* is to engage, through poetics, with "the unspeakable, the uncertain, [and] the obscure" in such a way as to forge new modes of relationality in the world.[3] In an era in which the "social corsets" communities have constructed to make sense of an unruly world are loosening, an era in which individuation, or the "liberation of the

'I,'" dominates social life, literature, Chamoiseau argues, should abandon the attempt to tame existential disorder, to press it into a tidy narrative arc; instead, literature should embark on an exploration of this chaos and uncertainty, focusing on the indeterminable, the incalculable—the poetic dimension of existence that gives vibrancy to life.[4] Against the "desiccation" of a neoliberal world lived through an economic reductionist lens[5]—the desiccation, that is, of a life reduced, like Robinson Crusoe's is so often taken to be, to quantifiable calculations and the tyranny of basic needs, as well as the isolationism of every-man-for-himself doctrines—*L'empreinte à Crusoé* seeks to re-world Defoe's scenario, to harness the life-affirming, world-remaking force of literature and participate in fashioning a new "ethicopolitical horizon," to use Pheng Cheah's terms.[6]

Within such a horizon, Chamoiseau's counterintuitive interest in individuation as a pathway out of the large-scale human and ecological disasters produced by racial slavery and Western imperial models of sovereignty and individualism becomes clearer. Chamoiseau's amnesiac begins his solitary adventure as an ill subject, one who suffers from an unhealthy form of individuation—*une maladie de l'individuation* (247)— mistaking self-sufficiency for plenitude and the island on which he awakens for a desert, a prison cell that walls him off from the world. His initial response to his terrifying estrangement is to focus intently on rescue and return—pacing the beach obsessively in hopes of spotting a ship that might come to his aid. Feeling himself imprisoned by the hostile forces of sky and water, Robinson then turns to organizing his physical and mental environment to conjure away chaos and ensure his survival. Like Defoe's hero before him, he builds up fortifications, stockpiles supplies, and practices vigilance to protect himself against all eventualities and surprise attacks. The unrecoverable yet painful past that lives on in his body similarly prompts him to fill his memory void with inventions, beginning with the name he adopts as his own, as well as the "armure intérieure" or "internal set of armor" (31) he creates for himself by inventing himself a phantasmatic genealogy, a family tree made concrete through portraits he has sketched of his ancestors, as well as a cosmology complete with gods and demons.

L'empreinte à Crusoé stages a passion for the human, asking its readers: What is proper to the human? What, if anything, distinguishes it from other beings in the world? Is it dominion over the nonhuman? Is it the affirmation of the self's sovereign will? This first section of the book bears the retrospective title "The Idiot," a time in the protagonist's life contrasted with two phases of growth that follow, "The Budding Person" (*La petite personne*) and "The Artist." "Idiot" takes on an ironic cast here; Crusoe is indeed isolated, without memory or a name of his own, without the possibility of speaking with others, of sharing an idiom, yet it is at this stage of his life on the island that he is most deeply marked by traces of a previous symbolic order. In his efforts to immunize himself from harm, to create order in his surroundings by drawing up a Constitution and codes, implementing daily rituals, assigning place names, capturing and domesticating animals for his own use, and declaring himself to be Robinson Crusoe, "sole lord and master, after God, of this island," Chamoiseau's Crusoe seems every bit as much the "good Englishman" as Defoe's hero before him, to use Karl Marx's disparaging terms.[7] Upon discovering a footprint in the sand, Chamoiseau's protagonist fears it belongs to a cannibal native to the tropics, or worse, a cannibal who has landed on the island with a horde of intruders. His amnesia has not made of him a blank slate; rather, he is libidinally committed in this state to a humanist image of self. Crusoe preserves and protects the idea of the human from avatars of the nonhuman—animals and savages: "The life of a man only has meaning when he holds his living to the highest possible requirements: to be neither an animal, nor one of these savages with which the world is infested" (22). Announcing that his task is "to restart civilization" (23), Crusoe displays the reflexes of a categorizer and colonizer suspicious of the "uncivilized" other and ready to eliminate him at the first sign of attack.

From this era of instrumental exploitation, desire for mastery, and heterophobia, this murderous fear of the other, Chamoiseau's protagonist moves on to a period of longing during which he unsuccessfully searches for the owner of the mysterious footprint and slowly rediscovers the island through new eyes, the imagined eyes of this fetishized other whom he now yearns to befriend and honor. In the phase of blossoming personhood, exteriority permeates and takes over the self. The footprint both indexes irreducible alterity, a check on Crusoe's cognitive powers, and inaugurates a new way of life, opening Crusoe up to onto-ethical preoccupations. His realization that only he himself could have created the print intensifies his embrace of estrangement, spurring him into dialogue with the opaque internal alterity he comes to call Sunday (*Dimanche*) along with the natural presences that surround him. His identification with the outside becomes almost absolute: "I was living outside [au dehors]—no doubt as an outsider, even [*en* dehors]—I ate outside, endeavored outside, slept outside, dreamed outside, pissed and defecated outside; I kept clear of hideaways, remaining acutely exposed" (89). No longer preoccupied with immunizing himself against the external world and its dangers, Crusoe now practices an ethics of the outside. *Vivre en dehors* fosters alternative modes of relating and making kin. Crusoe has transcended the prison house of sovereignty, where vigilance against threats of loss and cannibalism rules the day.

Bénédicte Boisseron teases out the implications of this shift by bringing to light the Sartrean paradigm underpinning Chamoiseau's recasting of the self/Other relation: "Chamoiseau's parable carries a strong Sartrean resonance, except that in Chamoiseau, the *pour-autrui*, the specular 'for-the-other,' is not alienating but rather all encompassing. The idea of the Other is not simply about the other human being but rather about the outside of oneself, namely the surrounding environment, the *Umwelt*. The realization of the Other frees the narrator from all enclosures."[8] Chamoiseau's vision of alterity resonates perhaps even more strongly with Emmanuel Levinas's account. For Levinas, "it is not the I who resists the system [...]; it is the Other."[9] It is the face of the Other that is irreducible to any system's economy of sameness. Levinas's emphasis on the Other's radical exteriority (the subtitle of *Totality and Infinity* is "An Essay on Exteriority") reconfigures the ethical scene. Ethics does not lie in the self's agency but emanates from the (human) face of the Other. In line with speculative realists, new materialists, and object-oriented ontologists, Chamoiseau generalizes this insight, extending ethical agency to nonhuman actors who exceed the self's preexisting horizon or totality, jolting the self out of its hermeneutic comfort.[10] Such an ethics of the outside redirects Crusoe's care to the world at large, dissolving the phantasmatic boundaries between himself and the island. His libidinal impulse is no longer to master his environment but to learn to live with the island, to relate to it as a living organism: "I constantly repeated to myself that it was a living organism, not a deserted island; not a hostile prison but a life that had managed to bring itself forth from the soulless lava" (180).

This evolution in Crusoe's way of being in the world thus relies on a recognition that his isolation is not one. He may be the only human in the immediate space, but he lives in relation with animal, vegetable, and mineral others that make demands on him, that surprise him and escape his grasp. In Glissantian fashion, this Crusoe comes to see the island as connected by air and water to the world around, as an integral part of this whole-world rather than an isolable entity cut off from contact, to the extent that when Captain Robinson Crusoe and his crew return to the island, he receives them happily but without surprise or impatience. A certain conception of isolation—an anthropocentric notion that the human is isolable from and isolated by nature, and that impregnable sovereignty is possible and desirable—proves to be a fallacy. Crusoe and the island are no longer ontologically separated, and the imperative to domesticate animality, to order and control what lies outside the self, melts away. We might say that the passion for the human opens to the unsovereign. In this new phase, the phase of the "Artist," Crusoe enters a state of intense lucidity and attentiveness, free of illusions, which he describes as a sort of "brute availability" or "raw openness" (*disponibilité crue*) to whatever may come, to the "infinity of the possible," without constraints of particular expectation but with a readiness to engage, to "sustain an open relationality" (204, 218).

Yet Chamoiseau retains a distinction between isolation and solitude that suggests the latter is not simply an illusion to be dispelled, quipping, "The worst thing about isolation is when it fails to open onto any solitude" (249). Solitude, aloneness, or loneliness—the French *solitude* bears all of these valences—remains an important motor or element of the character's transformation, and it figures prominently in one of the novel's epigraphs, a quotation from Michel Tournier's *Vendredi, ou les limbes du Pacifique*: "And my solitude not only attacks the foundation of things, it digs away at the very foundation of their existence" (*Et ma solitude n'attaque pas que le fondement des choses, elle mine jusqu'au fondement même de leur existence*). Solitude involves confronting and accepting the instability of being or what Chamoiseau describes repeatedly in his workshop notes and interviews about the text as "l'impensable," the unthinkable, which he links to the unpredictable, the unknowable to which we should open ourselves up. This confrontation is solitary in that it involves a form of amnesia, or rather *anamnesis*, more radical than Crusoe's initial memory loss: a willingness to let social strictures fall away, to dig away at their foundation to uncover the instability below—a willingness to live with the sublime terror and excitement of the unthinkable and construct ourselves without the aid of "social corsets" that both constrain and support, those "crutches" that purport to tame the world, to predigest it for us and make it meaningful.[11] Solitude occasions an implosion of ontology, of the attempt to fix being.

Within such a horizon, individuation serves as the basis for solidarity with the other rather than its antagonist. Individuation might best be understood here as a process of becoming singular, un-repeating and un-repeated—an island in an archipelago, both irreducibly singular yet cohabiting with others, in relation to others. This move involves not the total abandonment of prior models—even in his amnesia, Crusoe retains language and habits of thought traceable to various European and African traditions—but rather a kaleidoscopic decontextualization and recombination of these models. Like Derrida, who describes such a self as "a divided, differentiated 'subject,' who cannot be reduced to a conscious, egological intentionality,"[12] a subject whose freedom serves as the condition not for an impenetrable autonomy but instead for relationality with the other,[13] Chamoiseau's Crusoe describes his subjectivity as

> an errant availability densifying every day; nothing was happening, but an adventure was unfolding without my understanding a bit of it; nothing was wrong with my mental life or the health of my mood; no melancholia dimmed my eye; neither order nor disorder; neither ascendancy nor conquest, neither indifference nor attachment: *going forward* openly [*l'aller qui se fait disponible*] was my only presumption; this is what I want to name: a freedom without concessions that no longer confined me to anything at all, but which offered me up to myself and to my surroundings; *an entering-into-relation* [. . .] (214)

Such a relation "brings [him] closer" to everything around him "without clarifying anything"; in other words, he continues, it puts him into intimate contact with the "irremediable opacity with which I had to come to terms," or, literally, the opacity with which he has *to compose* (*composer*), to make do with and also to make—co-create—with.[14]

Crusoe comes to this Glissantian understanding of being and Relation through repeated meditations on opaque fragments of writing by Parmenides and Heraclitus that he has rescued from the wreck offshore, and that he sets into dialogue with one another by haphazardly copying the legible bits of Heraclitus's washed-out text into the margins of the sturdier volume containing quotes from Parmenides. This winking nod to popular contemporary representations of Heraclitus as the philosopher of flux and Parmenides as his opposite, the metaphysician who proposed that Being is one and unchanging, opens a dynamic reflection on impasse and becoming. In his workshop notes, Chamoiseau conveys his penchant for Parmenides's "Whatever is, is," not, as one might expect, for its identification of being and thinking but rather for its "indefinite neutrality": "Being as 'impotent' potency. It's too bad, such a negatively charged term for so much plenitude. I flirted with 'impassive' [*impavide*], but it's not really better. Parmenides's 'is' is still the best: indefinite neutrality" (244). This philosophical idea that "Whatever is, is" takes prominence in the narrative to the extent that it is the first quote from Parmenides that Crusoe cites: "il faut dire et penser: *il y a* être [One should both say and think: being *is*]" (170). This quote is immediately preceded by Heraclitus's "Je me suis cherché moi-même [I searched out myself]" (170). The juxtaposition invites speculation. What is the relationship between an aphorism that evokes an epistemic orientation (engaging in the pursuit of self-knowledge) and a statement that is ontological in nature (attesting to the metaphysical contours of the natural world)? To be sure, other citations from Heraclitus bear witness to ontological concerns, confirming his reputation as a philosopher of becoming, always attentive to the flux of existence, famously captured by the claim that "no man ever steps in the same river twice" (qtd. 181). And yet it is not insignificant that the amnesiac Crusoe would be drawn to Heraclitus's epistemic preoccupations. Flux breeds unpredictability, but flux itself, as a permanent feature of existence, is predictable: "the only thing that is constant is change" (178). Moreover, in Crusoe's narrative, knowledge of self and knowledge of the world are increasingly intertwined with questions concerning the ontological makeup of the island, including its nonhuman beings. Heraclitean becoming contaminates Crusoe. Not unlike Heraclitus, who earned the epithet "The Obscur," Crusoe undergoes an alchemical transformation. In becoming-obscure, the question "Who is Crusoe?" becomes inseparable from the (changing) nature of his Relation.

Expressing what we might call a passion for the pre- or post-colonial—an authentic account of the colonized, liberated from Western domination—Kathleen Gyssels faults Chamoiseau here for not returning his invented protagonist to his African origins. In this compromised rewrite, the reader never hears the Other's voice nor the voices of his kin: "his imagined protagonist and narrator has indeed no memories of the lost motherland, that is the African continent, nor of his tribal ancestry or local culture, but finds solace in Greek philosophers."[15] On this reading, Greek wisdom restricts the frameworks through which Crusoe (and Chamoiseau) can imagine relation, support, and salvation; "this new tale imprints a moral lesson on the reader: the individual must find retreat in his own Self, helped by Heraclitus's and Parmenides's philosophies."[16] Certainly, in any text grappling with the violence of Western epistemological and moral traditions, the role of Greek philosophy in this current, and in today's politics of citation, cannot go uninterrogated. At the same time, Heraclitus and Parmenides do not so much represent for Crusoe the founders of a modern, systematized, Cartesian egology as they do poets of the fragment and thinkers of *physis*—nature—the external world of living things.[17] For these authors, Being cannot be posited as ontological abstraction, as a separate and higher order rising above the merely ontical. To isolate Being from beings, and from becoming, is a murderous enterprise. Like Heraclitus and Glissant, Chamoiseau envisions Being and becoming as deeply entangled, as if each were one side of a Möbius strip. In these authors, Being is never logically opposed to becoming; rather the former poetically fuses with the latter.[18] Thinking Being constantly generates its others (such as beings and nonbeing).[19] *L'empreinte à Crusoé* stages the generative character of this struggle of opposites, which should not be understood as discordant, but rather, following Glissant, as constituting a form of "plastic harmony."[20] On the island, accordingly, Crusoe's senses take on a new priority. Civilization is no longer aligned with intelligibility and cognitive superiority; the sensible undergoes transvaluation.

The poetic conversation between Heraclitus and Parmenides transmutes into a generative poem that prompts first a desire to understand them, to decipher their given meaning, before deciding that they are fully opaque—attesting to their "right to opacity," as Glissant would say[21]—and should be appreciated as such, as musical objects one can worship without grasping. These two movements produce a third, however, a relation to this recomposed book as a harbor of infinite possibilities generated in the encounter between him and these voices, an encounter that leaves no trace on him, but imprints him nonetheless, so to speak, by shaping his openness to solitude, to the absence of pre-given meanings that serves as the condition for encounter itself.

While Crusoe describes "the place of encounter" as "cleared of any form, language, image, or narrative," he cannot fully escape discursivity, as the very text we are reading comes to us as discourse. Rather than achieving a nondiscursive life of fusion with the elements around him, what Crusoe comes to embrace as the artist is his own status as a *mapian*, a term used by the enslaved meaning "a wound that never heals" (220).[22] In this, Chamoiseau's poetics of solitude functions in a way we might describe, with Fred Moten, as paraontological. Paraontology, to recall, names, along with Blackness in Moten's thought, a form of *marronage*, or fugitive againstness, a resistant movement of disruption working alongside or apposite to ontology's form-giving, meaning-making schemas. This marooning alchemy operates on and through the given, preventing it from congealing into fixed form.

What emerges from Crusoe's meditations, then, is a mode of unsettled and unsettling relationality that Moten characterizes as "a rhizomatic voluntarity" or "involuntary consent of the volunteer," a non-sovereign form of freedom admitting unforeseeable multiplicities—in short, he notes, quoting Glissant, a "consent not to be a single being."[23] This alchemical undoing-recreating of the self is experienced as a generative solitude. In this sense, amnesia, in Chamoiseau's text, both illustrates the effects of social death—the dizzying, painful loss of relationality—and figures its remedy. For Glissant, following Deleuze and Guattari, the rhizome, as Alexandre Leupin recalls, is at once an "'antigenealogy'" and "'a network, an alchemy'" that "transforms the lead of the true and the real into poetic and imaginary gold."[24] When "one consents not to be a single being and attempts to be many beings at the same time," when we consent to "lose" ourselves to mutability, accepting multiplicity as an enrichment rather than an impoverishment and loss of sovereign mastery, we experience an anguish or vertigo that cannot be healed but that we can create with. This is a state of openness that Chamoiseau's Crusoe characterizes as full: "I was borne up," he says, "by a plenitude neither beatific nor worrying, but filled with itself, spherical and powerful [. . .] that always accompanied any eruption of beauty for me now; after twenty-five years of this motionless adventure," he continues, describing to Captain Crusoe what he experienced at the sight of his ship, "you and I were coming full circle, bridging the ultimate gap in an immense encounter" (221). Solitude and plenitude are brought together in this closing opening of possibilities.

Amnesiac meditations produce Chamoiseau's Crusoe as a weak sovereignty, a "*sovereign without sovereignty,*" as Derrida defines it.[25] However, this weak sovereignty comes up against the dominant sovereignty of Western civilization, embodied by the original Captain Crusoe, and the final loop in this text ends on a more questioning note, for Ogomtemmêli does not survive the encounter. Invited on board the ship, he once again becomes horrified at the cries of pain coming from the captives in the hold, and is shot dead by Captain Crusoe and his crew. Living as an amnesiac has enabled Ogomtemmêli to overcome another, antecedent disremembering: the naturalization of anti-Blackness brought about through the foundational violence of colonialism and slavery. European nation-states that celebrate their discovery and settlement of "new" worlds do so by obfuscating all traces of their founding violence. As Derrida argues,

All Nation-States are born and found themselves in violence. I believe that truth to be irrecusable. Without even exhibiting atrocious spectacles on this subject, it suffices to underline a law of structure: the moment of foundation, the instituting moment, is anterior to the law or legitimacy which it founds. It is thus *outside the law*, and violent by that very fact. But you know that this abstract truth could be illustrated [. . .] by terrifying documents, and from the history of all States, the oldest and the youngest. Before the modern forms of what is called, in the strict sense, "colonialism," all States [. . .] have their origin in an aggression of the *colonial* type. This foundational violence is not only forgotten. The foundation is made *in order to* hide it; by its essence it tends to organise amnesia, sometimes under the celebration and sublimation of the grand beginnings.[26]

Ogomtemmêli's affective response to seeing his human kin in chains discloses a raw and deeply unsettling exposure to anti-Blackness that his internalization of Western values—which initially enabled him to enjoy the rewards of sovereignty, at least partly—is no longer able to neutralize. Ogomtemmêli now exercises his "right to refuse what has been refused" to his fellows,[27] to reject rewards of inclusion that come at the expense of the enslaved. This refusal does not simply originate from a self-transparent, masterful "I"; rather, Ogomtemmêli's affective doing cancels the possibility of any return to the ship, of any re-inclusion in humanity or normalcy.

The text ends where Defoe's begins, with Robinson Crusoe condemned to live the fate he had imposed on Ogomtemmêli in a kind of karmic twist. Sophie Fuggle rightly observes that "Chamoiseau's Crusoe is a story of what will have been, the future anterior. His version is both a postscript and preface to Defoe's Crusoe."[28] To paraphrase Alexandre Leupin, Chamoiseau returns to the origin of Western civilization to produce the future of (un)sovereignty.[29] What the text asks us to consider, then, is how to enact a break with the logic of the Robinsonade, to dig away at its futurology and colonial enclosures. What would Robinson Crusoe, the paradigmatic figure of modern sovereignty, become if we, and Defoe's hero, were to take his unsovereign predecessor seriously?

Hungers for Blood

If Chamoiseau's Robinson must experience solitary meditation and a gradual opening to new modes of relation in order to unlearn damaging social norms that persist even in his amnesia, Shori's injury, by contrast, points up the vacuousness of a life devoid of memory and severed from social bonds. "I awoke to darkness. I was hungry—starving!—and in pain. There was nothing in my world but hunger and pain, no other people, no other time, no other feelings," Shori says of her first moments of semiconsciousness following an attack that, as she learns later, has left her blind, her body burned, her lungs scorched, and her skull broken (1). She is reduced to the instinctual life of physical sensation and a survival drive that enables her to react to heat, cold, hardness, softness, and excruciating hunger but nothing more. The slow recovery of language serves at first only to heighten her disorientation: "I had to look at these things, let the sight of them remind me what they were called—the hillside, the rock face, the trees—pine?—that grew on the hill [. . .]," she recounts of her experience surveying the landscape outside her cave. "I saw all this, but still, I had no idea where I was or where I should be or how I had come to be there or even why I was there—there was so much that I didn't know" (3). As she heals enough to wander the surrounding woods, she must rely on vague feelings of satisfaction, dissatisfaction, and restlessness, on an intuitive sense of what is "right" and "wrong," to sort through her confusion. Discovering that her hair is missing startles her, as does "a misshapen place" on her skull, which strikes her as "even more wrong" than her baldness (4). Coming upon the charred ruins of a "little village" (her mothers' compound, she learns later), she comments:

> I thought the place must once have provided comfortable homes for several people. That felt right. It felt like something I would want—living together with other people instead of wandering alone. The idea was a little frightening, though. I didn't know any other people. I knew they existed, but thinking about them, wondering about them scared me almost as much as it interested me. (5)

Amnesia throws into question all but the most basic of Shori's needs—eating, sleeping, and avoiding pain. Even her yearning for contact with others—which, she learns later, is not merely a higher-order desire but essential to her survival—hovers in front of her as a question, a source of both longing and fear. Without social encounters, without communication beyond her own thoughts, Shori remains unable to name and understand her needs, to survive as anything other than a bundle of reflexes.

When she does begin interacting with people again, however, it is with fresh eyes and a newly sharpened attentiveness to the reasons people behave and organize their lives as they do. Though she has retained language and recognizes most everyday objects, many terms expressing identity, cultural symbolism, and normative judgments about sexual behavior—such as "vampire" and "crucifix" but also "jailbait," "harem," and "pimp"—have become unfamiliar to her. Shori's confusion and questions work to defamiliarize readers as well, making assumptions about sexuality, race, dis/ability, and identity itself—its qualities and its persistence over time—visible and available for critical scrutiny. These include both human conventions and values dominant in the twenty-first-century United States, where the story is set, as well as Ina practices that come into view as contrasting examples. Human investments in heteronormativity, monogamy, racial distinctions and hierarchies, individual rights, the adversarial legal system, and incarceration as a solution to crime diverge from Ina bisexuality, group mating practices, cross-species interdependency, sex-segregated households, inquisitional justice system, and collective, family-based legal judgments and penalties. Readers are invited to reassess, with Shori, these practices' raisons d'être, their normative force, and their desirability.

In comparison to present human arrangements, the fictional Ina community with whom Shori's ties are first severed and then rebuilt appears in some respects to represent a transhumanist utopia, a possible future in which genetic engineering perfects organisms, improving their physical well-being and their bonds with others, sexual liberation multiplies and enriches ways of being together in the world, and racism disappears, along with the notion of race itself. This vision of ideal community is one in which both interdependence and individual will carry great value and are viewed as mutually strengthening rather than antagonistic forces. Ina mating and living arrangements revolve around interdependent sibling groups and multigenerational support structures, creating, together with the multiple symbiotic relationships each Ina develops, intricate, extended kinship communities practicing mutual aid. Within these communities, Ina-human bonds are particularly cherished and held inviolable. The Ina and their human symbionts become, through the exchange of blood and venom, physiologically and psychologically dependent on one another, to the extent that the death of either one threatens the life of the other. Because symbiosis is a life-altering commitment, the Ina love and protect their human partners fiercely, while Ina ethics require informed consent from the humans they seek to join with. This respect for individual minds also dictates that Ina should allow their human symbionts to live their lives, once bonded, as they wish, pursuing the careers, activities, and relationships with other humans that help them flourish—an ethical principle made more important because Ina venom diminishes agency by rendering the bitten highly suggestible. Once bitten they must obey; if ordered to carry out two contradictory actions, they can die.

The Ina vision of a good life takes the presence of others to be essential, and, notably, stresses the desirability of certain forms of normativity to mitigate interpersonal tensions and ensure freedom. Yet while the contrast between human and Ina worlds most often functions as a critique of modern Euro-American modes of life, it also puts Ina values under scrutiny, for these are neither universally upheld by the community—the antagonism at the center of the novel involves both racist-speciesist violence against Shori's families as well as breaches of both Ina written law and unwritten ethical codes—nor self-evidently perfect in themselves. To accept symbiosis, for the humans involved, is to consent irrevocably to a relation of dependency that might best be described, as Chuck Robinson puts it, as "willing servitude";[30] one human symbiont explains that the arrangement sounded at first to him "more like slavery than symbiosis," but the pull of the venom and its benefits was too powerful an attraction to pass up (204). The text does not, then, simply elevate an imagined Ina social order over a current Western human one; rather, its juxtapositions point to the contingency of social values, which appear in this light then as matters of interpretation and judgment, not matters of fact.

Stretching over the final third of the novel, the Council of Judgement held among Ina families to inquire into the truth of Shori's accusations against the Silk family and adjudicate the conflict serves as a stage on which such interpretive battles play out. Though Shori's allies argue strenuously for the superiority of the Ina's inquisitional justice system over the Anglo-American adversarial courts that appear by comparison to disregard fact-finding in favor of petty gamesmanship, Shori's success in convincing the council members of the Silks' guilt hinges not only on the facts but also on her ability to speak the language of the court, to abide by its customs and respond to the double binds such a requirement entails. Attacked for her human-Ina hybrid status, Shori must prove her humanity has not weakened her ability to hold her temper, respect the law, and reason dispassionately. "You, more than anyone, must show that you can follow our ways," Shori's host advises her. "You must not give the people who have decided to be your enemies any advantage. You must seem more Ina than they" (266). Yet, having lost her entire family—and, during the Council, a symbiont who is murdered to throw her off kilter—Shori must at the same time prove that her humanity has not dulled her senses and emotions, particularly the excruciating, incapacitating grief that Ina in mourning experience. "Your scent, your reactions, your facial expressions, your body language—none of it is right," one of her detractors charges. "You say your symbiont has just died. If that were so, you would be prostrate. You would not be able to sit here telling lies and arguing. True Ina know the pain of losing a symbiont. We are Ina. You are nothing!" (272).

The violence directed at Shori and all those who protect her stems from an impulse to immunize the Ina against racial and species contamination, to preserve Ina-ness as is, in a static and putatively pure form. As Russell Silk implies in his closing statement to the Council, Shori and her families deserved to die for having adulterated essential Ina nature and the qualities inherent to it:

> They [humans] destroy one another by the millions, and it makes no difference to their numbers. They breed and breed and breed, while we live long and breed slowly. Their lives are brief and, without us, riddled

with disease and violence. And yet we need them. [...] We could not live without them.

But we are not them!

[...] Nor should we try to be them. Ever. Not for any reason. Not even to gain the day; the cost is too great. (291–2)

This contempt for humankind, and for an ontologized Blackness, comes out more crudely in the furious insults that escape Russell's mouth after the Silks are found guilty and condemned to dissolution as a family: "Murdering black mongrel bitch... [...] What will she give us all? Fur? Tails?" (300).

In placing race and species difference together at the center of these arguments over how best to live our relationality, the novel blocks the racist conflation of Blackness with species difference while also frustrating a reading of species difference in the text as simply a fictional allegory for racism. It does so, moreover, by foregrounding rather than skirting biology as a key concern and site of struggle in ontological and ethical arguments over kinship and its responsibilities. Shori's enemies regard her not only as a biological threat but as doubly degraded—by her human DNA, which they disdain as a source of immunological dysfunction and violent inclinations, and by her Blackness, which they reject as an oddity and social disability. "You want your sons to mate with this person. You want them to get black, human children from her," a council member states with contemptuous disbelief to Shori's host. "Here in the United States, even most humans will look down on them. When I came to this country, such people were kept as property, as slaves" (272). Against such a view, the novel re-ontologizes skin color as a protective evolutionary trait, portraying melanin not simply as a superficial characteristic but as a desirable pigment to be cultivated for its benefits, while recasting behavioral tendencies as questions of species-level needs and socialization.

The word "questions" is crucial here, for if *Fledgling* does not assume species essentialism to be the driver of behavior, neither does it take species difference and biological necessities to be trivial concerns we could easily dismiss as of secondary importance or even irrelevant to social life. What connections, the novel asks seriously, should be drawn between the biological and the social, the ontological and the ontic? To what extent is the meaning we give to the notion of "living well" circumscribed or determined by our bodies and their essential needs?

Ina elder Joan Braithwaite confronts this question directly in explaining to Shori how deeply symbiosis binds the Ina to their symbionts:

It's extremely difficult for us to kill or injure our bound symbionts. It's hard, very hard, even to want to do such a thing. [...] I think it's an instinct for self-preservation on our part. We need our symbionts more than most of them know. We need not only their blood, but physical contact with them and emotional reassurance from them. Companionship. I've never known even one of us to survive without symbionts. We should be able to do it—survive through casual hunting. But the truth is that only works for short periods. Then we sicken. We either weave ourselves a family of symbionts, or we die. Our bodies need theirs. But human beings who are not bound to us, who are bound to other Ina, or not bound at all . . . they have no protection against us except whatever decency, whatever morality we choose to live up to. (270)

With these few words, Shori reflects with surprise and gratitude, Joan has "just told [her] more about the basics of being Ina than anyone else," and indeed, Joan's concise lesson offers at once a picture of Ina identity—what the Ina are, fundamentally—of the kinship structures that emerge from this essential nature and a suggestion that Ina moral responsibilities arise from instinct but extend beyond biological necessity (270). In her naturalization of the Ina's being-with-symbionts, Joan foregrounds the libidinal dimension of feeding. This nourishment is simultaneously a need and desire, something more than nutritional sustenance but resolutely anchored in the materiality of being Ina. Yet Shori's own extraordinary example—her hybrid status and amnesiac condition—casts each of these propositions in a new light by revealing being as fundamentally a becoming, a becoming open to alternate futurities. If Joan's account clarifies the being of Ina, the Ina as *doer*, Shori's amnesia reorients our attention away from the standardization of Ina-ness and toward her becoming-Ina, toward Ina *doing*.

Shori's very existence as a human-Ina hybrid proves what Milo Silk fears: that Ina nature, like all organic life, is malleable and always evolving, subject both to natural selection and to genetic engineering. Milo's anxious response to instability is to assert control, to attempt to fix Ina being and maintain Ina sovereignty over humans. His anxiety perhaps also stems from the Ina-specific epidemic illness that had threatened the species' existence. Shori learns of this historic event through her surviving relatives, who frame hybridity as a survival strategy in a time of duress: "Everyone took in orphans and tried to weave new families from the remnants of the old. We suffered long periods of an Ina-specific epidemic illness that made it difficult or impossible for our bodies to use the blood or meat that we consumed, so that we ate well and yet starved" (189). This collective trauma arguably conditions Milo's inhospitable horizon of filiation and his fear of genetic degradation. Though the lesson one might take from the epidemic is that creative kinship and recombination save lives, Milo foregrounds instead the presumed singularity and superiority of the Ina, the purity of a stock in danger of dilution: "May we remember always that our strength flows from our uniqueness and our unity. We are Ina! That is what this Council must protect" (232–3). In his attitude toward humans, he displays a mechanical ethics, instinctively protecting his own symbionts but regarding others as disposable tools. Milo cherishes his symbionts because self-preservation requires it but remains uneasy and wary of his own dependence on them. As Joan notes, "he resents his need of them, sees it as a weakness, and yet he loves them. He would stand between his symbionts and any danger" (270). For Milo, symbiosis represents a dangerous exposure to movement and multiplicity; his bonds with others are experienced as a dispersal of a self that must be vigilantly guarded, lest it slip away. The singularity of Ina-ness—embodied in its difference, distinction, or purity—must be defended. The blood of his kin—the basis for "the substance of the community"[31]—is at stake. Accordingly, Milo champions, as Chuck Robinson argues, what Deleuze and Guattari characterize as a majoritarian stance, devoting himself to preserving, through force, the dominance of a static Ina identity revealed to be a phantasmatic, abstract ideal.[32] Non-symbiont humans become in this imperialistic framework instruments through which Ina like Milo seek to reestablish mastery and invulnerability. They occupy the position of a degraded and precarious alterity that must be preserved as such if "Ina-ness" is to retain a semblance of coherence and superiority.

By contrast, Shori continually operates in the novel as an agent of minoritization, or "becoming-minor," a "vital, often virulent, force."[33] She does so first, Robinson observes, through her status as Ina (a minoritizing influence in a human-dominated world) and then more intensively through her genetic hybridity, which further opens up unprecedented modes of living. Finally, throughout the novel she continually resists "conventional filiation," forging bonds with unlikely symbionts and forgoing customary adoption into another family in order to set up her own household "on her own terms."[34] Her care for others extends even to those human symbionts used as tools to attack her family, to those she must bite casually to ensure her survival but to whom she feels responsible by virtue of her position of power. In her continual "movement away from normal,"[35] then, Shori instigates what could be described as an alchemy of abnormality. To Milo's model of the masterful doer behind the deed, Shori opposes a queer doing through which identity coheres temporarily, only to be set in motion again. To Milo's phobia of attachment and the exposure to pain and unsettlement it may bring, Shori opposes a willingness to risk libidinal investment in her new articulations of kinship. This becoming-Ina stresses, as Jasbir Puar would put it, "the impossibility of linearity, permanence, and end points."[36] Each new symbiont Shori takes on reshapes her self and kindles a new need-desire for them in their singularity that is "something beyond hunger," as she explains (37). Each new symbiont increases her vulnerability to loss and grief and strengthens her urge to protect them from harm, yet she becomes more and more resolved to allow them to make decisions for themselves and participate as active partners in constructing a new family.

At first forced by amnesiac ignorance to rely on her humans for knowledge and protection, Shori learns from them to cultivate interdependence as a value. "You need to touch us and know that we're here for you, ready to help you if you need us," says Brook, a symbiont whom Shori takes over from her murdered father, "[. . .] And we need to be touched. It pleases us just as it pleases you. We protect and feed you, and you protect and feed us" (177).

Shori's struggles to navigate the demands of feeding, however, demonstrate how power, far from dissolving here into a symbiotic utopia of symmetry and equality, persists concretely in mutualistic social structures, necessitating an ethics of relation. As Zakiyyah Iman Jackson observes, there is never in Butler's works "an unqualified endorsement of symbiosis, as some feminist posthumanists have claimed"; what Butler's fiction does instead is to stage "a complex meditation on the promise and perils of symbiogenesis, symbiosis, and parasitism under conditions of unequal power."[37] Her alchemical art "*radicalizes and transforms* the aesthetico-affective-cognitive politics of embodied difference rather than attempt to overcome (the movement of) differentiation."[38] Countering the impulse to fetishize, Butler situates and discloses the extent to which "received ideas about species are always a question of power, which as Donna Haraway puts it, 'reek of race and sex.'"[39] For the same reasons, becoming-minor is also not to be fetishized. "For Butler," Robinson argues, "becoming-minor is the sole vector of futurity—for better or for worse—and majoritarian identity begets only stagnation and annihilation." But, he adds, "I use this last term with due deliberation: Butler's becomings-minor can be violent or invasive, but these forms of violence are productive eruptions, propulsions of life into the future, rather than reducing to nil the majoritarian identification that wishes to remain in stasis and eliminate change."[40] What Shori's amnesia ultimately lays bare is the irreducibility of her biochemical needs and the inequities that arise from the material differences inherent to embodied life. These latter cannot be addressed merely by adhering to an ideal of free and informed consent in the abstract. Against an ethics premised on transcendence, on the denial of bodily needs, Butler's novel argues, an ethics of eating well must pass through the body's messy materiality and demands. If Milo reduces ethics to such needs alone, fostering a mechanical model of eating as biological necessity, in which care for the other can blossom only when it aligns with self-preservation, Shori accepts the vulnerabilities and responsibilities of ontological entanglement that Milo seeks to minimize and cover over. Kinship for Shori, more than any other Ina, must be deliberately forged, not just happily found. In both fashioning new symbiotic bonds and in extending care to those who fall outside the family circle—those who are not "hers," in Ina parlance—Shori continually queers, minoritizes, or alchemizes the notion of blood relation and the duties we owe "our own."

Filiation's Futures

If Chamoiseau's Ogomtemmêli comes to adopt an anti-genealogical orientation toward the self and relation, rejecting all preconceived foundational frameworks that would contain the self's inventive unruliness, Shori might better be described as embracing an alter-genealogy, an investment in particular forms of remembrance as generative of worthwhile futures. As she makes clear in *Fledgling*'s final paragraphs, Shori mourns irreparable loss and remains concerned with fighting historical erasure: "I couldn't bring anyone back, not even myself. I could only learn what I could about the Ina, about my families. I would restore what could be restored. The Matthews family could begin again. The Petrescu family could not" (310). While family attachments represent in *L'empreinte à Crusoé* a constraint on individuation, a yearning for foundations that must be forgotten in order to unlock the inexhaustible multitude and resource for relation that is the self, family in *Fledgling* infuses individuation with multiplicity, representing a mode of relation to be cultivated when it enhances mutualism through the admission of new blood or rejected when it fixates on bloodline as a singular and static essence to be preserved and protected from change.

Together, *Fledgling* and *L'empreinte à Crusoé* stage amnesia and history as most inventive when they enter into dialogical relation with one another. If amnesia represents at once a response to shock-experience and a coping strategy, history also allows the self to reorient to the absence of foundations that amnesia instantiates and represents. Speculating about Shori's trauma, Joan suggests, "I wonder if that's part of why your memory is gone, not just because you suffered blows to the head, but because of the emotional blow of the death of all your symbionts, your sisters, and your mothers—everyone. You must have seen it happen. Maybe that's what destroyed the person you were" (267). Traumatic memory cannot be sustained without devastating the self and its ability to relate to others. To directly remember the losses she has lived is to condemn her to a form of traumatic repetition, a memory so vivid that it cannot be lived as memory, only as a continuous, unbearable present. Amnesia removes both the pain of this injury and the secure assumption that her prior self, like Ogomtemmêli's, is both founded on clear origins and foundational for her life projects. This loss of memory opens up the possibility of new and future orientations to the world, creative genealogies, and queer filiations. Yet this reorientation, both novels suggest, depends on a persistent commitment to history, understood both as an ethical obligation to the dead and as a crucial resource for reorientation. Shori looks to history as instructive example rather than determining foundation; Ogomtemmêli tells a history of self that likewise reorients readers to a Robinson so often read as a figure of human nature, as an incarnation of human selfhood in its pure state, as if this Robinson had no history or precedent himself, no debt or obligation to others, and, in particular, no dependence on the non-European. If amnesia interrupts the naturalization of history and descendance, history disrupts the amnesiac lure of unfettered new beginnings, the fantasy of a self-invention that could unfold in isolation, without relation.

3

Future Ancestors

In giving voice to a yearning for being, for knowledge of the real, the essential, as a ground for possible futures, the amnesia plot, as we saw in Chapter 2, can work to radically reshape this desire. Patrick Chamoiseau's and Octavia Butler's texts do so by advancing a vision of being as becoming, a doing never fully unfettered yet open to refashioning. What amnesia reveals in these narratives, then, is not being in some raw, unmediated state, but rather the ways in which being, as becoming, is itself always mediated by its past. The future thus finds its beginning in being but not its origin; the trajectory of becoming gives shape to our fashionings but does not foretell our destiny.

This chapter takes up works that share this vision of futurity's openness but turn to the speculative and the impossible as resources and guides for alchemical invention. Speculative fictions typically foreground the explicitly counterfactual—alternative worlds, pasts, and futures that recognizably depart from our own and draw attention to that fact. As a world-making activity, speculative fiction shapes horizons, but its key mode—speculation—differs markedly from the extrapolative reasoning at work in genomics and the worlding projects that take genetic information as their foundation. "Where extrapolation is grounded in probabilistic reasoning," writes Steven Shaviro, "speculation is rather concerned with *possibilities*, no matter how extreme and improbable they may be."[1] To extrapolate is to follow a trend, that is, to extend the normative logic governing relations between points in a series, staying within its groove. By contrast, "speculation picks up just at the point where extrapolation falters and fails [. . .] speculation seeks to imagine what happens when a trend *exceeds* its potential, and pushes against or beyond its own limits."[2] Speculation's capacity to remake worlds hinges on its very status as invention: "Without the speculative lure of false propositions," suggests Shaviro, following Alfred Whitehead, "we might never be moved to change anything. Speculation attracts us and unsettles us, encouraging us to think and act in ways that we might not have done otherwise. In sum, even though speculation does not lead us to higher truths, it works in a positive manner by taking the form of *fiction*. Its import is aesthetic, rather than epistemological."[3] Philosophical speculation points up the inseparability of the cognitive and the affective, the interdependence of reason, feeling, and imagination. In so doing, it queers a normative sense of futurity (the expectation that the world as we know it today will be the same tomorrow), moving us to recast the world and relationality in a new mold.

How to read the past—how to scan the past for seeds of that which will or could come—remains a central question for both extrapolative and speculative engagements with the real, even as the latter's investment in an alternative future, in a break with the world as it is, might seem to require putting history to rest. What is at stake, rather, is precisely the "how"—how should we read the past's bearing on the present and future? Speculative fiction in particular, because of its very "departures from imitating consensus reality,"[4] serves as a fertile resource in struggles against the inertia of history, one consequence of which is the persistence of race thinking and race-based violence. Fictions that return to the slave plantation itself, like Octavia Butler's *Kindred* or Patrick Chamoiseau's *Old Man Slave*, often do so to explore its function as a crucible operating a kind of alchemy—the conversion of human kin into commodities—whose effects stretch into the present, while many others (Butler's work, again, and Samuel R. Delany's stand out as two well-known examples) envision alternative presents and futures that point up both the racial logics at work in our current world and the ways in which we might structure reality differently. Our present world remains diseased, or morbid, to use Frantz Fanon's term; the "complete lysis" Fanon called for over seventy years ago has yet to be fully accomplished, although social realities have also been altered by centuries of resistance and reimaginations.[5] Fiction has a key role to play in the ongoing work of transforming social relations, for intrinsic to the processes of emancipation or decolonization is the poetic act of reworlding, the act of setting time in motion again. Such processes require a new approach to past, present, and future. "Disalienation," Fanon famously declared, "will be for those Whites and Blacks who have refused to let themselves be locked in the substantialized 'tower of the past'"; for those who suffer in the present, "for many other black men," it "will come from refusing to consider their reality as definitive."[6] This work of poiesis, of creative invention, happens in dialectical relation to our social and material conditions. Poiesis is founded in human existential freedom, a freedom that, as beings-for-others, we can only realize in relation and therefore in language.

To speak of a poetics of disalienation is thus to draw attention to both the creative dimension of worlding and the specific ways in which linguistic and aesthetic form matters to its achievement. What speculative fiction contributes more specifically to this effort is a creative reimagination of the past capable of dwelling in the counterintuitive and exploring the productive frictions between the factual and the counterfactual. Often, speculative fiction shows us, it is through the counterfactual that reality can be apprehended anew and common understandings of the past's bearing on the present upended. Such an approach requires rethinking our understanding of the past but also of historical causality more broadly, as Slavoj Žižek notes:

> According to the standard view, the past is fixed, what happened happened, it cannot be undone, and the future is open, it depends on unpredictable contingencies. What we should propose here is a reversal of this standard view: the past is open to retroactive reinterpretations, while the future is closed, since we live in a determinist universe [. . .]. This does not mean that we cannot change the future; it just means that, in order to change our future, we should first (not "understand" but) change our past, reinterpret it in a way that opens up toward a different future from the one implied by the predominant vision of the past.[7]

Speculative historytelling, in other words, aims not at recovering ("understanding") the past as if it could be grasped within a singular and definitive narrative but rather at unsettling our very understanding of what we take historical interpretation itself to be. The future cannot change without looking anew at the past, without achieving what Édouard Glissant terms a "prophetic vision of the past,"[8] a queer and creative revisioning of history, a denaturalization of the past that expands consciousness and opens up new modes of being.

This chapter examines three works that mine speculation for its prophetic, alchemical potential: Fabienne Kanor's 2006 novel *Humus*, Damon Lindelof's 2019 HBO series *Watchmen* (a sequel to Alan Moore and Dave Gibbons's groundbreaking 1986 comic), and Ryan Coogler's 2018 *Black Panther* (a film adaptation of the Marvel comic). Each of these works stages conflicts over the meaning of lineage and inheritance in the afterlife of slavery. Each also sets its critiques in an uncanny reality, where the familiar returns to the audience in a strange and heightened echo, and the surreal tests the boundaries of futurology and its interpretive vision. In what ways and to what ends, this chapter inquires, do the fantastic, the impossible, and the aspirational shape imagination and affect, meaning and desire? Considering the weight given to genealogy and kinship in these works, I also ask here how such narratives upend and rewrite understandings of the body and birthright in a contemporary landscape shaped by a passion for redemption and the heroic, and proliferating with superhero stories of extraordinary feats but also biological constraint.

Violent Inheritances and Reparative Promise

Like the works discussed in the previous chapters, *Black Panther*, *Watchmen*, and *Humus* all take the afterlife of slavery—the wake of violence rippling through the present, in which "black lives are still imperiled and devalued by a racial calculus and a political arithmetic that were entrenched centuries ago"[9]—as the object of their alchemical transformations. This engagement with slavery is most direct in Fabienne Kanor's *Humus*, which revolves around a historical event, the collective revolt of fourteen Black women who leaped overboard together from the deck of the slave ship *Le Soleil* on March 23, 1774. Though set in an alternate historical timeline, HBO's *Watchmen* also uses its fictional tale of costumed vigilantism to engage a referential reality, white supremacy, and the elusiveness of racial justice in the United States. *Black Panther*, which showcases the cultural, political, and technological brilliance of the people of Wakanda, a fictional African nation, differs markedly from these two pieces in its exuberant tone. Yet while the film's Afrofuturist vision can seem to turn viewers' attention away from the past, it, too, takes the afterlife of slavery, and the possibilities of repair, as central concerns, both in its plot and in its function as a cultural product. Premiering in early 2018, Marvel Studios' *Black Panther* touched a sharp need among its audience, and particularly among Black American viewers, for legitimation, joy, fortification, and visionary imagination. Donald Byrd, for *Crosscut*, praises the film's "awe-inspiring Afrofuturistic vision of a technologically, eco-sensitive advanced civilization." He adds:

> Seeing it, I was filled with emotions. Here was a Black-attributed civilization, a culture unpolluted by chattel slavery and colonialism created using its own natural resources that had been protected from the theft and exploitation of the West. My eyes filled with tears. It was as if some unknown corner of my psyche had been unearthed. Sitting in the darkened theater with my Black extended family, I realized why I had rebelled all those years ago [against the pressure to conform to a world defined by elite, white norms]—I had been unconsciously dreaming of, longing for, Wakanda. In that moment, I felt a kind of nostalgia, a yearning for something that never was, that had never existed. There was a glimpse of what might have been, and I felt sadness.[10]

This mixture of joy and sadness attests to what could have been, to a passion for an Africa untouched by the evils of the Middle Passage and to Afrofuturism's power to spark meaningful cultural and aesthetic responses to anti-Blackness. In the words of Kodwo Eshun, Afrofuturism offers "a program for recovering the histories of counter-futures created in a century hostile to Afrodiasporic projection and as a space within which the critical work of manufacturing tools capable of intervention within the current political dispensation may be undertaken."[11] Steven W. Thrasher writes of the genre in *The Guardian*: "Afrofuturism allows black people to see our lives more fully than the present allows—emotionally, technologically, temporally and politically."[12] With its celebration of Africanity, *Black Panther* functioned for many to reparatively nurture "Black zeal" (*l'enthousiasme noir*), the sustaining and inventive energy that Fanon credited the Négritude movement for awakening in its audience.[13]

The specificity of the historical moment of *Black Panther*'s release, marked in the United States by a rise in racist hate crimes and Trump-emboldened white nationalism, but also by the continued growth of the Black Lives Matter movement and antiracist solidarity actions, also explains the intensity of viewer interest and responses to the film. "In the midst of a regressive cultural and political moment fueled in part by the white-nativist movement," wrote Jamil Smith for *Time* magazine, "the very existence of *Black Panther* feels like resistance. Its themes challenge institutional bias, its characters take unsubtle digs at oppressors, and its narrative includes prismatic perspectives on black life and tradition."[14] This growth in white violence and coming to power of a reactionary presidential administration, Smith observed, helped explain the palpable, "almost kinetic" enthusiasm surrounding the film:

> *Black Panther* parties are being organized, pre- and post-film soirées for fans new and old. A video of young Atlanta students dancing in their classroom once they learned they were going to see the film together went viral in early February. Oscar winner Octavia Spencer announced on her Instagram account that she'll be in Mississippi when *Black Panther* opens and that she plans to buy out a theater "in an underserved community there to ensure that all our brown children can see themselves as a superhero."[15]

Writing for *The New York Times Magazine*, Carvell Wallace also highlighted the importance of the film's timing while situating the excitement of its reparative promise in a longer cultural and political history. "'Black Panther' is a Hollywood movie, and Wakanda is a fictional nation," noted Wallace. "But coming when they do, from a director like Coogler [whose acclaimed debut feature, *Fruitvale Station*, recounted the police killing of Oscar Grant], they must also function as a place for multiple generations of black Americans to store some of our most deeply held aspirations."[16] Recalling *Black Panther*'s predecessors on screen and in print, as well as Black traditions of communal support and public affirmations of love, Wallace reads the film as taking up the baton in a relay of resistance and resilience, one in which Black audience members act not simply as spectators but as co-creators:

> Beyond the question of what the movie will bring to African-Americans sits what might be a more important question: What will black people

bring to "Black Panther"? The film arrives as a corporate product, but we are using it for our own purposes, posting with unbridled ardor about what we're going to wear to the opening night, announcing the depths of the squads we'll be rolling with, declaring that Feb. 16, 2018, will be "the Blackest Day in History."

This is all part of a tradition of unrestrained celebration and joy that we have come to rely on for our spiritual survival. We know that there is no end to the reminders that our lives, our hearts, our personhoods are expendable. Yes, many nonblack people will say differently; they will declare their love for us, they will post Martin Luther King Jr. and Nelson Mandela quotes one or two days a year. But the actions of our country and its collective society, and our experiences within it, speak unquestionably to the opposite. Love for black people isn't just *saying* Oscar Grant should not be dead. Love for black people is Oscar Grant not being dead in the first place.[17]

In this passage, Wallace situates joyous Black responses to the film in the context of life under the unremitting threat of death. The vigilant alertness to a danger one cannot fully predict or avert and the toll such heightened tension takes on the self and on one's relationships to others necessitate countervailing efforts to repair and sustain a sense of oneself as worthy and capable of persisting. Moreover, these survival strategies must also remake social bonds broken not only by violence itself but also by white accusations of paranoia—the denial that Black fears of future anti-Black violence or even mere assertions that such violence has already been done have reasonable grounding. As soon as he describes Black lives as expendable, Wallace can hear the defensive protests and calls to soften the statement that are sure to follow ("Yes, many nonblack people will say differently. . ."). The murder of Oscar Grant, the subject of Coogler's first film, inhabits the viewing experience of *Black Panther* as the opposite and ground for its joy, so to speak. It is the unquestionable—yet continually questioned—evidence of the pathological character of our "morbid universe," a social world built, as Frantz Fanon put it long ago, on "worm-eaten foundations,"[18] in which alienation passes for health and sound suspicion of the social order is passed off as paranoia. As Richard Wright pointedly observed, "I know I am paranoid. But you know, any black man who is not paranoid is in serious shape. He should be in an asylum and kept under cover."[19]

Black Panther's particularly intense appeal can be attributed not only to its celebration of Black strength and dignity in a time of resurging white supremacism but also to its plot, whose central conflict revolves precisely around the wisdom and politics of paranoia as an interpretive stance and orientation toward the future. As Eve Kosofsky Sedgwick explains, following Melanie Klein, paranoia can be understood as a position and mode of reading distinct from the reparative stance with which it is imbricated. These two modes foster different affects, favor distinct hermeneutic procedures, and importantly, produce varying political consequences. While the paranoid stance draws heavily on critical distancing and analytical dismantling, reparative practices involve relating and building up. If paranoia names "a position of terrible alertness to the dangers posed by the hateful and envious part-objects that one defensively projects into, carves out of, and ingests from the world around one," the reparative process mitigates anxiety and involves instead "us[ing] one's own resources to assemble or 'repair' the murderous part-objects into something like a whole—though, [Sedgwick] would emphasize, *not necessarily like any preexisting whole*. Once assembled to one's own specifications, the more satisfying object is available both to be identified with and to offer one nourishment and comfort in turn."[20] Paranoid and reparative readings can both produce truths, but, as Sedgwick puts it memorably in describing the former, each "knows some things well and others poorly."[21] What futures, *Black Panther* asks, can be opened up when the paranoid anticipation that past violence will reproduce itself gives way to the reparative hope for change?

Coogler's film, co-written by Joe Robert Cole, begins in darkness, with the voice of a young boy asking his father for a story: the origin story of Wakanda or, as the child names it, "the story of home." The word of the African father brings the story to life for his American son across time and distance, illuminating the screen with the blue light of vibranium, a strong, precious substance hurtling toward prehistorical equatorial Africa in a meteorite. Figures emerge from dust to illustrate the history of the five tribes who settle on the site and name it Wakanda, and of the Black Panther, a warrior shaman who puts an end to warfare among the tribes after the Panther Goddess Bast leads him to a heart-shaped herb endowing him with "super-human strength, speed, and instincts." Passed from one ruler to another upon victory in ritual combat, the power of the herb and mantle of Black Panther come with the responsibility to maintain the peace and protect the realm from harm by upholding a common vow Wakandans took to "hide in plain sight" from the outside world. While other nations endure chaos and war, Wakanda prospers in secret, using its vibranium to grow into the most technologically advanced country in the world while camouflaging itself as a poor, agrarian society that refuses foreign aid. "And we still hide, Baba?" says the boy at the conclusion of the tale. "Yes," replies his father, to which the child responds, "Why?"

This question, which goes unanswered, encapsulates the driving conflict of the film, which pits the orphaned boy N'Jadaka, son of Prince N'Jobu, now grown into the elite Navy SEAL operative known as Erik Killmonger (Michael B. Jordan), against his cousin T'Challa (Chadwick Boseman), the ruling Black Panther charged with maintaining Wakanda's isolationist tradition. Following his father—a spy sent to the United States who becomes convinced, witnessing African Americans' suffering, that Wakanda must share its resources to help the wretched of the earth—Killmonger successfully challenges T'Challa for the throne, then launches an operation to arm Wakanda's ring of war dogs and begin a worldwide revolutionary uprising. Wakanda's luxurious prosperity, Killmonger points out to the king's court, comes at the moral cost of neglect for others and thus complicity in their oppression. "Y'all sittin' up here comfortable. Must feel good. It's about 2 billion people all over the world that looks like us," he upbraids the court, "but their lives are a lot harder. Wakanda has the tools to liberate 'em all." Killmonger's political victory is short-lived; he is fatally wounded by T'Challa in combat, and his weapons' transport ships are shot down, preserving Wakanda's secrecy. In his final act of resistance, Killmonger refuses T'Challa's offer of medical care, suspecting that he will be healed only to finish his days in prison. "Just bury me in the ocean with my ancestors that jumped from the ships," he demands instead, "'Cause they knew death was better than bondage."

Killmonger is not the only character to question the morality of Wakanda's defensive policies. T'Challa's love interest, Nakia (Lupita Nyong'o), herself a covert operator, similarly argues in favor of revealing Wakanda's power, though what she wants to share is not weapons, but "aid, and access to technology, and refuge to those who need it." Though T'Challa will come to adopt her views by the end of the film, his initial reaction repeats the wisdom of his ancestors: "If the world found out what we truly are, what we possess, we could lose our way of life." This paranoid suspicion of outsiders and their potential to exploit vibranium for nefarious purposes leads Wakanda to erect an elaborate system of self-defense and secrecy-preserving techniques—a high-tech camouflaging dome concealing the country's development; a buffer of farming huts and pastures on the border providing an image of rural poverty to outside journalists; an advanced global network of human spies and surveillance technology; cloaking systems allowing airships to travel the world undetected; hidden, inner-lip tattoos providing a sure and rapid means to distinguish Wakandans from outsiders, and, of course, the Black Panther's impenetrable protective suit—that both alleviates and feeds Wakanda's anxieties while shoring up the narrow definition of selfhood on which their national identity rests. Wakandans are Wakandans by blood, and as the royal head and embodiment of this people, T'Challa is sworn to protect his subjects alone, over and above all others. "It is not our way to be judge, jury and executioner for people who are not our own," T'Challa argues to Killmonger. "I am not king of all people. I am king of Wakanda," he further retorts when Killmonger proposes a much more expansive understanding of Wakanda's responsibilities: "But didn't life start right here on this continent? So ain't all people your people?" T'Challa presents his non-interventionist position in language suggesting respect for others' political self-determination. But Killmonger sees a weakness in this argument, which uses the rhetoric of choice and due process (the right to choose and live by one's own codified laws and not be subjected to arbitrary judgment or force) but thereby obfuscates the exclusionary hereditary lines dividing insiders from outsiders in Wakanda, as well as absence of choice or process for those on the outside, who are denied insider standing and have no means to appeal the injustices done to them.

At the end of the film, T'Challa determines to reveal Wakanda's secrets to the world and provide aid to those in need through peaceful technology and information exchange programs. In championing this journey from isolationist secrecy to transparent philanthropy, *Black Panther* tells on one level a story about overcoming paranoia, about embracing vulnerability and opening oneself up to potential harm for the sake of fostering justice and reducing the pain of others. Significantly, what prompts T'Challa's decision is in part the failure of Wakanda's paranoid hermeneutics to anticipate Killmonger's threat. In Derridean terms, Wakanda is thrown into an autoimmune crisis. Its attempts to immunize itself—its communal sovereignty—against all possible dangers, to wall itself off from the outside world, turn self-destructive. The isolationism intended to protect Wakanda has made it paradoxically more vulnerable to trauma. T'Challa discovers that in sacrificing one of its sons and leaving Erik to fend for himself in America, all to stave off contamination (mixing with the wretched of the world), Wakanda has turned its own self-protective mechanisms against itself, against its people, undermining its identity as Wakanda: a utopia safe for *all* its people, a place where Wakandans can enjoy their community and technological inventions in tranquility.

Though Wakanda's orientation to the world stresses the anticipation of attack and constant attention to dangers lurking below innocuous appearances, this process of "vigilant scanning," as Sedgwick calls paranoid practice, fails for T'Challa to fulfill its "first imperative," namely, "*There must be no bad surprises.*"[22] Overcoming Killmonger and taking back the throne thus represents on the one hand a way for T'Challa to close a broken circle and reestablish containment: restoring Wakanda's sovereignty, safety, and self-enclosure. This "monster of our own making," as he describes his cousin, whose embrace of violence as a tool for liberation disrupts Wakanda's monopoly on the use of force and offends T'Challa's sense of right and wrong, must be eliminated to preserve Wakanda's "way of life." Yet T'Challa's shock at discovering that the father he reveres lied to him about his uncle's disappearance and his cousin Erik's very existence—having in fact abandoned the child in the United States after killing Prince N'Jobu to protect Wakanda's secret—throws his understanding of his duty irremediably into question. N'Jadaka/Erik's dual African and American heritage troubles Wakanda's understanding of national belonging, revealing the porousness of the line separating "our people" from those Wakanda's forefathers would cast out. This "bad surprise" shakes T'Challa's foundations, leaving him vulnerable but thereby able to be touched by his cousin's pain. Autoimmunity—which prevents paranoia from delivering on its hermeneutic promises—engenders a life-changing shift in Wakanda's Black Panther. It discloses the need to rethink the values ascribed to both immunity (a paranoid sovereignty) and autoimmunity (a compromised sovereignty). As Jacques Derrida points out,

> Autoimmunity is not an absolute ill or evil. It enables an exposure to the other, to *what* and to *who* comes—which means that it must remain incalculable. Without autoimmunity, with absolute immunity, nothing would ever happen or arrive; we would no longer wait, await, or expect, no longer expect one another, or expect any event.[23]

Paranoia fails but its failure—allowing Killmonger to penetrate Wakanda's community—proves beneficial rather than purely destructive. If Wakanda's community dreams of absolute immunity, displaying a fear of traumatic disruption and a paranoid disposition toward the external world, T'Challa not only learns the impossibility of absolute immunity but also comes to view it as undesirable. Just as witnessing suffering abroad did for Nakia and for Prince N'Jobu before her, T'Challa's exposure to surprise—the very experience paranoia strives to foreclose—compels him to question his prior refusal to engage in sociopolitical struggles that are putatively not "his own," to abandon suspicious withdrawal and to reach out in love. Breaking with the extrapolative futurology of paranoia, the film holds out the promise of alternate endings for the story of anti-Blackness currently scripting Black bodies into unending violence.

For Carvell Wallace, understanding African Americans' relationship to Africa, or more precisely to an "African dreamscape" sculpted anew by each generation, is key to understanding the impact of *Black Panther*'s hopeful futurism and its particular reparative meaning for Black American audiences. "From Paul Cuffee's attempts in 1811 to repatriate blacks to Sierra Leone and Marcus Garvey's back-to-Africa Black Star shipping line to the Afrocentric movements of the '60s and '70s," writes Wallace, "black people have populated the Africa of our imagination with our most yearning attempts at self-realization."[24] Though these imaginings ("populated by KRS-One, Public Enemy and Poor Righteous Teachers") took a different form of expression for his generation, Africa represented an object less to be discovered than to be assembled, offering nourishment and comfort through the exercise of creative imagining:

> Never mind that most of us had never been to Africa. The point was not verisimilitude or a precise accounting of Africa's reality. It was the envisioning of a free self. Nina Simone once described freedom as the absence of fear, and as with all humans, the attempt of black Americans

to picture a homeland, whether real or mythical, was an attempt to picture a place where there was no fear. This is why it doesn't matter that Wakanda was an idea from a comic book, created by two Jewish artists. No one knows colonization better than the colonized, and black folks wasted no time in recolonizing Wakanda. No genocide or takeover of land was required. Wakanda is ours now. We do with it as we please.[25]

Wakanda embodies the imagined vibrancy of African lives untouched by the European colonizer's political ontology, by the anti-Blackness at the core of Western modernity, "an era in which an entire race appears, people who, prior to any transgressive act or losing a war, stand as socially dead in relation to the rest of the world."[26] This "recolonization" infuses the socially dead with new life; it functions as a form of decolonization of the mind, if the mind is understood not just as a set of interpretive dispositions or cognitive frameworks but also as one with the feeling, sensing body, subject to fear, despair, and loathing as well as ease, joy, and hope. Elaborating on the consequences these differing interpretive positions have for our understanding of the past and our future possibilities, Sedgwick explains that "to read from a reparative position is to surrender the knowing, anxious paranoid determination that no horror, however apparently unthinkable, shall ever come to the reader as new."[27] It is to surrender the need to project the present into the future (which must unfold along anticipated lines if we are to avoid being caught unawares), to retroject current realities into the past in the goal of better preparing for their future perpetuation. Letting go of anticipation involves an often-terrifying exposure to uncertainty. "Because there can be terrible surprises, however, there can also be good ones," Sedgwick continues, noting further that such surrendering opens the past up to new readings on which to build different futures:

> Hope, often a fracturing, even a traumatic thing to experience, is among the energies by which the reparatively positioned reader tries to organize the fragments and part-objects she encounters or creates. Because the reader has room to realize that the future may be different from the present, it is also possible for her to entertain such profoundly painful, profoundly relieving, ethically crucial possibilities as that the past, in turn, could have happened differently from the way it actually did.[28]

To read *Black Panther* reparatively, then, is to read it for sustenance and as a springboard for imaginative thought. Yet the film's ability to represent Black realities also plays an extremely important role for Black American viewers who stress the cultural work that film can do when it presents complex, wide-ranging characters, debates, and interests in a cinematic tradition in which Black experience has often been overdetermined, depicted in one-dimensional terms and linked to violence or historical trauma, when not simply left out of the frame altogether. *Black Panther*'s politics of representation redeems Blackness, rejecting the superhero genre as a white privilege. It recasts Black bodies as dynamic agents of their destinies. As one moviegoer noted, "I'm excited to see people that look like me as superheroes on the big screen. I think there's a lot of narratives around Blackness that have to do with slavery and history, but this is more like Afrofuturism."[29]

That moviegoers value the film for both its mimetic elements and its imaginative leaps, its celebration of joy and its critiques of violence, points to the multiplicity of the "murderous part-objects" to which viewers are relating. Hollywood's representational traditions are one such object, and one frequently cited by the audience, that Coogler's team and majority-Black cast "repair" to provide spectators with more fortifying models of identification and nourishment. In so doing, they also extend a similar tradition of rewriting and renewal present in Marvel Comics' multiple print runs on *Black Panther*, which each reenvision the character, his supporting entourage, and the challenges he faces. But it is also worth dwelling on the ways Africa represents in Coogler's hands not merely an antidote to whiteness but itself a complexly hateful part-object requiring repair before it can provide such nourishment. Africa in this film is at once a rich historical legacy, bursting with inspiration for future possibilities, and the lost homeland to which one cannot return, the patriarch who denies paternity and turns away kin. Indeed, in centering a confrontation between a Wakandan king and an orphaned African American child who identifies more strongly with his enslaved ancestors than with the African royalty responsible for his exile, *Black Panther* stages and invites debate over Black natal alienation in the aftermath of slavery, the part elite Africans played in abetting the Atlantic slave trade, and the consequences of this history for the present-day diaspora.

"The most universal definition of the slave is a stranger," writes Saidiya Hartman in her powerful account of her travels along the slave route in Ghana in search of historical memory. "Torn from kin and community, exiled from one's country, dishonored and violated, the slave defines the position of the outsider."[30] For African Americans estranged from historical memory and unable to feel at home in the hostile land of their birth, the yearning for reconnection and kinship with a Black, pan-African family is sharp, but also, Hartman cautions, an aftereffect of the Atlantic slave trade, which created the color line on which the notion of Blackness and Black solidarity rests:

> Contrary to popular belief, Africans did not sell their brothers and sisters into slavery. They sold strangers: those outside the web of kin and clan relationships, nonmembers of the polity, foreigners and barbarians at the outskirts of their country, and lawbreakers expelled from society. In order to betray your race, you had to first imagine yourself as one. [. . .] It was

not until the sixteenth and seventeenth centuries that the line between the slave and the free separated Africans and Europeans and hardened into a color line.[31]

Consequently, "the vision of an African continental family or sable race standing shoulder to shoulder" sprang from the hearts of "captives, exiles, and orphans"—not from those who remained free behind. "The slave and the ex-slave," Hartman continues, "wanted what had been severed: kin. Those in the diaspora translated the story of race into one of love and betrayal."[32]

This history is condensed in *Black Panther* in the figure of Killmonger,[33] son of royalty via his father and descendant of slaves through, the film insinuates, his absent mother, of whom we see and know nothing, save that she was an American Erik's father fell in love with. The story of this mother is eclipsed by the tale of fathers and sons, of Killmonger's attempt to reconquer the throne to carry out a mission whose contours drift from imperial conquest ("The sun will never set on the Wakandan empire!," he declares) in the name of racial solidarity with those "2 billion people who look like us," as he puts it, to a radical anticolonial uprising of "oppressed people all over the world," from London to New York to Hong Kong, armed to "kill those in power, and their children, and anyone else who takes their side." If the film elicits some sympathy for revolution, it also blocks it at the same time. It does so first, in a positive sense, by foregrounding the will of the collective over the desires of an individual ruler. As Lewis R. Gordon argues, the film draws an important distinction between a politics based on legitimate power and a tyranny drawn from strength:

> Super strength, achieved through a scientific energy source, does not entail power, which is instead achieved through character of leadership, the support of public opinion, and the general will of the people. The narrative thus distinguishes legitimate force from violence. The Black Panthers, except for the one embodiment of a tyrant, use their powers for justice, reparations, or addressing strife. Villainy comes from using instrumental force at the expense of others.[34]

More troublingly, as Racquel Gates observes, the film codes Killmonger in stereotypical terms as "the angry, loud, violent, yellow-gold-wearing Black man who is introduced in every scene with hip hop."[35] Moreover, it paints his ideology in overly broad brushstrokes while also inscribing his fervor in a specific, personal family betrayal which, transmuted into allegory, effectively narrows the history of slavery's aftermath to a tale of paternal sins visited upon the sons.[36] Gates questions the impact of this framing on our understanding of injustice, inquiring what it does to the audience to locate the source of Killmonger's resentment and anger exclusively in personal loss and the psychic trauma of slavery, and *not* in the reality of the cultural and socioeconomic privileges of his Wakandan relatives in comparison to his own life and experience. Is there a way that we could begin to really talk about the tensions between Africans and Black Americans without reducing them to either an absent father or the original sin of slavery?[37]

What Africa, we might ask, does *Black Panther* ultimately offer its viewers for nourishment and comfort? Into what sort of object is Wakanda reparatively fashioned?

T'Challa's vision for Wakanda's future global role, while inspired by a shocking discovery of broken kinship ties, extends Wakanda's care to all the world's peoples. "We must find a way to look after one another," exhorts T'Challa in an address to the United Nations, "as if we were one single tribe." Choosing the United Nations as the venue for announcing Wakanda's new policy stresses the transidentitarian, humanistic principles underpinning T'Challa's determination that Wakanda now serve as a beacon to the world, but also throws into question the film's conception of politics and political change. As Leslie Lee perspicaciously remarks, *Black Panther* is symptomatic of a broader trend in Marvel Comics that showcase Black heroes, where "the task of fighting for a better world is left to the villains, as the crimes of a mad scientist or alien invader ultimately pale in comparison to those of the United States."[38] Though *Black Panther* pushes the audience to imagine a world in which Black people occupy positions of power and, unlike currently dominant nations, live up to the responsibility of ensuring justice for the weak, the film remains invested in referentiality and thus in giving voice to the abjection of Blackness in the referential social order. This curious dynamic results in the fictional Black hero successfully completing the superhuman job so often demanded of people of color in the real world: according to the logic of whiteness, it is the minority other who must bridge the gap, who must anticipate and accommodate white paranoia, defuse imagined dangers, soothe white discomfort, and, of course, renounce any form of critique or resistance that might be construed as violent. For non-Black audiences, T'Challa seems to propose a reassuring vision of oneness, a hand extended in peace and philanthropy, offering change through gifts of resources and community centers focused on education, leaving political structures inside and outside Wakanda intact.

Framing this outreach, and the world's collective responsibilities, in terms of kin-keeping—insisting that Wakanda must serve as an example of how "we, as brothers and sisters on this earth, should treat each other"—allows T'Challa's speech to resonate with multiple audiences for different reasons. The language of kinship, as Hartman argues, became the idiom of racial solidarity for captives and their descendants because this language "both evidenced the wound and attempted to heal it."[39] For the diasporic orphan, the new Wakanda—located in the geographic center of Africa, dazzling on screen with topographies, art forms, visual patterns, and written alphabets commingled from across the continent—offers ancestral recognition and inclusion, the "African continental family" from whom the exile has been severed. *Black Panther* offers such kinship in word even as T'Challa kills his cousin; indeed, the price of kinship for those who remain seems to be the excision of a particular kind of "monstrous" memory of grievance and the renunciation of forms of violence Killmonger views as cleansing. Extending kinship to those who have been denied recognition and to those non-Black neighbors who demand—without reciprocating—brotherly treatment as their due, Wakanda can thus remain both a symbol of a thrilling new social order for the dispossessed, the prodigal father who returns humbly to the abandoned son, and a non-threatening dreamscape for those who enjoy the status quo, whose world would be unsettled if wealth and justice were in fact redistributed in this world.

Because of the reparative energies it does offer, critiquing Wakanda and the future histories it offers can seem like a perilous enterprise. "Beloved texts that create such affective joy in audiences—and Black audiences specifically—certainly engender careful responses," comments Kristen J. Warner in her *Film Quarterly* conversation with Racquel Gates. After first laying out their positive reactions to the film, Warner quips only somewhat jokingly, "Whew. Now that we've established that we are not enemies of joy, I can continue trying to identify the feelings I've had while listening and watching all of the conversations around *Black Panther*."[40] What Gates and Warner parse sensitively in their dialogue is the difficulty in acknowledging the friction or magnetic repulsion that arises between reparative and paranoid modes of reading while at the same time refusing to treat them as mutually destructive opposites. Considering the relationship between them to be dialectical or interdependent—Sedgwick views them as "infusing" one another, as being at times necessary to one another—shifts us away from the logic of temporary suspension, from the notion that joy requires the suspension of critique and critique the suspension of joy. "A truly 'reparative' view of paranoid theory or radical politics," argues George Shulman on this point, "would have to value and sustain ambivalence, a tension between the hermeneutic of suspicion and quest for deep truth that characterizes 'critique,' and a generosity that seeks and welcomes possibility, in the form of unexpected changes, actions, attunements."[41]

Bringing such a perspective to *Black Panther* and its reception leads us to question both the dimensions of the film that first went uncriticized amid the celebration—the seemingly untroubled embrace of the CIA as Wakandan ally; the commercialization and disarming of the Black Power movement in the film's marketing strategies; the treatment of Killmonger as the true villain, rather than imperialism, capitalist exploitation, and anti-Blackness[42];

the celebration of African characters and culture set antagonistically against the negative portrayal of African Americans—but also those relationships to the film too quickly dismissed as uncritical. Black viewers, Gates argues, may, for example, experience the film through the dual lenses of double consciousness, responding to its pleasures with joy while also "deliberately performing a type of fandom to signify the film's prestige and importance as a Black representation on the global stage."[43] These public displays of joy and excitement—on social media, in commentaries, in dressing up for the viewing, and in showing up, in all senses of the term—are understood by moviegoers as functioning under the white gaze and serving as an expression of Black presence, solidarity, and collective political and cultural strength. Viewers may revel in the reversal of the Black sidekick trope which makes of white CIA agent Everett Ross a loyal, puppy-dog partner to the Wakandan regime yet also question the reach of this irony and whether it manages to unsettle viewer allegiances to an organization responsible for the brutal suppression of anticolonial and anticapitalist governments and resistance movements all over the globe.

Yet to read Wakanda from a position of double consciousness is not merely to hold competing views in mind simultaneously—with the friction and sorrow that accompanies life in the veil—but to adopt the type of second sight that Du Bois also calls a gift and that opens out onto possibilities beyond the horizon of the given. Such a stance allows paranoia to inhabit reparation and reparation to inhabit paranoia. A reparatively infused paranoia refuses to lock the Black subject in a Manichean universe of Us versus Them (the temptation of Killmonger and those who view his death as necessary); it is directed inward as well as outward in view of the need to inhabit rather than deny our relationality, our solidarity with the *other* wretched of the earth. Rereading Wakanda reparatively is to counter a paranoia that adopts a dystopian hermeneutic stance, self-assured and vindicated in its pessimism (the certainty, for instance, that the CIA *will* betray T'Challa, Agent Ross's supportive veneer notwithstanding). The paranoid subject splits self and other, reifying friend and foe. This paranoid subject determines with confidence who stands with and against Wakanda (or Blackness in general).

A reparatively infused paranoia dialectizes hope; it confronts the perils of racial hopelessness (yes, the CIA *might very well* betray T'Challa) while resisting the apolitical impulse to despair and retreat. Political inventiveness emerges from within and despite the suffocating horizon of anti-Blackness; its reparative mode of hope effectively breaks with futurology, a totalizing "forecasting of the future from the present trends in society."[44] A paranoid reparation also tempers an Afrofuturistic penchant for unqualified utopia, the risk of reinforcing phantasmatic imagery of wholeness and plenitude—a reified time prior to colonization—in the attempt to think the future otherwise than the present. It admits surprise, good and bad, as well as the necessity of prediction as a survival strategy. Such a stance also works to stave off the equation of repair with the type of purity so dear to paranoia, with its desire for safety and wholeness. In this, it can be likened to a kind of "anti-anti-Utopianism"[45]: skeptical of the search for plenitude but wary of intractable forms of pessimism, committed and life-affirming in an uncertain time of death.

Origins and Reckonings

Both Lindelof's *Watchmen* and Alan Moore and Dave Gibbons's 1986–7 *Watchmen* before it similarly center these questions of determinism, pessimism, and the past's relationship to the future in their creative retellings of history. Moore and Gibbons's tale takes aim at American nationalism and its exceptionalist ideology by transposing the politics of the Reagan era onto a fictional but uncannily familiar world. In this alternate history, a chance nuclear accident has given the United States a Vietnam War-winning weapon in the form of Dr. Manhattan, a godlike superhuman with the power to rearrange atomic particles and to experience all moments in time simultaneously. The presence of this deterrent has not prevented tensions between the Americans and the Soviets from rising, however, and when the story opens in 1985, with fifth-term president Richard Nixon at the helm, the two nations are on the brink of nuclear war. It is against this backdrop of a ticking doomsday clock that the history of the Minutemen, a group of once fêted and now outlawed masked vigilantes, is related in flashbacks, assorted documents, and the present-day interactions of the retired "heroes." *Watchmen* is replete with self-reflexive *mises en abyme* and intertextual references to 1930s and 1940s comics that work to critique a patriarchal and often xenophobic war-time patriotism idealized in superhero narratives. Through these techniques, Piatti-Farnell has argued convincingly, *Watchmen* "unveils the very understanding of history as a potentially subjective, disjointed narrative."[46] Thus, while deeply invested in a demystifying realism that can appear fatalist in its grimness, Moore and Gibbons's *Watchmen* cautions against any passion for the real that would eschew interpretive uncertainty and reduce reality to a single determinate (and determining) core or key.

The HBO series, authored by a cross-racial team of writers and foregrounding Black characters,[47] can be described as both a sequel to the original comic book and an adaptation, in that it picks up Moore and Gibbons's story of America's masked crusaders thirty years later and extends its plot, while also redeploying many elements of the original's narrative structure in order to focus its critical lens on a different sociopolitical issue: white supremacy and the elusiveness of justice in the racist United States. In highlighting the centrality of racial violence to America's founding and national narratives through an "expanded writing of a history across temporalities and locations (galactic or otherwise)," argues Michael Boyce Gillespie, following Aimee Bahng, *Watchmen* makes brilliant use of the resources of speculative fiction, "'a genre of inventing other possibilities'" that "often concentrates on measuring the conditions of the present through an excavation of the remains of yesterday and tomorrow."[48] As Emily Nussbaum similarly notes, the show "reorders the fictional universe, writing buried racial trauma—from slavery to lynching—back into comic-book mythology, as both its source and its original sin, stemming from the Ku Klux Klan, a group reawakened, back in 1915, by the original masked-hero blockbuster, 'The Birth of a Nation.'"[49] Creator Damon Lindelof credits Ta-Nahesi Coates's essay, "The Case for Reparations," and the way it "shifted [his] perception of United States history," as the inspiration for this choice, explaining,

> What's the equivalent now of impending nuclear war? What's creating the big cultural anxiety? For me, it's the anxiety of a reckoning. Not because there are white supremacists, but because I am complicit in white supremacy. Because I'm a white man, I've gotten to take this entirely different path through life.
>
> So that reckoning, that process, the identification of white supremacy as a bad guy in a superhero comic book that could not be defeated — the Klan wears masks, but why are they never the villains in a superhero story? Those ideas felt like natural fits for "Watchmen." The original is provocative, it's dangerous, it's groundbreaking, it's political, it's unsafe. The idea for the show had to check all those boxes.[50]

Though characterized by Lindelof here as a "superhero story," *Watchmen*, like its source material, takes a skeptical view of heroism, which, so often fetishized, functions ideologically to smooth over the troubling gaps and conflicts between law and justice. "Quis custodiet ipsos custodes," or "Who watches the watchmen?"—the Juvenalian refrain appearing repeatedly as a graffiti tag in Moore and Gibbons's New York and cited as a postscript on the comic's final page—has become the creed of the Tulsa, Oklahoma police in the HBO team's reenvisioning (who answer the question in call-and-response fashion with "Nos custodimus," or "We watch"). Following an attack on law enforcement by the white supremacist organization the Seventh Kavalry—an event dubbed "the White Night" by the news media—Tulsa's police now work incognito, concealing their identities with costumes and masks. While characters central to the original—notably Dr. Manhattan himself (Yahya Abdul-Mateen II)—play key roles in this adaptation, the sequel foregrounds Angela Abar (Regina King), a Black police detective born in Vietnam (now America's fifty-first state) and orphaned as a child when her parents are killed in a freedom fighter terrorist attack. When the series opens, Angela has returned to Tulsa, her family's hometown, where, having survived the White Night, she fights crime under the identity of Sister Night. Angela and her colleagues particularly relish rooting out Seventh Kavalry members, with the help of racist psychology-detection technology as well as more brutal beating tactics, procedures widely practiced on the force and sanctioned locally, although, it is hinted, they may not be lawful.

How, *Watchmen* asks, can the white supremacist foundations of American life be reinterpreted in such a way that new futures open up? Can the arc of history be bent and ongoing injustices repaired? The *Watchmen* universe provides a fitting stage for these questions because of its attention to the fragile boundaries between law enforcement and vigilantism, justice and state-sanctioned repression, democracy and tyranny. On that stage, the 2019 sequel sets competing modes of world-making, inviting viewers to weigh their animating logics and desires and to contemplate the horizons they open up or shut down. This competition is embodied particularly starkly in two characters' plans to kill Dr. Manhattan and appropriate his extraordinary powers of destruction and creation for themselves. In one corner is the Seventh Kavalry white supremacist militia, secretly headed by Senator Joe Keene, Jr., who purports not to be a "racist," but rather a patriot rectifying the unjust reforms and humiliations the nation has suffered under liberal President Robert Redford. In the other is Lady Trieu (Hong Chau), a scientific and entrepreneurial prodigy out to save humanity from the traumas of its past and move it "gloriously into the future," merging the dreams of her subjugated but unbroken Vietnamese mother with the talents of the wealthy employer from whom the latter surreptitiously steals a vial of sperm—Adrian Veidt (Jeremy Irons), aka Ozymandias, the genius who "saved" the world in 1985 by engineering a common enemy against which Cold War foes could unite: a giant squid, dropped on New York in what is made to look like an alien incursion, killing half the city.

At the center of this battle over national identity, lineage, memory, and power sits *Watchmen*'s extraordinary tale of Angela's orphaned family history—a tale that opens onto an alternative genealogy of the past and history of genealogy through its intensely surreal imbrication of fact and fiction. The first episode begins with "something I thought I'd never see on television," writes philosophy professor and relative of one of the victims, Lawrence Ware: "the depiction of a dark day in American history that not many know about—the Tulsa massacre."[51] In 1921, white mobs murdered over 200 African Americans and burned down Tulsa's thriving Greenwood District, known as "Black Wall Street," destroying entire square blocks of businesses and homes. It was "the country's most significant incident of racial terrorism," writes Nussbaum, and "a true story that will be left out of schoolbooks, mislabelled a 'race riot,' and deliberately forgotten."[52]

As Victor Luckerson explains, "Many Tulsans, both white and black, stopped talking about what happened. A brutal invasion became a victimless crime, then a repressed memory, then a hazy urban legend that few people had even heard about."[53] And yet, Luckerson adds,

> some of the people who remembered—black people on the outskirts of recorded history—never stopped talking about it. [. . .] The reason we know what happened in Greenwood at all—the reason that the massacre is tangible enough for Hollywood to re-create in a glitzy prestige cable show—is because folks in Tulsa kept talking about their memories, even when the conspiracy of silence was deafening.[54]

Watchmen not only revives this suppressed history but also depicts its vulnerability—"the way that history itself is so susceptible to manipulation, distortion, and erasure"[55]—from its very first scenes, which frame historical narratives as the product of struggles over representation. The series begins with a sound, rather than an image: the click of a film projector beginning to roll. The "Watchmen" series title then flickers unsteadily on the screen, while the dramatic piano accompaniment and the images that follow signal that we are watching a silent movie from another era. A white man in a white suit and cowboy hat appears riding a galloping white horse and firing a pistol over his shoulder at his pursuer: a hooded man clad in black, astride a black steed and wielding a lasso. As the chase crosses a grassy plain and reaches a church, the pursuer succeeds in dismounting his target, who wears a lawman's badge. A congregation of shocked white folk pours out and the preacher mouths a question. "Ho! What have you done to our Sheriff?" reads the intertitle. The hooded figure declares that the sheriff is a cattle thief unworthy of the badge, prompting a new question: "And who might you be, STRANGER?" In lieu of a response, the figure, silhouetted against the sun in a low-angle shot, casts off his hood, revealing a Black man wearing a badge of his own. The camera cuts back to a jubilant young white farm boy among the congregants, who makes an emphatic declaration. "Dontcha know who this is?" the belated intertitle reads, "BASS REEVES! The Black Marshall of Oklahoma!" As the Marshall proudly displays his Oklahoma Territory badge to the cheering crowd, the camera pans to the theater, which is vacant, save for one enthralled young Black boy and the pianist. On screen, the congregants' thoughts turn to retribution; they demand the thieving sheriff be lynched. The child has seen the movie before and gleefully voices the Marshall's climactic pronouncement in sync with the actor: "There will be no mob justice today! Trust in the law!"

The room is empty, it happens, and the pianist, the boy's mother, is in tears, because this is the Greenwood District's Dreamland Theater in Tulsa, 1921, and outside the building the massacre has begun, creating an ironic and horrifying contrast with the action on screen. This opening scene uses the conceit of the silent movie in several important ways. The portrayal of Bass Reeves (a former slave become US Marshal in real life as on film) through this medium illustrates, first, the gap between historical event and narration, between the voices of the past and the belated interpretations that mute them or make them speak anew, that any account of history must grapple with. What we are watching when we begin *Watchmen* is a filmic representation of a historical event, the Tulsa Massacre, told through the eyes of a fictional child who is watching a filmic representation of a historical figure before being rushed to escape through the carnage by his parents, under a barrage of bullets from rioters and aircraft. However, beyond reiterating the point that history is story, involving critical analysis and construction rather than simple discovery or unveiling, what *Watchmen*'s opening does is to dramatize the particular struggles that have shaped histories of racism in America and also to ask what role fiction can play in engaging the major conflicts and questions at issue here—racial antagonisms and violence; law and its role in restraining or abetting mob rule; the ability of the lasso to bring down the more heavily armed forces of injustice; and the troubling likeness between the lasso and the noose.

These conflicts are explored across the season through an intricate and richly drawn plot centering on Angela Abar's childhood, her marriage with Dr. Manhattan (who has temporarily blocked his powers in order to live the human relationship she desires), and her present detective work as Sister Night. Angela uncovers piece by piece the deeply rooted secret white supremacist society that has been working among the ranks of government and law enforcement for decades. Her quest begins when she finds her beloved boss, Judd Crawford (Don Johnson), mysteriously hanged, and an elderly, wheelchair-bound man (Louis Gossett, Jr.) claims responsibility. The elder's identity and life story—he is the young child from the Dreamland Theater and, moreover, the grandfather Angela never knew she had—are only revealed to Angela and to the audience in episode 6 when she swallows a bottle of his "Nostalgia" pills (a pharmaceutical designed to aid patients with memory loss). Having been orphaned during the massacre, we learn, the boy took the name Will Reeves and eventually joined the police force in service of Bass Reeves's heroic creed. Will discovers, however, that the law is not to be trusted when his colleagues subject him to a mock execution for asking too many questions about their racist practices. And so, shaken, he turns the lynching hood and noose used to terrorize him into a protective disguise, passing as a white man under the identity of "Hooded Justice," the inspiration for a generation of costumed vigilantism, in order to eradicate corruption. One such corrupt official is Judd Crawford. When Will warns Angela that Judd had skeletons in his closet, Angela takes the phrase literally, stealing a moment at Judd's wake to slip into his actual closet, an elegantly appointed space where she discovers a hidden compartment holding a full Klan robe with a lawman's badge pinned to it. Her quest to solve his murder leads back to the grandfather, who has been openly telling her the truth. He has turned the secret society's mind control tactics against Judd, compelling him to hang himself—with his own rope, we might say.

The details of *Watchmen*'s portrayal are worth dwelling on for the ways in which the show explores the problem of a racism at once carefully closeted yet also hiding—or rather parading—in plain sight. The series' blend of speculative world-making and historical reenactment provides a means for re-familiarizing viewers, through uncanny estrangement, with a reality from which too many too often turn away while also immersing the audience in a world where reality can unfold otherwise. That "otherwise" remains a horizon of possibility requiring interpretation and enactment, rather than a clear path to a sure, anti- or non-racist future. This dialectic between speculation and extrapolation, between fictional meditations on alternative pasts and futures and the reality check of obstacles to change, is set in motion from the first minutes of the show. As we've noted, the opening scenes point up the friction between the reality of murderous, racist violence outside the theater and what appears from the perspective of 1921 as one of the broken promises of Reconstruction—the possibility, remembered on screen, of a world in which a strong Black marshal is the object of white admiration and the law serves as a bulwark against arbitrary judgment and extrajudicial executions. This friction is reframed in the following scenes, which jump ahead in time to 2019, fading from the dirt road where the young Will Reeves regains consciousness to a contemporary, paved road stretching toward the lights of the modern city. A seemingly routine traffic stop on this road presents the state of policing and race relations in this contemporary universe: a Black police officer covering his nose and mouth with a mask questions the white driver of a pickup about the load he is hauling. Glimpsing a contraband Rorschach mask in the glove compartment—Rorschach, the morally rigid and psychotic vigilante killed in the original comic has, we soon learn, been reappropriated as a martyr for the Seventh Kavalry—the officer returns to his vehicle and radios a request that his supervisor unlock his service weapon. Approval is delayed, the remote release malfunctions, and the scene turns deadly; the pickup driver, donning his mask, opens fire on the police vehicle, critically wounding the officer. After a moment of silence, a brassy, upbeat orchestral music begins; as the shot cuts to the next scene, a medium close-up of a smiling singer, we realize it is the title song to the musical *Oklahoma!*, which is being performed by an all-Black cast in period costume in the Dreamland Theater. This time, the theater is full, save for two empty seats. The camera pans over an attentive, multiracial, African American-majority audience. On stage, Curly and the chorus sing, "We know we belong to the land / And the land we belong to is grand! / And when we say / Yeah! A-yip-i-o-e-ay! / We're only sayin' / You're doin' fine, Oklahoma, / Oklahoma, O.K."

Inviting comparison between the two historical moments, this cut from past to future suggests at first that much has changed for the better in Tulsa. Electric vehicles have replaced gas-powered cars, police access to firearms has been significantly restricted in this world (presumably as a corrective to police brutality), and African Americans wield state power (as police officers) and cultural capital (as artists and patrons). But despite these progressive reforms, the body that is violently gunned down in 2019 is still Black, and the agent of that violence is a white supremacist. The vision championed by the color-conscious casting of *Oklahoma!*, that of a postracial nation to which all can claim belonging—"We know we belong to the land / And the land we belong to is grand!"—remains, at best, aspirational, as well as uneasily equivocal, since "to belong to" means both "to be included in" and "to be the property of." Like the superhero comics whose conventions the original *Watchmen* redeploys ironically, *Oklahoma!* serves as a springboard and a lens through which the HBO series punctuates and reframes the unfolding plot.

Oklahoma! is set in Indian Territory, on the eve of Oklahoma's statehood, although, as critics have pointed out, the musical makes no mention of Native Americans, the seizure and contraction of their lands, or the legislative history leading up to the merger of the Indian and Oklahoma Territories in the new state that entered the Union in 1907. Beyond simply skirting this issue, the Rogers and Hammerstein production arguably actively effaces the Native American elements of its source material, *Green Grow the Lilacs*, by Cherokee playwright Lynn Riggs.[56] Angela maintains an ironic distance from the production being staged at the Dreamland Theater, as we learn in episode 1 when she jokingly chides Judd for failing to inform her immediately of the Seventh Kavalry's attack on her colleague ("I know why you didn't call me. [. . .] You were mad that my sitter bailed and you had to suffer through Black *Oklahoma!* without having someone to roll your eyes at!"). Angela's own relationship with US settler colonialism is complex. As the daughter of a serviceman stationed in Vietnam and a police officer herself, she is socialized to view state power favorably and she participates herself in its exercise and its incursions on individual liberties and collective claims to sovereignty. As her family history reminds us, though—her father and great-grandfather are both war veterans who are violently killed, the elder by rioting whites in Tulsa, the other by Vietnamese insurgents, while her grandfather narrowly escapes death at the hands of his fellow officers—the path to military service is not always freely chosen, and African Americans have been disproportionately exposed to combat risks and treated as expendable in various conflicts.

While *Watchmen* represents some of this forgotten history directly on screen—memorably in a sequence in which German forces air-drop a propaganda flier on American Black regiments during the First World War asking pointed questions about the US' hypocritical promises of democracy for its citizens of color—Native American history is mainly present as an absence, indexed through allusion. "Little Bighorn" serves as the police pager code indicating an emergency, and in Judd's house, directly after Angela discovers her boss's hidden Klan robe, she passes a painting: George Catlin's 1834–5 *Comanche Feats of Horsemanship*, depicting Comanche warriors on a grassy plain practicing a difficult battle maneuver in which riders slide down the side of their horse, using the animal as a shield.[57] The artwork takes on several meanings here. Judd's possession of this piece (which also inspires the title of the episode, "Martial Feats of Comanche Horsemanship") calls to mind American mythologies touting white appropriation of Native American dress and guerrilla tactics during the Revolutionary War. As a prop in his cultivated public image, the piece suggests he is a tolerant friend to minorities. But if Custer's Seventh Cavalry Regiment lost the battle of Little Bighorn, the Plains Indians lost territory a year later, and *Comanche Feats of Horsemanship* begins in that light to look like a private joke, a perverse victory trophy whose status as such would only be recognized by Judd's secret supremacist inner circle. Judd's identification with the warriors further echoes the appropriation of Native symbols by recent extremist groups nostalgic for hegemonic whiteness, who style themselves victims of an unfair dispossession.[58] While Angela, trying to slip out of the house unnoticed, glances furtively at the painting without turning her head, the camera lingers on the image, slowly zooming in for an extreme close-up. As Angela leaves and the guests are occupied elsewhere, the camera (and by extension the show's viewers) becomes the sole audience for the painting, drawing attention to a pre-contact world and its often marginalized story—a story of past and ongoing struggles over sovereignty, land, and belonging.

In Judd's closet also appears a framed black-and-white photograph of a man and a child, presumably of himself as a youth with his grandfather (who, we learn later, was also a lawman). The reverence given to this patriarchal lineage recalls Senator Joe Keene, Jr.'s coded description of America as a country which has forgotten the "principles upon which it was founded," that is, the principle of white power. Judd and Joe's vision of America is one in which their power, the ease with which they move through the world, is an inherited and indivisible right; Joe complains that it has become "extremely difficult to be a white man in America now," while Judd's wife Jane, in the guise of a joke about her husband's dissatisfaction with the *Oklahoma!* actors' performance, states what turns out to be a bald truth: "He's just jealous because he played Curly in high school" (Season 1, Episode 1). This fear of white removal and "replacement," a staple of racist discourse, reflects a rigidly hierarchical notion of power as a possessable quantity and due inheritance linked to blood, understood to be the substance of white community.[59] Power cannot be shared; if some have it, by this logic, it necessarily follows that others do not. It can be taken away from whites but only unrightfully.

Against such a backdrop the stealth self-insemination Lady Trieu's mother carries out appears on one level subversive. Adrian Veidt sees it that way when Trieu reveals her identity to him and attempts to enlist him in her plan to take Dr. Manhattan's power and use it to "fix the world, disappear the nukes, end starvation, clean the air—all the things he should have done." "Your genius wasn't given," he retorts, "it's stolen" (Season 1, Episode 9). Trieu's mother sees it as an act of liberation as well, quoting her daughter's legendary namesake when she declares, "I want to ride the strong winds, crush the angry waves [. . .] remove the yoke of slavery. I will not bend my back to be a slave" (Season 1, Episode 9).[60] But this alternative world-making vision relies first on a notion of genius as heritable and, perhaps more importantly, on a sense of the future as predictable, controllable, and independent from the past. Explaining why she engineered the memory drug Nostalgia, one of the few failures she admits, Lady Trieu comments:

> I gave people the means to visit the past so they could learn from it. So they could evolve and transform and better themselves. Instead, they became fixated on their most painful memories, choosing to experience the worst moments of their lives over and over again. And why? Because they were afraid. Afraid that once unburdened by the trauma of the past, they would have no excuse not to move gloriously into the future. (season 1, ep. 7)

The lesson Lady Trieu takes from this failure is not that past traumas cannot simply be overcome and set aside, but rather that humans lack willpower—they make excuses because they are fearful of their freedom—and the solution to this lack is transhumanist engineering. The means to achieve this glorious, suffering-free future is to transform herself into a heroic, godlike superhuman and exercise her willpower unfettered, on behalf of the world. That she goes to great lengths to resurrect her dead mother through body and memory cloning, and to retrieve her father Adrian from his exile on Europa, a moon of Jupiter, so that he can witness her achievement, gives the lie to her stated belief that one must "unburden" oneself of the past. Lady Trieu on the contrary remains rooted in her desire for parental recognition—recognition that she has achieved her mother's dreams and proven her father wrong about her potential. This rootedness proves to be a fatal flaw in her plan, as she is ultimately killed by Adrian before she can transfer Dr. Manhattan's energy into herself.

The crack in Lady Trieu's vision is alluded to earlier in the series in a surreal scene in her clinic, where Angela has undergone treatment after overdosing on her grandfather's nostalgia pills. As she recovers the capacity to distinguish between her own memories and Will's, which she has relived in painful and vivid detail, Angela's main goal is to find her grandfather and make him answer why he has turned up so suddenly and thrown her life into upheaval. Convinced that the intravenous fluids she's receiving are coming from Will, she follows her tubes down a hallway, only to discover she is attached to an elephant, sprawled prostrate on its side. Personally reliving her own childhood traumas as well as her grandfather's life history, marked by multiple incidents of racial violence, has not "unburdened" her of the past, or dispelled the literal-metaphorical elephant in the room, which appears here at once as a life reduced instrumentally to human needs, as a symbol of Lady Trieu's power and ambition (her namesake's iconography often shows her riding an elephant), and also as a weight or distress borne but also perhaps relieved through relation. While Angela's impulse is to rip the IV from her arm and run from the building, the scene suggests that heroic individual action or therapy is not enough; interdependence requires a different, collective approach to memory.

The surprise created by the image of a human intravenously connected not to another human but to a nonhuman animal known for its memory and its ability to feel grief also raises questions about blood relations more specifically and their importance or insignificance for world-building. *Watchmen* delves right into the heart of the contemporary passion for the body as an encoded map to the past and future, a microcosm of time. The show's engagement with this hunger is most evident in its treatment of Will Reeves's irruption in his granddaughter's life and in its reinterpretation of the character of Dr. Manhattan, a figure whose life outside of time provides a thought experiment through which to explore the shape of unmediated access to knowledge. When Will appears in 2019, a centenarian in a wheelchair claiming to be "the one who strung [her] chief of police up," Angela is understandably skeptical and so deploys an interrogational trick to get a clearer answer to her question, "Who are you?" (Season 1, Episode 2). She fixes him a coffee, then bags the mug as evidence and heads to the Greenwood Center for Cultural Heritage, a museum devoted to the 1921 Tulsa Massacre and an approved application site for reparations under the Victims of Racial Violence Act signed by President Redford.[61] Passing a dozen protestors at the entrance chanting "Redfordations are an abomination" and "You got a sorry, now you want a handout?," Angela enters and approaches a line of computer terminals, mug in hand, where she is greeted by an interactive service featuring US Treasury Secretary, Henry Louis "Skip" Gates, Jr. In real life, of course, Gates is a renowned professor and the director of the Hutchins Center for African and African American Research at Harvard University, as well as the host of the popular PBS program *Finding Your Roots* discussed in Chapter 1.[62] Like *Finding Your Roots*, *Watchmen* points up the importance of genomic research to peoples like Angela's, whose histories have been suppressed. DNA analysis can fill in certain gaps and serve as a counter to histories told from the perspective of dominant groups and supportive of that dominance. In *Watchmen*'s America, for example, survivors of the 1921 massacre and their descendants—or, more precisely, "only survivors of the 1921 Tulsa Massacre and their direct descendants"—can receive compensation for their trauma.⁶³

Yet *Watchmen* also prompts viewers to question the uses and limitations of genomic analysis as a tool for social justice in several ways. Beyond raising questions of data security and ethical governmental uses of genomic information (we are, after all, watching not just an orphan discovering her untold roots but also an officer of the law carrying out an extrajudicial investigation with DNA obtained from an unlawfully detained and disabled man), *Watchmen* stages a debate over identity and the agency that knowledge of identity enables (or not) through an exchange in episode 2 laden with irony. In possession only of the man's first name and his DNA traces, Angela passes herself off as Will to Gates's automated avatar, who greets her with the question, "Hello, Will, what can I help you with today?" When Angela says, "I need to know who I am," Gates replies, "I'm sorry I can't help you with that. But I can check your eligibility. Would you like me to do that?" Her request and Gates's response both take on double meanings. What Angela wants is to identify her suspect. What she needs, but does not know that she needs, the scene suggests, is to know who she is, in a broader sense. DNA testing service cannot produce a name; it can only compare the sample to an existing database and tell the applicant the probability that the donor is a relative of anyone in that data set. But DNA testing also cannot tell her who she "is" in a more profound sense. And since it cannot, the show prompts us to ask, what does it really mean to "be," and to know, who you are? On what is identity founded?

Watchmen continually foregrounds the idea that lives are defined by projects rather than essences, be they biological (blood) or techno/historical over-determinist (inexorable forces evacuating human agency). Angela and Cal's strong bond with their three adopted white children (the children of her police partner killed during the White Night) frames kinship as a cultivated relationship, rather than a "natural" one; similarly, Angela teaches her son, Topher, that racism is a practice rather than a fixed identity. Reacting to Topher's defensive justification ("He's a racist!") for punching a classmate who used a slur, Angela quips, "He's not racist. But he's off to a good start" (Season 1, Episode 1). Yet as this very struggle over the project that is America shows, we do not operate in the world with fully unconstrained creativity. The questions the series raises, then, are to what extent we can know these constraints, how we judge them desirable, unchangeable, or unacceptable, and how we go about either working within them, reshaping them, or dispelling them.

These questions are perhaps raised most clearly in the show's reinterpretation of Dr. Manhattan. Educated in nuclear physics, Jon Osterman becomes the entity government publicists call Dr. Manhattan when an accident vaporizes him and transforms him into a superhuman who lives life on a quantum level. He exists in multiple moments at once, so that past and future no longer have the same meaning to him, and he is capable of such feats as creating and destroying life through atomic manipulation, traveling instantly through space, and teleporting others at will. His altered condition makes it difficult, however, for him to identify with finitude or human concerns ("A live body and a dead body contain the same number of particles. Structurally, there's no discernible difference. Life and death are unquantifiable abstracts. Why should I be concerned?"[64]). Nor is Jon omniscient (his vision can be blocked by tachyon interference), and though others assume him to be omnipotent, able to use his foreknowledge to change the course of events, Jon himself insists he is not God and, moreover, that he is incapable of changing the future, because "to [him], it's already happening."[65] At the end of Moore and Gibbons's comic, Jon has regained some interest in human affairs but declares he will leave the galaxy, perhaps in order to create new humans elsewhere. His existence allows the comic to stage questions of free will and fatalism, and what becomes of morality when human conceptions of life and death are translated into equivalent material states and thus deemed inconsequential.

Chronologically, *Watchmen* picks up Jon's story again at a bar in Vietnam in 2009, when "a god walks into Abar," as the episode title quips, and the two fall in love. Jon takes on a new appearance (that of a Black man) and name (Cal), as well as a tachyon implant blocking all memory of his identity and powers. "Like Hooded Justice," Luckerson comments, "[Jon/Cal] uses blackness as a shield of anonymity in a world transfixed by white heroes. But because he agrees to give up his powers and memories to save his relationship, blackness also robs him of his ability to alter history with the snap of his fingers."[66] The two leave for Tulsa to make a fresh start where they live happily married until the Seventh Kavalry's and Lady Trieu's plots to kill Jon prompt Angela to remove the implant and bring his memory back.

What Jon's figurative death as superhuman—followed by his final, bodily annihilation at the hand of Lady Trieu—does, however, is to cut the strings holding the human actors whose actions he has been orchestrating. Or rather, his death makes their status as actors, as agents rather than puppets, more visible to them. *Watchmen* literalizes this metaphor at the moment of Jon's death, when the explosion of his energy lifts Angela off her feet and seems to throw her back into history itself; in a slow-motion shot, the camera focuses on the horror on her face as she looks toward the site of the murder while her body is propelled in the opposite direction, framed by a looming poster for the production of *Oklahoma!* (Season 1, Episode 9). Taking refuge in the Dreamland Theater, Angela finds her grandfather watching over her children, teleported out of harm's way before the drama and now asleep on the stage. Jon's absence is felt strongly in the moment of silence that follows, as well as in the obtrusiveness of the stage as a stage, set for a play but quiet and unlit. The children, symbol of futurity asleep among the straw bales, lie still—what is to come remains uncertain, a potential as yet unshaped. Reflecting on his own experience as Hooded Justice, and what he wishes her to understand about his "origin story" and her own future, Will tells his granddaughter, "You can't heal under a mask, Angela. Wounds need air." History can wound—sometimes fatally—but one can also heal. What ties the two of them together is not descent, but rather a shared investment in healing, in justice, and a shared interpretation of the past from which a future can emerge. As the new family leaves the theater to return home, we survey the devastation of Greenwood accompanied by Frank Sinatra's haunting a cappella rendition of "Oh What a Beautiful Morning," the song that opens *Oklahoma!* The Greenwood District persists, though damaged; this beginning is an ending and this ending a beginning. Whether the future will simply repeat the past remains an open question.

Revealing to Angela that Jon had wanted to die, Will relays, finally, a puzzling message from her husband: "He wanted me to give him up. He told me you'd try to save him, but this was the way it had to be. You can't make an omelet without breaking a couple eggs." The meaning of this enigma only becomes clear back at Angela's house, as she notices a single intact egg in a mess of broken shells left behind in the chaotic moments before Jon is taken away to be killed. Angela suddenly recalls a playful exchange between her and Jon the night they met, when she asked whether it would be possible for him to give his powers to someone, like his children. After declaring that he would never "pass [his] abilities on to someone without their consent," he concedes that it might be possible. "I suppose I could transfer my atomic components into some sort of organic material," Jon states with careful exactitude. "If someone were to consume it," he continues, "they would inherit, as you call them, my powers." "So," a skeptical Angela pushes him, playing along with what she still believes to be a game, "you could put them in this egg, and if I ate it, I could walk on water?" "Theoretically, yes," Jon responds (Season 1, Episode 8). The series ends on this very question. In the final sequence, Angela walks slowly out to her swimming pool, cracks open the egg, and swallows it raw; just as her foot touches the surface of the water, the screen cuts to black. "I am he as you are he as you are me and we are all together," we hear as a cover of the Beatles' "I am the Walrus" plays over the credits.

The egg in this final scene acts as a microcosm for the series and its questions as a whole but also as a playful explosion of the very notion of the microcosmic. The series has primed us with egg imagery in multiple episodes and so eggs are both overdetermined—laden with meaning wherever they appear—and underdetermined, since potential meanings abound in the show, thwarting any single symbolic reading: we see eggs forming a smiley face in a nod to the original *Watchmen* comic's motif; eggs as disguise in Angela's cover story (that she has quit the police to run a bakery); eggs as a symbol of fertility lost and found again; eggs being fixed by Cal as an act of care for his kids; eggs being fixed by Will (who asks Angela if she likes them "hard-boiled," alluding slyly to her skeptical detective attitude); eggs in Jon's musings about chicken-and-egg causality paradoxes; and finally, two repetitions of the saying "You can't make an omelet without breaking a couple eggs," itself an "Easter egg" (an insider reference to the original comic). This saying is first uttered in Moore and Gibbons's piece by the character Rorschach. During his own private interrogation of a suspect, Rorschach has eaten a raw egg and dropped the shell on the floor as part of his intimidation tactics. The "suspect" knows nothing, and Rorschach apologizes for the mess with the remark about omelets; his conflation of the metaphorical omelet and the concrete eggs reflects the rigidity of his personal moral code, which admits no compromise and must be followed to the letter, not just in spirit. In the HBO adaptation, this line is placed first in the mouth of Ozymandias, in a joke told by Laurie Blake, where it symbolizes the hubris of a man who believes firmly in his own vision of the greater good and is willing to do significant collateral damage in order to achieve it. It reemerges in the final episode, as Jon's last word to his wife.

As a message from Jon, relayed by Will, "You can't make an omelet without breaking a couple eggs" evidently points to Jon's death as the necessary sacrifice for the omelet, the new acts of worlding, Angela is poised to make. But what sort of worlding is she meant to undertake? What is the nature of the powers she may (or may not) "inherit" by consuming Jon in the distilled and fertile form of a chicken egg? Has Jon given her the capacity to reappropriate this symbol of Rorschach's single-mindedness and Ozymandias's hubris and turn it to different ends? The cut that ends the series dangles the possibility that Angela has become a new, superhuman force of justice to reckon with. But in refusing to answer the question definitively, in making such a cut to black in mid-action, the series also ejects us from the alternative universe back into our own, just as Angela is thrust upon the death of her husband back into *Oklahoma!* and all of the unresolved dilemmas it embodies. The one force who would seem capable of making the impossible possible did not bring about a fully just world. What sort of reparative work, then, will be needed to bring forth the truly nonracial world that *Watchmen*'s *Oklahoma!* gestures to but does not achieve?

"He was a good man," Will says of Jon to Angela in his final line of the series, "I'm sorry he's gone. But, uh, considering what he could do . . . he could've done more." The first question Will's thought prompts is, what more will Angela do? But what Will's statement also suggests is that what Jon has passed down to her, and to viewers, is not a superhuman power to save the world on her own, but rather the power to consider what she, and we, can do, in the very absence of foreknowledge and omnipotence—the power, that is, to speculate, to reconsider the impossible as a possibility, the kind of queer speculation so needed to break the normative path of extrapolative reproduction and bring new futures. If the Seventh Kavalry are wedded to organic, blooded hierarchies, and Lady Trieu's world-making vision rests on a single conductor, a masculinist master planner following an infallible map to glory, *Watchmen*'s vision of world-making insists on the messy interconnectedness of I and he and you and me and we, all together, the potential (for success and failure) enabled by uncertainty. Such a vision stresses the importance of incorporating the past in its materiality—acknowledging what was broken, what cannot simply be put together again, as if it never happened—but also of breaking the egg that is the belief in organic wholeness and certain futures, the belief that the future, like the past, surely belongs to the heirs apparent.

Rebellious Foresisters

Like *Watchmen* and *Black Panther*, Fabienne Kanor's *Humus* finds in speculative fiction a means to break with the "consensus reality" of anti-Blackness and envision possibilities of living otherwise by working with and through the entanglement of reason, feeling, and imagination. *Watchmen*'s rejection of mechanical and identitarian models of birthright, driven by blood ties and collective fantasies of racial superiority, achieves its force through its sensitive portrayal of the differing wounds we inherit from history, refracted through the lens of a not-quite-reality where hitherto unforeseeable, unimagined bonds and healing projects materialize as collaborative possibilities. Like *Watchmen*, *Black Panther* takes aim at current realities of anti-Black violence but does so by portraying what might have been, in the absence of colonial conquest and exploitation, as a richly detailed and vibrant world that could still come about. Wakanda's effervescence fills the screen, taking on power not by denying current inequities but by portraying the ways in which this other future might expand to push them out of the frame. At the same time, it resists optimistic closure by making of its antagonist, Erik Killmonger, an ambivalent enemy, the motor for T'Challa's change of heart and a manifestation of unhealed historical traumas and erasures that cannot be repaired, only remembered and honored. Killmonger's final words—"Just bury me in the ocean with my ancestors that jumped from the ships. 'Cause they knew death was better than bondage"—haunt the film as both a warning against compromising on liberation and a reminder that resistance cannot always avoid violence.

Devoted entirely to a group of women who took such a leap, *Humus* prolongs the resistance of those who chose the ocean over the hold, alchemizing the potent traces of this act left by the very archival inscription that strives to contain and defuse it. Sparked by a chance encounter with the captain's logbook documenting the event, *Humus* aims to give voice to these women, bringing texture to these lives treated meagerly as merchandise in the scant record reproduced as an epigraph to the book:

> On the 23rd of March last, fourteen black women apparently leaped overboard, from the poop deck into the sea, all together and in one movement. . . . Despite all possible diligence, with the sea extremely choppy and the wind blowing a gale, sharks had already eaten several of them before any could be hauled back on board, yet seven were saved, one of whom died that evening at seven o'clock, being in very bad shape when rescued, so in the end, eight were lost in this incident.
> —Excerpt from the logbook of Louis Mosnier, captain of the slave ship *Le Soleil*[67]

Composed of twelve chapters named after their narrators' social identities—"the mute woman," "the old woman," "the slave," "the amazon," "la blanche," "the twin sisters," "the employee," "the little one," "the queen," "the-one-who-flies," "the mother," and "the heiress"—*Humus* "delivers a 'chorus' in fourteen voices" that comingle yet remain distinct, forming a collective that "noticeably resists a perfect unity or total harmony," as Doyle Calhoun puts it well.[68] This resistance manifests itself in the disparate experiences and paths that lead each to this leap, in the sea chanty snippets that surround each chapter like a net, recounting the adventures of "Big Jehan of Nantes, topman on *Le Soleil*," in the fragmentation and disorienting juxtapositions of the women's memories and manner of speaking them, and in the text's explicit struggle, as the narrator warns in her prologue, with the annihilating violence of slavery and suicide, "where the human being, plunged into the darkness of a bottomless blue-black sea, must confront the cruelest trials that exist: aporia and the death of the spoken word" (9). Woven into the text too, in its final chapter, are the pains the narrator faces, as "heiress" to this historical memory, in her endeavor to nevertheless make the impossible possible.

The aporia *Humus* faces arises from the nature of the jump itself, a contradictory choice between death by drowning or the living death of slavery, the spirit murder of captivity that kills speech in its own way.[69] Each of these violences consumes the witnesses who could give their own account of it; those left to speak come up against the inadequacies of narrative itself, of giving an orderly form to such destruction, at the risk of falsely redeeming it, making of it a tale either edifying or titillating. "Abandon all hope, you who think a story of slavery will be a novel of adventure," exhorts the narrator. "An epic tale, a heroic, tragic story filled with rape, pillaging, brawls, and death. [. . .] Grandiose. Exotic. Unimaginable. Unheard of" (9). To speak of this history requires a form of narrative that is not one—that is not narrative, and that is not singular but multiple. "This story is not a story, but a poem," she explains, emphasizing at once the orality, nonlinearity, and absence of conventional arc or closure in the pages to come. It is a "story that repeats itself like a chant, prefers new chapters to endings, the surest stammers to sharp conclusions," a "story that is not a story, but an attempt at a shift in a space where there are no longer witnesses to speak" (9).

A "shift in a space" suggests both an affective transformation and a change in readers' conceptual, ethical, and political dispositions. It is a task reminiscent of the one undertaken by Chamoiseau's figure of the Warrior of the Imaginary, who makes of fiction an exploratory encounter with the marvelous, the surprising, and the unpredictable that unsettles silent, insidious forms of domination.[70] Where *Humus*'s narrator wants to take us is stated both negatively—we will move away from the excitement of adventure and pathos of tragedy—and affirmatively, counterintuitively, as a passage to the "familiar and familial": this story will not contain "vivid description [. . .] to make you see it, as if I'd been there. I wasn't there, that's all I can say for sure. But any one of us could have been there, so universal are the ordeals. Familiar and familial, by our very existence." Moreover, the narrator forewarns, "you will be taken captive. Chained to the words against your will. [. . .] Like these shadowy figures put in chains long ago," she continues, "the reader is condemned not to move from this moment on. Just listen with no other distractions to this chorus of women. At the risk of losing your bearings, hear once more these hearts beating" (9). To describe this recognition of the familiar and familial as paradoxically disorienting, as well as painfully captivating in a literal sense, is to point to the role of disavowal—the psychic move to unknow what we know, to turn away from the discomfiting—in confrontations with slavery's history and afterlives. Colonial disavowal is a problematic response to white anxiety; it divides the ego between knowing and not knowing. While allowing new information to be admitted into consciousness, its symbolic impact has nevertheless been neutralized and "not really integrated into the subject's symbolic universe."[71] This denial manifests itself not only in ignorance but also in the turn to the vicarious experience of adventurous action stories, stories that give a protective illusion of having been there, of having lived a tale with a beginning, middle, and end, a book whose cover we can close and walk away from, sated and purged of horror and obligation.

In a countervailing effort to respond to the past, and to the particular event of the captives' jump, Kanor's *Humus* keeps open the wounds of the Middle Passage, refusing the illusions of closure and collective healing that dominate perceptions of slavery in France, as she explains in an exchange with Gladys M. Francis:

> In the United States, there is a place for these enslaved women, there is a place to listen to their testimony. There, it is not a time gone by or a settled matter. We must live in the footsteps of this history, for we are its product. Whereas it is a truth that can be told and shared in the United States,

however, France continues to proclaim itself as a post-racial Republic, which makes it difficult to have these necessary conversations.⁷²

While the topics of slavery and its ongoing impact on the present continue of course to meet resistance in the United States, France's institutional and cultural investment in color-blind ideology, part and parcel of its passion for the ideal of an egalitarian French Republic in which citizens are and should be treated in public life as raceless and genderless, poses its own specific challenges that Kanor conveys through the metaphor here, too, of space. Space—public, archival, rhetorical—must be shifted in order to make a place, a space of belonging for "the truth of a French colonial past that continues to be subdued"⁷³ and a situation of address in which this truth can be both articulated and heard.

Underlining the insufficiency of "amnesia" as an explanatory metaphor for this suppression of the colonial past, colonial historian Ann Laura Stoler argues that "aphasia" better describes the conditions giving rise to "the political, personal, and scholarly dispositions that have made the racial coordinates of empire and the racial epistemics of governance so faintly legible to French histories of the present."⁷⁴ Aphasia, Stoler continues,

> is a dismembering, a difficulty speaking, a difficulty generating a vocabulary that associates appropriate words and concepts with appropriate things. Aphasia in its many forms describes a difficulty retrieving both conceptual and lexical vocabularies and, most important, a difficulty comprehending what is spoken.⁷⁵

Colonial aphasia, a condition of "dis-ease"⁷⁶ disordering individual and communal speaking and listening, motivates the project of *Humus* and also shapes the way that Kanor inscribes articulation and unease into her re-membering of these women. Kanor mobilizes what Saidiya Hartman calls "critical fabulations," speculative narration that functions simultaneously as invention and intervention, a creative attempt to bear witness to the forgotten lives of the enslaved, represented in the archives by only "'a meager sketch of [their] existence.'"⁷⁷ *Humus* insists on their realities while proceeding cautiously, enacting the "narrative restraint" Hartman advocates by resisting the impulse "to fill in the gaps and provide closure."⁷⁸ Narrative joints connecting sundered stories and bodies protrude in *Humus*, as does their absence. Each chapter links together pieces of spoken memory, visually marking leaps in time, train of thought, vantage, and speaker with spatial gaps, asterisks, and typographical modulations. Shifts in rhythm, voice, and speculative mode similarly work toward the narrator's stated "desire to swap," to "trade away technical discourse for the spoken word" and tell "this story of men" differently, "otherwise," so as to "upend the reader's expectations" (9). Throughout the text, the force of aphasia is made visible, as are the characters' efforts to grapple with it, to speak in light of and through the tensions that inhabit (post)colonial situations of address.

The "mute woman"—whose naming itself signals the paradox of voicing the voiceless, of speaking beyond the woman's silencing first in life and then in death—is the first of the captives to share her recounting. Her speech takes shape first as a de-creation story testifying to enslavement's destruction of the word and the being that flows from it: "In the beginning there was absence. Say nothing, be nothing. Nothing but a thing they use. Use up until its insides break" (13). Destroying the word does not destroy witnessing, but it disables exchange, rendering the woman mute and cutting her off from any who would listen. "I saw everything," she affirms, but continues, "Don't ask me what. Lost words are lost forever. To speak all that is in my mind, I'd have to invent" (13). Her loss—what she has lost herself, and our loss of her, those of us who come after—is irreparable. But the women of *Humus* nevertheless invent; in Lauren Berlant's terms, they respond to the imperative "to make language do what it cannot yet do,"[79] notably by transforming the dislocations of aphasia—the disassociation of "appropriate words and concepts" from "appropriate things," to recall Stoler's words—into a form of poiesis. "One night, they ate my belly," says the mute woman of the captors who raped her, translating this violent reduction of the body to flesh, a sexual instrumentalization that ungenders, by transposing an act of brutal penetration into a language of voracious consumption. Vomiting, or the forceful refusal to digest, also comes to figure cruelty for "the slave," who speaks bitterly of the moment "the sea spit us back up on the deck" (52). In displacing the agency of the sailors who haul the women out of the ocean, indicting instead the water itself, the slave implies that the hopelessness of this reimposition of captivity remains strictly unspeakable—the captors' imperviousness to what they treat as commodities can only be confronted indirectly, through the ironic personification of the inhuman sea. Yet this move also allows the slave to challenge the terms of what Captain Mosnier misnames a "rescue" and to preserve her own creativity, to shunt the sailors to the margins of her story and figure it in her own way.

Driven to psychosis by the agonizing reification and sexual violence of enslavement, La Blanche similarly takes up a double-edged language that bears the marks of the irreparable yet continues to signify inventively. Her vivid hallucinatory descriptions of rats and serpents entering her thighs stand side by side with her loving conversations with the flower she identifies as her baby, while her disjointed phrases refuse to create seamless transitions where there are none: "Moldy, me vomited, spoiled, thrown away. Me rancid. Dirty. Salty. Without. Alone" (90). These verbal splinters prefigure the dismemberment La Blanche undergoes as she is torn apart by a sugar cane mill. Yet this final mutilation liberates her, restoring a more flowing, though no less horrifying grammar:

> In the room where they had so often seen me dance, I was galloping, I-blanche, the body ravaged. A dress without ruffle or thread. Vast. Finally free. From my smile, which the unrooted head had somehow held onto, they figured I must have been happy. I had fallen asleep, surrendered to the monster, my little hands feeding him even more. Until the rollers had pulled me in and crushed me.
>
> In the vat of sugar juice floated my thing.
> I still don't know what they did with it.

In this deliverance, the fragmented phrase—"Vast. Finally free"—takes on a new valence, transforming from index of nightmare to declaration of liberty. The mute woman similarly forges newness from fragmentation in her telling of the jump:

> Call them whatever you want, I no longer hold their names in my head. Barely even their faces, turned toward the ocean, facing it, laughing. So was I.
>
> I did.
> I.
> We jumped.
> Together. We.
> Jumped. Sea. Jump!
> We
> Did it. (15)

Erupting into free verse, the mute woman re-members the dismembered and dis-remembered, arranging fragments into an order that remains irregular and opaque, yet by its very form as verse conveys intentionality, an agential capacity that enslavement would deny.

Who will hear these voices and respond to their retellings remains an open question throughout the text. The sea chanty verses that both link and separate each chapter remind us that the connections between these "sisters of the chain," as the amazon names them (59), are forged by contingency—enslavement throws together women of widely different origins, languages, beliefs, and social standings. The song of the sailors stands as a reminder of those "stories of men" that threaten to drown out the particularities of these women's lives and motivations, as well as the shared decision to revolt that solidifies their sisterhood. "Where are you?" asks the heiress herself, the writer of this text who has heard the women's call but struggles before the blank page as she travels from Paris to Nigeria to Guadeloupe in search of their voices. "The question hangs in the air. What must I do to set the memory in motion?" (178). Conversely, that the ballad (and the novel it closes) ends on an equivocal note—Big Jehan of Nantes, altered by his voyage, "now laughs no more [. . .] / in liquor he drowns [. . .] / Facing the river, fists raised with his screams" (189)—recalls that dominating discourses are never seamless; these women's lives made ripples and left traces that can be picked up and followed again by willing listeners. In this sense, as Kanor argues in an interview,

> We should understand this jump [. . .] as a pretext, the text that precedes the novel to come. It is because these women jumped that Captain Mosnier took up his pen, and that the novel can begin. They jump not because they no longer have anything left to say, but precisely because they need to tell everything that happened. And I use this jump to dive into the narrative, to bring closure to it as well as to rekindle it. [. . .] It is never a period, but works instead as a comma, an opportunity for speaking [*une possibilité de parole*].[80]

The jump disrupts the smooth functioning of the slave trade, which aims to produce pliant, docile, laboring object-subjects whose speech is not speech, but rather an extension of the masters' words, a reflection confirming what they desire to hear. The indocility of their collective act disrupts, at least momentarily, the social coordinates of an anti-Black world. The jump speaks otherwise, unpredictably, prompting a response and thus setting exchange in motion. The interlocutor may well shut down that exchange, putting a period on the end of the story; they may, like Captain Mosnier, reassert narrative control, reiterating, through the telling, the terms of the existing grid of intelligibility. To read the jump instead as a comma is to tarry with its (im)possibility, to embrace a queer temporality, to reopen the telling and linger on how this leap might breach those terms.

One such matrix that *Humus*'s retelling importantly challenges for contemporary readers who find themselves "chained to the words" of the novel is the framework through which acts of resistance, and agency itself, become legible to us as such. *Black Panther*'s Killmonger hints at such terms in reading death and bondage as the two opposed options facing the enslaved and the contemporary freedom fighters who are their heirs. To jump is to choose death over capitulation; suicide represents the final act in the heroic fight that has led up to it. If Killmonger's invocation of his ancestors makes visible anew a tradition of Black radicalism often overlooked or misunderstood in hegemonic Euro-American accounts and memory, the ancestral line he draws also flattens their history and reinforces a phallic model of historical recognition grounded on the solitary individual's exceptionality and worthiness. To claim one's ancestors as ancestors is in this model to claim an affiliation that begins and ends in a desirable quality, a muscular, masculinist heroism untainted by compromise. Such an account also risks feeding what Hartman describes as an "obscene" project, "the attempt to make the narrative of defeat into an opportunity for celebration, the desire to look at the ravages and the brutality of the last few centuries, but to still find a way to feel good about ourselves,"[81] particularly because Killmonger's story is presented for the viewers' sympathy and then subsumed into a liberal celebration of development through beneficent foreign aid.

Kanor tells suicide's contribution to the Black radical tradition otherwise by queering the eventalization of the suicide, foregrounding, in turn, the collective and unfinished character of the jump. In *Humus*, the amazon, a Dahomey warrior "prepared to defend the kingdom at any cost [. . .] hack off heads [. . .] burn, torture," shares Killmonger's militant view, and it is she who convinces her fellow captives to jump, urging the fearful with the words, "Let me tell you loud and strong, it is better to flee than to submit. Death before slavery!" (60–1, 65). Yet even for the amazon, death itself is not the aim, the final option at the end of the battle, but rather a risk worth taking; she jumps willing to die yet determined to swim to shore and fight. And indeed, though she is recaptured, she escapes, successfully, when the ship lands in Haiti, then joins a maroon rebel who recalls to readers the promise of revolution that hangs over the events of the novel and continues to haunt the present. The queen, as well, makes a similar wager, risking death in hopes of returning home and regaining her throne. In lingering on their stories, Kanor reminds us vividly, as Cedric Robinson has stressed, that the "cargoes of laborers" traversing the Middle Passage "contained African cultures, critical mixes and admixtures of language and thought, of cosmology and metaphysics, of habits, beliefs, and morality"[82] that motivated rebellion and shaped the alternative social structures they aimed to pursue. "These," Robinson continues, "were the actual terms of their humanity," a humanity that racial capitalism strove to obliterate but could not fully erase.[83] "Slavery," in other words, "altered the conditions of their being, but it could not negate their being."[84]

Humus testifies to this "preservation of the ontological totality," as Stefano Harney and Fred Moten describe it, the persistence of an Africanness "more or less than African and otherwise than being," through its engagement with the anti- or "ante-heroic" character of a Black radical tradition that achieves "what should have been impossible" but "nonetheless exists"— the survivance of an African peoplehood without peoplehood, a heroism without heroes.[85] Considered from this angle, the women of *Le Soleil*, in Kanor's telling, can be seen as participating, like Nanny Grigg and Nat Turner, in keeping alive and passing down this collectivity that is not one:

> Nanny Grigg or Nat Turner, Robinson teaches us, keep something going through their certain deaths, keep something going that cannot win under the rule(s) of the hero and his people, but survives in something more exhaustive. There is something unheroic about this, the failure to win, and something other than heroic about it, too. Under the law of the hero,

even tragic heroes are remembered despite their own fall or death through the victory of *a* people. They are monumentalized for having fallen on the road to success. Or, at least, this is the way a white hero is conceived. But the black anti- and (ante)heroic is condensed and dispersed in sacrifice for the victory of the people by the ontological totality in its antagonistic relation to a people.[86]

As Robinson stresses, to conceive of Black radicalism in this way is to recognize that "is about a kind of resistance that does not promise triumph or victory at the end, only liberation. No nice package at the end, only that you would be free."[87] And it is not insignificant that, to help his audience grasp the point, he turns to a work of fiction, Julie Dash's 1991 film, *Daughters of the Dust*:

> *And I guess the most poetic representation of that I've ever seen is when Eula tells her story in* Daughters of the Dust *of why Ibo Landing has its name. Do you remember the story in* Daughters of the Dust? *The Ibo were brought here in chains, and in chains they were marched from the big boats and conveyed in smaller boats to the shore. They looked at this land and they saw what their future was, and they turned around . . . and walked back into the ocean.*
>
> *Only the promise of liberation, only the promise of liberation!*[88]

Kanor invites us to reimagine the temporality and meaning of success, failure, and the heroic by probing the nuances, dynamism, and tensions of Black being, this ontological totality, multiplying and elaborating the varying circumstances that push each woman to jump while keeping ever present the chains through which they form and are formed into a collectivity acting as one. The slave, recognizing the queen she had served in captivity, follows her into the water only to kill her out of vengeance; the employee, a guard hired by the captain to spy on the captives, jumps on a spontaneous impulse, in envy and admiration, because "something broke inside [her]" at the sight of their resolve to be free (111). The mute woman jumps to end the unrelenting torture of slavery, while La Blanche does so out of despair at being rejected by her sailor lover. "Of all my characters," comments Kanor, "[La Blanche] is the one who shows that slavery did not solely produce heroes, that jumping overboard does not always equate to rebellion. [. . .] There were all sorts of people in these ship holds: bad folks as well as good ones, bastards as well as victims, cowards as well as warriors."[89] In recognizing and dwelling on the density and contradictions of these women's lives, *Humus*'s heiress works to rebuild their being, to reconstruct an ontology eviscerated, though not abolished, by the Middle Passage, but also flattened by romanticized portrayals of slavery's victims. To recognize oneself as an heir not only to amazons but also to "deeply human" women like La Blanche, "made up of great pettiness and ordinary paradoxes,"[90] is to reject both the notion that they, like the "wayward" women of Saidiya Hartman's counter-history, are "surplus women of no significance, girls deemed unfit for history and destined to be minor figures,"[91] and the belief that our present, or we ourselves, can be redeemed by celebrating the resistance of the past. To claim sisterhood with the women of *Le Soleil* is instead to affirm that innocence and heroism should not be preconditions for liberation, that one need not be superhuman to be worthy of life, attention, and care, and that ambivalent acts and collectivities do make history, do keep history in motion.

Kanor's project of radical imagination shares the commitments of what Stoler describes as "effective rather than idle colonial history," whose force stems not from "its timeliness" or "how well it fits current politics and the stories long rehearsed," but rather from "how deeply it disrupts the stories we seek to tell, what untimely incisions it makes into received narratives, how much it refuses to yield to the pathos of moral outrage or to new heroes, subaltern or otherwise."[92] *Humus* works in this vein, however, as a co-conspirator with such a history, precisely because it is a poetic fiction, not a historical novel in the conventional sense of a narrative steeped in mimetic realism. In Lacanian terms, Kanor's poetic vision translates the *extimacy* of our encounter with these familial yet unfamiliar others, whose truth is both external to us and intimate, existing outside us yet bound up with our internalizations. This extimate space of relation is the space Kanor's alchemy of voice works to "shift." The interpenetration yet mutual alterity of inside and outside, figured most starkly by the ship hold, marks our encounter with the Middle Passage. *Humus* emerges from the difficult realization, "after filling the page with symbolic marks [*signes*]," as Kanor puts it, "that there will never be enough signs to tell the story of the ship's insides"; what is needed to counter the void ("even the earth, even the sea seemed to have forgotten what happened") is nothing short of a spell to "ward off this fate" (*pour conjurer ce sort*)—an invention that takes account of its own inventiveness and the varying forms of truth that history and fiction offer.[93] As Kanor explains:

> Right away, the idea of "manufacturing" [*fabriquer*] a historical novel seemed illusory to me. I am a novelist, someone, that is, who lies, likes fables, and still believes in mermaids. Besides, I don't think it is always necessary to tell the truth in order to touch people; what matters is the characters' truth, their power, their psychological coherence. [. . .] The important thing was not that [the amazon] be an exact copy of her sister-ancestors [the women warriors of the Dahomey], but that she be an atemporal character who suffers, fights, and loves for real. And this is how I went about it for each of my women: first by doing my research and then by trying to forget everything I had learned. The idea was not to

say, "this is how it happened," but rather, "this is happening now, this is what people are experiencing."[94]

The experience of being present in the now is not to be confused, however, with the illusion of having been there, to recall the prologue's warning. Rather, it is to be called to witness. *What do these women mean to me?* we are asked. *What kind of world ignored them and consigned them to historical oblivion?* In making this history present, the novel also prompts us to respond to the question, *What future will spring from this present-past?* Threaded through the novel's choral repetitions and open-ended form, this question is also posed in different ways by the women of *Humus* themselves. "What good is freedom, when the past is heavier than chains?," muses the slave (51). The heiress's surreal chapter, traversing dreamlike sequences intensely real in their unreal quality, ends in Guadeloupe with the narrator pondering the future as she and an artist-friend fill his studio with black-on-white paint and words:

> When all had been said, and the walls of the room were covered, we felt inside us a deep silence. Vertigo. Then words. Finally, the cry, too long contained, muffled by the song of the seas and the discourse of men.
>
> "We are the *papa-feuilles*, the healers," Peter whispered to me.
>
> I stood up. Facing the book to come. Facing these walls where the ghosts nestled, ghosts who would soon fade away. (187)

The book to come is the physical book we hold in our hands, the one we stand face to face with, but also the future tellings, future healings or fadings, that will soon arrive. The title term, "humus," the rich soil that decomposition leaves in its wake, captures the conjoined decay and fertility from which the novel springs and which its prophetic vision of the past produces, a promise of radical memory and action with no guarantees. To claim these "sisters of the chain" as foresisters is to recognize oneself at once as their contemporary, sharing in a collective tradition of resistance, as an heir, who comes after and who cannot perfectly know them and their world, and as a future ancestor, one who may pass on a legacy or not. To claim these women as foresisters is thus not to inherit their qualities and experiences as a possession but rather to see oneself as "of the chain"—shaped by an inheritance we do not choose, but also custodians of an inheritance that we also shape. It is to allow that this past, their stories, have a claim on us, a rightful need of our response.

From No to Yes

Speculative fiction's peculiar power lies in its ability to point beyond what is, beyond the status quo. It performs its alchemy first in saying "no" to the known, to the immutable familiar. Speculation effectuates a critical parallax, a dislocation of vision and affect that brings the impossible into view. But it achieves this no by saying "yes": "yes" to an otherwise reality thrillingly or hauntingly vivid in its almost-but-not-quite nearness. To say yes to *Black Panther*'s Wakanda is to reparatively construct a fuller whole with which to sustain life and plan futures, a sense of the creative potentialities within the self and the social world that fortifies through its expansiveness. It is to say no to rigidly constraining self-fortifications and, even more importantly, the pervasive anti-Black violence that necessitates such measures of self-preservation in the first place. It is to say no in particular to disregarding the ways such violence orphans communities and individuals, disrupting the power of ancestral memory to serve as a resource to think with, accept, or reject, and quite literally kills life, stripping away kin. *Watchmen* dwells on this orphaning as well, but equally calls out the dangers of an attachment to bloodline as a source of self-worth and political legitimacy. Angela rejects mechanical and identitarian models of inheritance, driven by blood ties and collective fantasies of racial superiority. In letting her grandfather into her life, accepting him finally as her own, and claiming the inheritance Jon has left behind in shedding his immortality, she lifts her mask in recognition of her own wounds but also her capacity for healing.

Yet in ending on a question—What sort of healer or hero will Angela become? Will she do what Jon failed to, the "more" that her grandfather, Lady Trieu, and all those who remain racialized and colonized have been clamoring for?—*Watchmen* warns us that the future always remains undefined. "Yes" has the power not only to liberate but also to foreclose emancipatory change. If, as Kennan Ferguson puts it, the no, the negativity of refusal, "stands against consensus, against assumption, against presumption, against the easy passage," saying yes entails affirming a specific vision, a fixed, positive content.[95] To say yes is to risk halting imagination, settling down, or simply settling for less. When the "yes" enters politics, it does so as "a modality of power"; it "underpins the familiar demands that one cannot criticize without an alternative, that people who complain or refuse or block must build an entirely different world before that complaint or refusal or blocking can be considered valid, that every unhappy person proves responsible for his or her own unhappiness. [...] Yes is agreeable; yes is conciliatory; yes is complicit."[96] T'Challa's "yes" forecloses Killmonger's more revolutionary vision. This orphaned cousin can be claimed as an ancestor in the abstract, as an idea, a figure for the children to come whose fate T'Challa wants to change, but he must be denied and contained in the concrete here and now for the film to achieve the resolution it has set as its aim: the perpetuation of the global political system but with Wakanda at its helm. Angela's yes remains obscured, held in suspense, requiring us to spin our imagination in search of possible futures while also holding in mind both the legitimate grievances and counter-models for resolving them that the series vividly explores.

Humus foregrounds the entanglement of negativity and affirmation in its very title, in the fertility yet irreducible loss brought about in decay. *Humus*'s rebellious women say no to the living death of enslavement, while Kanor rejects their commodification and ungendering, the transmutation of their bodies into mere flesh. As she says of her desire to revive their voices and complexities, to attend to the facets of human existence that the Middle Passage simply sought to evacuate from their being, "I simply wanted to tell the tale of African women who are put in shackles but continue to be women: they grow old, wait for their periods, bicker with each other, tell each other stories, remember, think about their men, fall ill, go mad, or fall in love."[97] They continue to desire, to need, to connect with one another, to live messy contradictions. But to forestall the reifications of narrative rescue, to prevent her affirmations from congealing into inert substance, Kanor develops a yes of infinite accretion, an alchemical art of the "more than." These women are more than what racial slavery makes them out to be, more than the sum and summit of their collective jump, more, too, than what can be recounted, imaginatively invented, in *Humus*. To be chained to the novel's words is to be enjoined at once to acknowledge what cannot be undone, to break what can, and to add links. It is to accept our inherited history as a project, to make community with these ancestors as fore and future sisters.

4

Fugitive Belongings

The speculative fictions studied in Chapter 3 alchemize historical memory, embracing a form of storytelling that forges, in Glissant's words, a "prophetic vision of the past"—a creative re-visioning of history aimed not at recovering a "schematic chronology" or an inert givenness confining in its rigidity, but rather at engaging memory as a communal act through which we relate to the world in its becoming.[1] In such a Glissantian vision, "memory," Jean-Luc de Laguarigue argues, "is not the key to the past," a tool that unlocks meaning, releasing us from mediation, but rather "an essential condition for the expansion of consciousness we need to achieve," a consciousness of the world's "tout-possible," its utmost possibilities.[2] Speculative writing sparks transformations in memory by crossing the wires of the possible and the impossible, illuminating what might have been and what may yet still be.

This chapter takes up two works that similarly reenvision the past, but do so by confronting the inertia of the given, dwelling in the discomforting constraints of slavery's afterlife and furtively cracking open its fissures: Colson Whitehead's *The Underground Railroad* (2016) and Maryse Condé's *The Wondrous and Tragic Life of Ivan and Ivana* (2017). These novels can be said to favor a paraontological mode of unsettlement, a fugitive form of alchemy spurred by "a desire for and a spirit of escape and transgression of the proper and the proposed," to recall Fred Moten's words.[3] These two novels both revolve around fugitivity—around guerrilla acts of subversion and flight—and enact *marronage* on the level of narrative form, rusing with the generic conventions that they flee and deploying the critical energy of parodic repetition to convey the weightiness of anti-Blackness's persistence while working to alter its givenness. In training their lenses more precisely on fraught projects of national belonging, these texts engage the "genre of the human," along with the attendant notions of property, rights, and contract, through which French and American understandings of national community have been constructed. How, these works prompt us to ask, might we realize the paraontological dream of bringing forth new, disalienated social structures and modes of relationality from that "zone of nonbeing" to which Black life has been consigned since the advent of chattel slavery?

From the "American Imperative" to French Republicanism: States of Anti-Blackness

While approaching national belonging through differing historical and sociocultural angles—the antebellum United States and 2010s Guadeloupe, Mali, and France—*The Underground Railroad* and *The Wondrous and Tragic Life of Ivan and Ivana* both stage the entanglement of political and libidinal economies undergirding the French and American nation-states and their respective forms of anti-Blackness. Centered on an enslaved woman called Cora who flees a Georgia plantation on an actual underground train, Whitehead's novel makes vivid the interdependence of desire and matter, idea and substance, through its striking literalization of metaphor. The material dimensions of slavery and its post-Emancipation reincarnations—the bodies that labored and suffered under servitude; the energies, children, and life stolen from them; the raw materials the enslaved worked; the infrastructure built through their toil; and the products, economic rewards, and medical data extracted from Black folks under slavery and beyond—circulate in an economy driven at once by the inertia of its own material structure and by the ravenous will to possess Blackness. This latter is most vividly exemplified in the slavecatcher Ridgeway, who obsessively pursues Cora out of devotion to what he dubs "the American Imperative," the belief that possession is all and might makes right. Ridgeway embodies this "American philosophy" whose motto is genocidal: "'if you can keep it, it's yours,' and, 'if you can't keep it, why not destroy it?'"[4] Under such a horizon, figuring the underground railroad as a complex of subterranean stations, tunnels, tracks, and cars brings to life the intense force required to move these material mountains, the exertion needed to fashion not only the networks of escapees and allies who worked to bring captives to freedom but also the very notion that one can attempt such a feat. "Running was too big an idea," muses Caesar, Cora's companion in flight, on her initial rejection of his escape proposal; before you can even allow the thought to enter the mind, let alone "truly live" there, "you need someone else to help you along."[5] The American Imperative grips like an iron shackle, one that can only be broken or melted down with great collective effort.

The idealism, in both senses of the term, of French republican color-blind ideology is the object of Maryse Condé's scrutiny in her tale of incestuous twins driven to different ends. Written in response to a three-day series of coordinated terrorist attacks in and around Paris in January 2015, the novel traces the paths taken by Ivana, the docile sister and excellent student who sets outs to become a police officer in order to protect the weak and rectify injustice, and Ivan, the unruly brother who struggles to find a meaningful life plan and turns instead to militant revolt against an unjust world. The conceit of siblings locked in a passionate but lethal embrace allows Condé to translate the intimacy of terrorist violence and to hold up to scrutiny the public debates over nature and nurture, individual psychology and collective socialization, that are reopened in the West in the wake of each new attack. Transposing the incest trope with an exploration of racism, colonialism, and terrorism jars with lingering assumptions that erotic desire is a private and highly particularized affair with little bearing on the broader social foundations of political-religious conflict, and, conversely, that contemporary terrorism is fundamentally about an ideological clash between a progressive, secular, gender- and color-blind republicanism and a gender-regressive, communitarian Islamism. Weaving a story of radicalization into a tale of erotic passion and Black female martyrdom, the novel jolts into focus the tangled and mobile relationships between the particular and the contingent, on one hand, and the overdetermining gendered and racialized structures shaping global currents on the other. At the same time, the novel's picaresque form and repeated ironic jousts deflect attempts to settle on any interpretation of "radicalization" and its causes. What emerges from Condé's unseemly fable instead is a satiric portrait of French leftist debates over the causes of the 2015 attacks, where the neglected colonial dynamics and "white analytic" underpinning republicanism are laid bare for the reader.

While Condé's text scrutinizes the whiteness and partiality of French libidinal attachments to republican universalism, Whitehead probes the generalizability of Ridgeway's American Imperative, the extent to which the slavecatcher's peculiar formulation of this drive captures not only the ethos of slaveholders but a racial imaginary subtending the whole of America itself, from the belligerently racist states of Georgia and North Carolina to the more "welcoming" states of South Carolina and Indiana. Ridgeway characterizes this imperative "to conquer and build and civilize" as a necessary mission, "our destiny by divine prescription" whose rightfulness reveals itself teleologically, through the very destruction and reordering of the world that its exponents wreak (226). As Ridgeway and countless other white settlers reason, "If the white man wasn't destined to take this new world, he wouldn't own it now" (82). Stripped to its core, the American Imperative, "the divine thread connecting all human endeavor," is a ravenous will to possess, experienced as an ordained right and law of nature dictating "if you can keep it, it is yours. Your property, slave or continent" (82). In transmuting history into destiny this ideology comforts a passion for the real; it offers ontological security, stamping white power with the marks of authenticity and timelessness. For Ridgeway, the American Imperative represents "the true Great Spirit" (82), a genuine, fundamental grounding more solid even than the "iron facts" (76) he admires in the work of his father, a blacksmith who finds meaning and pleasure in manipulating the "liquid fire" that is "the very blood of the earth" (75). As the narrator relates, Ridgeway takes to the vocation of "ensuring that property remained property" for the promise of sovereignty that it offers, a sense of unfettered mastery and self-importance in his role as the essential motor of a vast social system (82). Coming into his own, "he finally left his father behind, and the burden of that man's philosophy. Ridgeway was not working the spirit. He was not the smith, rendering order. Not the hammer, not the anvil. He was the heat" (82).

The "heat" evokes the policing required to maintain the thingly status of living beings rendered property, the intense energy needed to produce and run the infrastructure and social hierarchies of "King Cotton's" empire—from nails, horseshoes, and shackles to entire communities, states, and national political systems—but it also conjures up the deep psychic, erotic pleasures—to say nothing of the large monetary rewards—taken in dominating another in the name of white power and American destiny. Ridgeway thrills to the hunt, "the only remedy for his restlessness" (78). "Charging through the dark, branches lashing his face, stumps sending him ass over elbow before he got up again," he relishes the exercise and proof of his manhood that the hunt provides; "in the chase his blood sang and glowed" (78). The American Imperative thus represents much more than a racist ideology. It is fueled by an anti-Black libidinal economy, an economy "of desire and identification, of energies, concerns, points of attention, anxieties, pleasures, appetites, revulsions, and phobias—the whole structure of psychic and emotional life—that are unconscious and invisible but that have a visible effect on the world, including the money economy."[6] Western modernity itself revolves around this libidinal investment in anti-Blackness; as Jared Sexton argues, anti-Blackness is not simply one instantiation of racism among others, but rather "an unconscious cultural structure, a grammar, a *weltanschauung*, a metaphysics."[7] It is a grammar that produces Blackness as fungible property and the human as property owner. Human subjectivity is fantasized as fully realized in the sovereign possession and disposition of Blackness, in the capacity to utilize, bend, and incarcerate Blackness at will.

In such a metaphysics, slavery is but one manifestation of the desire to possess and dispose, though it is the form that displays most viscerally the underlying continuity between those pleasures and appetites too often mistaken for counters to the revulsions and phobias at work in anti-Black racism, rather than their obverse. Ridgeway himself draws a line connecting varying libidinal rewards when he describes the dictate that is the American Imperative: "To lift up the lesser races. If not to lift up, subjugate. And if not subjugate, exterminate" (226). As a way of life, anti-Blackness sets the collective horizon that conditions white treatment of Black people, who can only, in this schema, be property: property to lift up (dressed up in the ideology of whiteness oblige), property to subjugate (exploit for profit), or property to exterminate (kill with impunity). In this respect, the American Imperative is the ideological articulation of white civil society's libidinal economy. If the libidinal economy unconsciously regulates white desires and phobias, the American Imperative articulates it in the open, legitimizing the production and circulation of anti-Blackness as the prerogative of white sovereignty. Radically opposed from the perspective of life, the acts of lifting up and exterminating nevertheless function as two sides of the same coin for white folks; both provide the titillations of a mastery secured by supremacist ideology and legal impunity, a self-possession only realized through the captivity of the other. Thus, if Cora's journey from Georgia to South Carolina, North Carolina, Tennessee, Indiana, and beyond takes her through what an underground station agent describes as a series of "states of possibility,"[8] it also thrusts her into varying experiences of anti-Blackness, or states of impossibility. On the Randall plantation in Georgia, Cora, like all the enslaved, is "reduced to a thing, to *being* for the captor," as Hortense Spillers puts it.[9] She is fungible property to be "enjoyed," in David Marriott's terms, "as a non-recognized thing, a *res* who can be used, put to work, killed and fucked as such (i.e., without any possibility of subjectivity or transformation)."[10] Cora's escape, like her mother Mabel's, is met by Randall, and Ridgeway too, with an obsessive fury that is driven by more than anger over their monetary loss. Her flight shakes the captor's being, revealing that his sovereignty is not absolute. As Ridgeway admits, he experiences Mabel's disappearance "as a personal injury" (226); her *marronage* is a scandal to him and his likes. He fixates on catching Cora as a way to repair his narcissistic wound and restore his white wholeness. North Carolina's exterminationist laws manifest a similar logic on a communal scale. In the world of the novel, the state has banned all Black people from its soil; its "Friday Festival" lynchings of discovered fugitives, accompanied by minstrel skits, bear the marks of scapegoating rituals designed to purge each community of imagined sexual predations and anxiously anticipated outbreaks of retributive Black violence—or rather, to revel in the theater of purging, since the ritual must repeat itself every Friday, without fail, and therefore the supply of lurking threats must never fully dry up. The illusion of white plenitude depends on the presence of a nameable otherness to identify, manipulate, and exercise mastery over.

Mastery generates at once sadistic pleasures—the thrill of torturing or killing—but also fantasies of virtue and deification. The continuity between these distinct white experiences becomes visible in North Carolina, where the community's genocidal commitment to extermination seems at first to conflict with the attitudes of Martin and Ethel, the reluctant allies who hide Cora in their attic. The distance separating the two positions shortens, however, as the novel shifts vantage points. Ethel sees no wrong in slavery

("Slavery as a moral issue, comments the narrator, "never interested Ethel"), reasoning teleologically, like Ridgeway, that "if God had not meant for Africans to be enslaved, they wouldn't be in chains" (199). She resents being made to risk her life, viewing slavery as an issue that does not, and should not, concern her or oblige her to any course of action. Martin subscribes to a similar view, making excuses for his wife's coldness that Cora effectively demolishes:

> "You understand she's scared to death. We're at the mercy of fate."
> "You feel like a slave?" Cora asked.
> Ethel hadn't chosen this life, Martin said.
> "You were born to it? Like a slave?"
> That put an end to their conversation that night. (171)

Ethel's change of heart when Cora falls ill—breaking her previous silence, she nurses Cora back to health and keeps her company during her convalescence—reveals itself to be rooted in an anti-Blackness of a piece with her neighbors' murderous drives. Cora's illness becomes for Ethel only an occasion to realize her Christian missionary dreams of finding "a savage to call her own" (200). Her childhood fantasy of proselytizing grateful Africans who "lift her to the sky, praising her name" (195) is a violent and narcissistic delight, a self-gratifying instrumentalization of the other that the novel explicitly likens to rape. Ethel can live her Christian humanism without dissonance only by denying Black claims to humanity. For her, Africans and their descendants are "sons of Ham," cursed and excluded from the Hebrew tribe (186); if it is sinful to enslave a fellow human, such treatment applied to Black folks is without blame and even ordained. Her desire to act as savior can only manifest itself as humane treatment of the nonhuman, as a surplus gesture, not a moral duty; only as such can it escape both altruism and obligation, and function instead to confirm her virtue and comfort her idea of self.

On a broader scale, the state of South Carolina similarly implements policies of "colored advancement" (93) that allow white folks to savor their roles as educators bestowing gifts of knowledge and controlling historical narrative or as doctors "lifting up" those in their care. In providing Cora, both literally and figuratively, with "the softest bed she had ever lain in" (96)—access to education, a paying job, comfortable room and board, and therapeutic social events—South Carolina keeps her, and all of its Black residents, in gentler, less obvious chains but chains nonetheless. The pleasure of the virtuous teacher toiling for the benefit of her charges is distinct but inseparable from the pleasure of the slaveowner, a continuity that the television series based on the novel translates well in its striking depiction of the curator at the Museum of Natural Wonders, who takes glee in cracking the whip in his diorama presentation of plantation life.

His enjoyment reveals what is *in him more than him*: an anti-Blackness that exceeds his symbolic representation of himself as a forward-thinking and benevolent educator.[11] His affect shatters the truth of his racially welcoming symbolic ego, unveiling, as it were, a slaveholder in every white subject, regardless of the state.[12] South Carolinians pride themselves on their enlightenment and their superiority to the likes of the brutish Ridgeway, but their paternalism springs not only from vanity but also from fear, a lethal combination that generates state-mandated programs carrying out forced medical experimentation, sterilization, and institutionalization. As Dr. Bertram confides to a white railroad agent he wrongly assumes to be sympathetic:

> America has imported and bred so many Africans that in many states the whites are outnumbered. For that reason alone, emancipation is impossible. With strategic sterilization—first the women but both sexes in time—we could free them from bondage without fear that they'd butcher us in our sleep. The architects of the Jamaica uprisings had been of Beninese and Congolese extraction, willful and cunning. What if we tempered those bloodlines carefully over time? (125)

Controlling Black bodies and futurity in this way allows South Carolinians to act the liberator without sacrificing white comfort and dominance, to eradicate all threats of a retribution while playing at being upstanding and just.

While Whitehead uses estranging anachronism to link varying historical manifestations of anti-Black oppression to a common libidinal economy, Maryse Condé makes a similar critique of racial progressivism through an ironic interrogation of contemporary France's color-blind ideology of belonging. In the aftermath of the murders at the offices of the satirical newspaper *Charlie Hebdo*—one in a three-day series of coordinated attacks in and around Paris in January 2015 that resulted in twenty deaths, including those of three assailants, and that motivated Condé to write *The Wondrous and Tragic Life of Ivan and Ivana*—mass demonstrations in France coalesced around the slogan "Je suis Charlie," reinvigorating a commitment to secular republican values and reigniting national debates over the causes of terrorism. Reviewing *Ivan and Ivana*'s mordant take on this handwringing search for origins, Maya Jaggi argues that "Condé's provocative fun cloaks a challenge: is there not more than a little bad faith in the way the west earnestly seeks the roots of jihadi radicalism while turning a blind eye to the flagrant ills that add rocket fuel to its meretricious allure?"[13] What skews these public debates more specifically, Alana Lentin has argued, is the "culturally singular vision"[14] of French republican wholesomeness that serves as its assumed ground and guide. This vision—or "white analytic" as Lentin puts it, following Barnor Hesse—takes white French majoritarian culture to be the neutral, non-racist, nonsexist, and nonreligious norm against which other cultural and religious practices, or identity-based organizations, become marked by contrast as partisan, racist, antifeminist, and anti-secular. This alignment of *laïcité* with antiracist neutrality forecloses the conclusion that critiques of Islam in France—in which debates over gender equality also come to serve as a wedge—could have anything to do with racism and whiteness as a culturally specific viewpoint. Reductive understandings of racism as a matter of "personal prejudice"[15] similarly lead such proponents of *laïcité* to mistake their particular interpretation of secularism for a universal, rational, and obvious reading of the law.[16] Viewed through such an optic, Lentin demonstrates, anticolonial and antiracist anger becomes illegible as a motive for terrorist violence. Charges of racism—such as the criticisms of *Charlie Hebdo*'s long practice of deploying racist caricature in the name of fighting racism—then incite puzzlement and the counterclaim that critics have either misread the complex context of France or that their judgment is itself clouded by their non-color-blind (and therefore racist) perspective.

Not only, however, does a commitment to color-blind *laïcité* make anti-Blackness difficult to identify in any form other than overt bias, obscuring the libidinal investments involved in an attachment to neutrality that itself passes for unemotional rationalism, but its ideological hegemony also overdetermines the shape of critique by focusing the debate on the republic's inclusions and exclusions or how best, in other words, to realize universalism's promise. What compelled Condé to write about the 2015 attacks were those dimensions of the violence that disrupted these prevailing analytical approaches. While the *Charlie Hebdo* murders dominated national and international news coverage as well as the language of protest that emerged in their wake, the events also involved the killing of hostages at a Kosher supermarket, as well as the shooting of a young police officer, Clarissa Jean-Philippe. It is this last death—the "blind slaughter" of a Black woman from Martinique by another Black French citizen, a man of Malian descent—that Condé describes as the "turning point" that spurred her to write this novel in response.[17] What struck her about this particular attack was the way it shattered existing understandings of cohesion and violence. As she explains, this killing gave the lie to the myth that racial identity creates sufficient affinities to give rise to anticolonial political solidarity among Black people. The unprecedented form of violence exercised against Jean-Philippe—"a violence without regard for skin color, family, or friends"—cannot be combatted simply by calling out the usual suspects, Condé argues.[18] "Rehearsing admonishments of colonialism and its aftermath is no longer enough," she states in an interview. "'Terrorist' attacks, as they're called, are drawing blood from the planet, affecting the world in its entirety: in India just as in Pakistan, in Turkey just as in Europe and America. Why are we in this situation? No one has clear answers. But what seems clear is that that literature's mission has to change in response to this new information."[19]

The unsentimental, even playful, approach Condé takes to terrorism in this work represents a startling intervention into a global problem Condé characterizes as a "human" one: a problem of "human and social dysfunction" giving rise to self-destruction, to a violent conflict between "one part of humanity [who] seems bent on destroying the other."[20] If the figure of the terrorist signifies for a Western audience the inhuman par excellence, the irrational and ruthless enemy of humanity and civilization—legitimizing, in turn, Islamophobia and an endless War on Terror across the Western world—Condé's novel prompts her readers to reconsider what it means to see and fear the enemy as (in)human and to allow the literary imagination to interrupt that knowledge. The need to think and do literature otherwise is urgent, if literature is to be capable of saying something about the globalized, inhuman world, if it is to help us enter into relation with the inhuman—those who break with accepted images of the human, with social codes of humanist belief and action. The newness of the situation, she suggests, requires not just a change in mission but also a change in the literary form of the Francophone Antillean novel, a change so necessary that she describes her approach to *The Wondrous and Tragic Life of Ivan and Ivana* as a pursuit of "innovation at any cost," a risky endeavor whose success is not guaranteed.[21] But the goal of literature, as Condé's terms suggest here, is not so much explanation as *response*, a response to the interpellation of global events. In fact, literature's challenge is an ethical one: it must respond and reflect in the *absence* of "clear answers," as well as in the absence of aesthetic blueprints. If literature is to interrupt knowledge of the inhuman—or more precisely the "white analytic" that drives the search for clear answers—it must carefully scrutinize the profound racialization of the human as such. It must work by recalibrating, rather than setting aside, anticolonial and antiracist modes of critical response.

Troubling the Human, Worlding Blackness

Beginning imaginatively with the twins' blissful unity in the womb, Condé's novel immediately throws into question what it means to trace a life's trajectory back to an origin that would explain its eventual telos. Elevated to mythic status already by the chapter title, with its Shakespearean echoes ("In Utero or Bounded in a Nutshell"), Ivan and Ivana's birth takes the form of a tragic fall from harmony dictated by uncontrollable fate: "besieged" in the womb by "an invincible force," they undergo a "horrible downward journey" through the birth canal and into a blinding light.[22] Yet while their separation into two distinct bodies disorients the infants, it is not only this parting in itself that the novel targets but also the hierarchizing forces of a white and heteronormative symbolic order that carves evaluative distinctions into their flesh as it individuates them. The twins' expulsion from the paradise of the womb begins even before they draw their first breath, as the corporate "they," expressed in French by the masculine plural "ils," gives way at once to the singular and to sex differentiation:

> They got the impression of being brutally dragged down and forced to leave the warm and tranquil abode where they had lived for many weeks. A terrible smell clung to their nostrils as they gradually, helplessly, made their descent [. . .]. The twin who had a button between his legs preceded the smaller less developed other whose sex was hollowed out by a large scar. He butted his way down the narrow passage whose walls slowly widened. (15)

To make the imaginative leap into the fetuses' untutored perspective, the narrator focuses on sensation—smell and touch—and approximates naive description with the use of nonspecific terms like *bouton* (a button, a flower bud, or pustule). Yet the impossibility of socially unmediated perception is brought sharply into view at the mention of the *balafre*—a long, liplike scar—marking Ivana as wounded and "hollowed out," always already castrated and seemingly destined to follow rather than lead. Observation is entangled with interpretation, and difference, as soon as it is noticed, is read as loss. Like the "a" at the end of "Ivana"—which we soon learn is merely "a feminine version" of the name Simone gives to her son (21)—the *balafre* functions as an excess that ironically signifies derivativeness and a presence that indexes an absence, an injurious cut (the French word designates both the scar itself and the wound that leaves this trace).

A new kind of scarring marks Ivana again at the end of the novel, seemingly bringing her story full circle. Killed by her brother during a Christmas attack on a nursing home for retired police, Ivana becomes a revered martyr in Guadeloupe. Something of a parody of the Christian nativity unfolds the December after Ivana's burial in her home village of Dos d'Âne (a name meaning, first, "donkey's back," evoking Mary's journey to Bethlehem, but also "speed bump"): three Haitians, following a bright star in the sky, make their way to her tomb, launching a tradition of annual pilgrimage to honor their "petite sœur de la blesse," or "little wounded sister" (249). Meaning "scar" or "wounded" in Creole, the narrator explains, the word *blesse* "refers of course to the scars dealt by life which are never erased and always remain a wound in both body and soul" (249). To sanctify Ivana this way is to retrospectively confirm the twins' predestination from birth, to see the meaning of Ivana's life as encapsulated by her original identity in the womb as the smaller, scarred sister. At the same time, the satirical portrait of this pilgrimage casts a skeptical light on this unbroken arc from birth to death. Moreover, the multiplication of wounds in the narrator's translation—the many scars life leaves—along with the shift back to a more melancholic tone in these concluding words place weight instead on the temporality of Ivana's story and the historical causes of such wounds. Wounds may never disappear, but they do appear; if Ivana is wounded, this condition is not a transcendental one completely outside of time. If Ivana's sex is a scar even in the womb, it is not because there is no cause for this condition, but rather that she is born into a woundedness that precedes her, a narrow channeling of her flesh and being into categories of legibility that leave a mark.

In this light, Ivana's natal scarring is reminiscent of what Hortense Spillers has described as a "hieroglyphics of the flesh," the traces left on the flesh by the "severe disjunctures" of slavery.[23] These traces of a violent ungendering and theft of the body, as Lisa Guenther comments, are "not outside of history, but not quite inside history either," in that they are passed on from generation to generation, in altered form.[24] Like slavery's hieroglyphics, which "come to be hidden to the cultural seeing by skin color,"[25] Ivana's scar becomes invisible as such to the eye steeped in French republican values—a color-blind ideology invested in the preservation of equal rights through the eradication of difference from the public sphere. "Ex utero," it is Ivan, rather than Ivana, who is assumed to be scarred and whose woundedness takes center stage in the inquiry into terrorism's causes. If Ivan's status in the womb is that of the developed twin, the one who butts his way down the birth canal, seemingly taking charge of his movements rather than passively submitting to the forces that are expelling him, his masculinity—the measure against which Ivana's body and initiative are judged lacking—is valued only when it is expressed through sanctioned pursuits: education, social courtesy, the enforcement of law and order. Every injury major and minor to Ivan's dignity and love for Ivana is scrutinized by the narrator as contributors to his radicalization, to his becoming inhuman; his story, like his sister's, is read through a "white analytic" from its telos backward, as a fall into demonic depravity. Conversely, as a model student and servant of the republic in the making, Ivana provides the foil of angelic wholeness to Ivan's damaged self.

A "Black analytic" by contrast brings to light race as a code for what Sylvia Wynter calls the "genre of the human," a construction in which the figure of the white (and in this case secular, French) citizen "overrepresents itself as if it were the human itself."[26] As Alexander Weheliye puts it, race operates not as a biological or cultural taxonomy, but rather as "a set of sociopolitical processes that discipline humanity into full humans, not-quite-humans, and nonhumans."[27] These "racializing assemblages" naturalize who truly belongs to the nation; they differentiate, hierarchize, and ban "nonwhite subjects from the category of the human."[28] France's republican framework, its "white analytic," masks this ideological division between the human and its racialized others by upholding abstract equality and casting critiques of this very abstraction as illegitimate attacks on equality itself destined to reproduce rather than eradicate racist practices.

Accordingly, when race and gender are thought intersectionally, the point is not only to expose the limits of white feminisms with the goal of gaining entry into its frameworks for the excluded but to question the human as such. Commenting on Wynter's transformative project, Weheliye notes the tendency (as exhibited by Judith Butler) to misread the force of her critique:

> Viewing Wynter's colossal project, with which Butler does not engage in any sustained way, both of critiquing the current western instantiation of the human as coterminous with the white liberal subject and of crafting a new humanism should not be reduced to observing the historicity of this concept with the aim of showing how women of color and other groups are excluded from its purview. Or to put it in Butlerian terms: Wynter is interested in human trouble rather than "merely" woman-of-color trouble, even while she deploys the liminal perspective of women of color to imagine humanity otherwise.[29]

Understanding the perspective of women of color in order to bring them into the existing fold is not sufficient; rather, Black feminism undertakes the project of *imagining humanity otherwise*, opening up an ethico-political horizon under which Black women can enact universality and be seen as agents of worlding.

In reading radicalization as a form of gendered racialization, the novel gestures to its own alchemical "world-forming" capacity.[30] It does so by indicting the disciplining of the human itself, connecting the expulsion of the terrorist from the realm of the human to the colonial structures that have similarly drawn lines between human and other throughout European modernity. If the novel's first pages evoke both the twins' fantasy of blissful union and Western onlookers' attempts to boil their story of terror down to a calculable cause that could then be contained, it also represents the kind of imaginative and affective work the novel will do throughout to unsettle the interpretive protocols characterizing the earnest Western search for radicalization's causes. Playing on the empty familiarity of birth—a universal but also universally forgotten personal experience—the "in utero" opening fills this void with a descriptive content that is evocative but also estranging, alluring in its offer of knowledge but also bitingly ironic.

"Ex utero," the novel portrays colonial ideology as a creeping force that can be held at bay only for so long. If the twins begin life enchanted—finding delight in their mother's beauty, in the touch of sand sifting through their fingers, and, most of all, in forming a unit, a "they"—this bliss depends in part on ignorance:

> They were at first filled with wonder by the ray of sun that entered through the shack's wide open window [. . .]. They rapidly remembered their names, pricking up their ears and waving their little feet at the

mention of these syllables so easy to retain. What they didn't know was that the priest at Dos d'Âne, a fat, dull-witted man, had almost refused to christen them.

"How could you give them such names," he shouted angrily at Simone. "Ivan, Ivana! Not only do they not have a father, but you want to turn them into true heathens!" (18–19)

If Simone holds firm and wins the battle with this church authority, her retelling of her victory to the twins becomes a reminder of their position as liminal, policed bodies whose inclusion in the circle of insiders is subject to the whims of the more powerful, those who draw lines between the believer and the heathen, the Christian and the *mécréant*, that ambiguously racialized "infidel" or "miscreant" whose alternate religion or atheism is portrayed as a negation of true faith and expression of savagery.

A seeming non-sequitur follows this exchange with the priest, sharpening the narrator's jabs at his dull-witted logic:

Simone's family was used to both multiple and singular births. In the nineteenth century, her ancestor, Zuléma, the first of a litter of quintuplets, had been invited to the Universal Exposition in Saint-Germain-en-Laye in order to prove what could become of a descendant of a slave when he breathed in the effluvium of civilization. Dressed in a tie and three-piece suit, he was a surveyor by trade. He had learned opera arias all on his own by listening to a program on Radio Guadeloupe called *Classical? Classical Indeed!* (19)

It would seem that what Simone's family is accustomed to is not just multiple and extraordinary births, but rather colonialist scrutiny of their bodies, their intelligence, and their reproductive decisions. The animalization of Zuléma (as the first of a "litter" of children) and his celebration, at the heart of empire, as an admirable prodigy are two sides of the colonialist coin, one that acknowledges and champions its own "civilizing" force without granting its colonized subjects full title to that civilization.

In these two brief anecdotes the narrator ties together the Christian fundaments of French colonialism, the heterosexual, patriarchal values of the same that continue to dominate contemporary culture, and the racialization of both religious and cultural difference that lives on in the ostensibly postcolonial and secular republic. Time and again the narrator draws attention back to this race-gender-religion knot as a key to understanding Ivan's path, from the twins' discovery, once they start school, "that they had no father in Guadeloupe," an absence their mother interprets as a contributor to Ivan's waywardness (23), to an argument with a woman selling fruit at the market, who derides the "miserably black" family—revealing to the twins that "they belonged to the most underprivileged category of the population, the ones anyone could insult as they liked" for "their skin was black, their hair kinky, and their mother worked herself to the bone in the sugarcane fields for a pittance" (27)—to Ivan's parroted critique of France (which the narrator describes tellingly as "blasphemy" [29]), in imitation of his primary school teacher's fury against a white, Western order responsible for the death of his wife and son, killed in the Middle East in a NATO bombing raid. As French citizens, Ivan and Ivana are abstractly and juridically fully human—they purportedly belong to the French Republic—but in practice their Blackness haunts them. They are periodically reminded of their status as *not-quite-human* (as nonwhites whose difference is never forgotten, they cannot fully occupy the ontological position of the human), a liminal condition constantly under threat of sliding into the *nonhuman* (noncitizen or denationalized others who fall outside the "protection" of French Law, like the refugees in limbo at Calais that Ivan eventually encounters).

At the same time, this haunting takes different forms as it intersects with their gendered positioning in France's civil society. "Heartbroken" by the fruit vendor's harsh words, Ivana vows to "avenge her mother and give her the gentler way of life she deserved," while Ivan is "filled with rage against life and against his fate which had turned him into an underprivileged subordinate" (27). For Ivana, education and a career in policing hold out the promise of an agency she is denied as a Black woman, and her docility helps her achieve it; being called "Snow White" at work appears to her a harmless inside joke, and she can only accept Ivan's conversion to Islam, a religion that "disgusts" her, as an act of social integration, not a matter of conviction (109). For Ivan, education and an apprenticeship in chocolate-making (the available position that career counselors deem him fit for, with ironic echoes of colonial Europe's tropical exploitations) represent submission to an emasculating and recolonizing authority that promises nothing but more of the same, while Islam eventually comes to represent for him the promise of changing the world. Ivana's path to success is reinforced by professors, colleagues, and friends who integrate her into their milieu and praise her choices, while Ivan drifts without much conviction from one ideology and brush with the law to another, influenced by various anticolonial activists, religious extremists, and other rebels against the status quo along the way. If Ivan progressively dissolves into the category of the nonhuman, the inhuman terrorist, joining the ranks of the wretched of the earth, Ivana grows closer to the French ideal holding out the promise of humanity/whiteness.

The novel interrogates this ideal first through its multiplication of the "causes" to which Ivan's participation in the attacks might be attributed, troubling the attempt to draw a line from his actions back to some essential core being. No less than three times does the narrator claim an explicit "beginning" to Ivan's radicalization, and the events that implicitly steer him toward his end are even more numerous.[31] Focalized in large part through

Ivan's perspective, while also ranging widely in tone, from melancholic sorrow to dispassionate analysis to caustic irony, the novel also pushes us to expand our affective dispositions and to allow curiosity and sympathy to flow alongside repulsion, frustration, and confusion. In this sense we might characterize Condé's novel as responding to a double bind: to understand the inhuman (the terrorist, the enemy) and to resist converting this inhuman otherness back into the familiar (the human). At stake in the double bind is, first, the relationship between an ethics of relation and a politics of justice, and the ability of each to remain in productive tension with the other. Slavoj Žižek's discussion of Mary Shelley's *Frankenstein* highlights the strengths of literature's humanizing potential but also the dangers of allowing the humanizing imagination to collapse this double bind. From a humanist standpoint, literature harnesses the powers of dialogue and transforms the enemy into something other than enemy, following the belief that "an enemy is someone whose story you have not heard." *Frankenstein* exemplifies for Žižek the power of aesthetics to transform relationality through the imaginative act of listening:

> Shelley does something that a conservative would never have done. In the central part of her book, she allows the monster to speak for himself, to tell the story from his own perspective. Her choice expresses the liberal attitude to freedom of speech at its most radical: everyone's point of view should be heard. In *Frankenstein*, the monster is not a "thing," a horrible object no one dares to confront; he is fully *subjectivised*. Mary Shelley moves inside his mind and asks what it is like to be labelled, defined, oppressed, excommunicated, even physically distorted by society. The ultimate criminal is thus allowed to present himself as the ultimate victim. The monstrous murderer reveals himself to be a deeply hurt and desperate individual, yearning for company and love.[32]

Through its appeal to the imagination, the novel works to expand our understanding and sensibilities, teaching us "to rid the mind of the narrowness of believing in one thing and not in other things."[33] *Frankenstein* performs an alchemical transformation by humanizing the monster, giving him subjectivity, creatively empowering him to speak in his own voice—in short, changing his being. As a consequence, Shelley's readers have a chance to believe otherwise, to believe in the creature's right to a livable life, in his right to narrate and not to be exclusively narrated by Victor. At the same time, Žižek pointedly observes that "there is, however, a clear limit to this procedure: Is one also ready to affirm that Hitler was an enemy because his story was not heard?" Diffusing the horror of an event through storytelling can obfuscate its injustice.[34] That is to say, this humanizing procedure is not generalizable to all cases of conflict; understanding cannot take the place of critical judgment and justice. It would be absurd, for instance, to ask: *Is*

Ridgeway Cora's enemy—a monster bent on terrorizing runaway slaves—because she hasn't heard his story?[35]

Allowing oneself to imagine the inner life of the terrorist in this aesthetic education does not, then, equate simply to rehumanizing Ivan. Rather, it involves imagining humanity otherwise, as at once humane, inhumane, and irreducible to predictable psychic or historical forces. Ivan's suicidal violence against elderly ex-officers is arguably detrimental to the cause of racialized communities, but it is also a response to the politics of racial indifference, reflecting anger and a desire to change the existing state of affairs. His act strikes back at a social order (symbolically manifested in the police retirement home) that deprives him of a meaningful life plan, yet it is also a nihilistic and escapist response to what Ivan experiences as a living death in the absence of his sister's love. Thwarted by his upbringing, which forbids the intimacy the twins desire, Ivan chooses murder-suicide. In this sense his turn to terrorism enacts the death drive as Freud describes it: "an instinct [. . .] inherent in organic life to restore an earlier state of things."[36] Ivan craves a return to his previous fusion with Ivana, and self-annihilation provides the only possible release from permanent alienation.

Condé's novel troubles the human further, and in unexpected ways, by inviting us to reconsider the death drive from Ivana's vantage point. Like her brother, Ivana chooses death: "It was the only thing to do," the narrator declares when Ivan fires on his sister, "the only act that had meaning to it. Ivana understood perfectly. Consequently she arched her breast in order to acknowledge the blessing from the bullets" (236). This self-sacrifice appears on the one hand a stereotypical example of feminine passivity and lovestruck loyalty; Ivana remains faithful to her brother to the end, to the point of subordinating her very life to his desires. At the same time, the novel's positioning of incest as a wrench in the Western story of radicalization politicizes her abrupt decision. Withstanding their attempts to deny it, the twins' incestuous longing for fusion hovers persistently over them as an ideal just outside their grasp, eventually overwhelming their story. Ivana's drive to succeed in her career and to conform to social expectations through marriage to a colleague suddenly mutates into a death drive disrupting her previous commitments and decentering the disciplined and disciplining police officer self she has been crafting. The death drive derails what Elizabeth Freeman dubs "chrononormativity": "the use of time to organize human bodies toward maximum productivity."[37] Freeman draws here on Dana Luciano's concept of "chronobiopolitics" ("the sexual arrangement of the time of life"[38]), referring to the temporal regulation of life spans through "teleological schemes [. . .] such as marriage, accumulation of health and wealth for the future, reproduction, childrearing, and death and its attendant rituals."[39] The death drive brings to ruins Ivana's socially forecast identity and sanctioned future projects.

Queer desire jams the disciplining of the twins' humanity, and the death drive in Ivana shifts cast, taking the form not simply of a return to a prior, biological death, but rather of "an uncanny excess of life" or "an 'undead' urge which persists beyond the (biological) cycle of life and death," as Žižek puts it.[40] "The ultimate lesson of psychoanalysis," he continues, "is that human life is never 'just life': humans are not simply alive, they are possessed by the strange drive to enjoy life in excess, passionately attached to a surplus which sticks out and derails the ordinary run of things."[41] What the death drive points to is a self-sabotaging principle,[42] an excess that lies beyond human mastery, "an excess that is ambiguous in the sense that it can be a source of constructive energy or it can be purely destructive."[43] To domesticate the monstrous, to bring the inhuman back into the realm of the human—in the name of understanding, giving voice, or otherwise—is to cover over this "abyssal dimension" of the subject and to misconstrue how the drive to enjoy functions.

This indocile force does not obey a cost-benefit logic. In thrusting herself into the bullets Ivana is no longer acting in her own interests: preserving her life and serving the republic. She rebels against the strictures shaping her future, because she is *more* than an agent of biopolitics in pursuit of symbolic whiteness. A death drive such as this, as Adrian Johnson notes, holds emancipatory potential: "Thanks to 'the death drive' (as disruptive negativity), the human individual isn't entirely enslaved to tyranny of the pragmatic-utilitarian economy of well-being, to a happiness thrust forward by the twin authorities of the pleasure and reality principles."[44] In this moment of decision, Ivana makes Antigone's choice, rejecting an order premised on the destruction of people like her brother and the love she bears him. Ivana's act jams the "white analytic," rejecting state power and its interpellative rewards.

But if Ivana's self-sacrifice momentarily troubles the sanctioned genre of the human, it is no heroic act that will change the world, nor even save the life of her brother. The twins' story escapes their grasp upon their death and like clay gets reshaped in the hands of those who remain. Ivan is reviled, and Ivana is revered, solidifying the line between human and monster. If the state works to erase Ivan from view, cutting him off from all visitors to his deathbed and hastily burying him in a common grave behind the hospital, Ivana's sympathetic admirers entomb her in sanctity, transforming her into a frozen statue of herself, everyone's and no one's "little wounded sister." Ivana is truly idealized only when she dies, when she becomes fully malleable to white desires and designs. Yet, like Ivana herself, driven by an undead urge, the novel outlives itself, pursuing an unending that is more than its ending and testifying to the uncontainable fecundity of Ivan and Ivana's story. The novel's conclusion proper ("More About the Uterus: There's No Escaping It") tracks the restless, dissatisfied storytelling that the twins spur, kept alive by the incomprehensibility of their love and death, and whets the appetite for more with the revelation that Ivan has left behind a lover pregnant with twins. A further epilogue chides readers for their narrowmindedness and revives the urge to reinterpret, to refuse to let the story lie, in both senses of the term—we cannot allow the story to rest, and we cannot help but question its relationship to truth. Rather than merely declaring Ivan and Ivana's tale inexplicable, the novel produces a proliferation of reasons for their actions, an aesthetic overabundance that keeps the work of meaning-making in play. Its caustic and sanguine demonstration of the persistence of race and gender formations is twinned with an indomitable drive to reshape the horizons of this world. We might say that the death at its center forms a talking scar, a trace that protrudes and impels new efforts at healing and worldling.

Rebellious Properties

The Wondrous and Tragic Life of Ivan and Ivana dislocates a "white analytic" through an affective alchemy. Its erotic proliferations work to reshape the libidinal dimensions of meaning-making, revealing that economies of anti-Black desire are not seamless and unchangeable, though their inertia is strong. Indeed, such a libidinal economy continues to propel the French state—which, as we've seen, effectively co-opts Ivana's death, gentrifying its disruptive potential, festishizing her martyrdom, and reinvesting her body with republican (race-free) values. To this practice of capture by assimilation, Condé's text opposes a monstrous fable, confounding in its narrative unruliness, in its tale of a fabulous destiny, or *destin fabuleux*, that refuses to stop at its foreordained destination.

Whitehead's *Underground Railroad* similarly confuses genres but does so to engage the obdurate violence of capture by possession. In figuring Cora's fugitivity as a continually thwarted effort, *The Underground Railroad* identifies, with Afropessimist thinkers, slavery's devastating evacuation of relation, its ontological transformation of Africans into objects to be possessed, things void of relationality, as a crucial problem for America's present and future. In turning genres on their head, the novel underscores the pervasiveness and persistent threat of capture; as critics have noted, *The Underground Railroad* uses fantasy as "a vehicle to expose the truths of history rather than to indulge in its negation"[45] and deploys counterfactuals to render racism "as simultaneously preposterous and real."[46] Yet the novel not only takes stock of slavery's ontological devastation but also continually highlights the untotalizing character of this imposed thingliness, the rebellious capacities of those who persistently refuse to act as the property to which they have been reduced. Cora is unwilling to remain anchored and docile. She survives her dispossession, not only by physically fighting and fleeing but also through her rhetorical jabs, using every symbolic weapon at her disposal. When Ridgeway exalts the American Imperative, Cora deflates him by replying, "I need to visit the outhouse" (226). To his self-serving discourse lauding American destiny and glory, Cora can only respond scatologically, calling bullshit, in plain terms.[47] Cora's mockery recognizes the overwhelming evidence that the enslaved are indeed cursed—condemned to their current reality—yet refuses to accept it as settled truth: "Maybe everything the slave catcher said was true, Cora thought, every justification, and the sons of Ham were cursed and the slave master performed the Lord's will. And maybe, he was just a man talking to an outhouse door, waiting for someone to wipe her ass" (228). Her next gesture—selecting a fugitive bulletin to use as toilet paper (227)—emphasizes the connection between symbolic and material revolt, as well as the force of small gestures: the force required to revolt in even the minutest of ways against conditions of desperation and constraint, as well as the life-sustaining power of small, even internal, acts of resistance.

In figuring *marronage* as a utopian fugitivity, as a continually renewed effort, the novel insists, with thinkers like Fred Moten, on the ways in which relationality—the ability to form kin, to form communal projects, and to refashion the self in relation with others—escapes to some degree the destructive forces aligned against it, forces that work to instrumentalize Black bodies. To some degree, because, as Moten points out, relationality in itself is not liberating; for the captive subjected to the captor, relationality can give rise to "an expression of power, structured by the givenness of a transcendental subjectivity that the black cannot have but by which the black can be had; a structural position that he or she cannot take but by which he or she can be taken."[48] Rather, to affirm the persistence of relationality despite slavery's and racism's objectifications is to affirm that the conditions by which one can be had, by which another can have purchase on your being—contact with and vulnerability to the other—are also the conditions that allow for movement, for resistance to one's ossification as an object, condemned to social death. Acts of taking flight and remaking kin and community persist, altering the given, what is.

As Nihad Farooq has argued, Whitehead's novel deploys flight to figure the political possibilities of utopia understood not just as a nonexistent place but as a flight from place itself, a flight from the values associated with rootedness, settlement, and stasis. Farooq notes that *The Underground Railroad* foregrounds movement, or *marronage*, as both "the cost and the gift of freedom."[49] It "untethers" freedom from the myth of American statehood and insists instead on freedom as a deterritorialized form of relationality, of striving, actively, with others.[50] In portraying Cora's struggle as precarious and unending, the novel is both clear-eyed about the deceptive falsehoods of American narratives of freedom, equality, and uplift that ignore the realities of racism, but also utopian in its openness to the possibilities of change, to "being otherwise."[51] Farooq draws here on Jameson's contention that utopia must remain a horizon, an impetus to action and rethinking, if it is to retain its political dynamism and avoid falling prey to "the myth of teleology, techno-rationalism, or settlement."[52] In *The Underground Railroad*, Farooq writes, "political subjectivity is not a reward for making it to the other side of slavery and joining a community of free people, but, rather, a constituent element of the journey itself."[53] Likewise, "utopia is presented throughout the novel as a necessary and perpetual yearning that is a fundamental aspect of present, collective survival—a striving *toward*, not a static realization *of*."[54] Utopia as fugitivity thrives on negativity, in its refusal "to be objectified or reduced."[55] It stages escape as "a permanent state of being that runs *from*, rather than *to*, and that refuses the refuge of home where home, freedom, and liberation have already been defined in white supremacist terms and in a dependent relationship with the notion of slavery."[56] Indeed, it is not just movement that is at issue here but the collectivity and the mode of thinking and being relationally that movement entails or figures. Movement, then, is not simply practiced by an autonomous subject in isolation, but rather by one whose maroon practice is born of interdependency and sustained through relation. Cora's flight takes shape on the suggestion of a fellow slave and her life depends on the others who aid her (and who are put to death in the process); more hauntingly, her ability to conceive of flight as a possibility is significantly shaped by her mother Mabel's earlier escape, an escape that painfully incarnates both the fact of human interdependence and the denial of that interdependence under slavery, a condition in which mothers and children are reduced to fleshly objects without the possibility of relation, objects whose bonds are persistently broken. Cora lives Mabel's departure as at once a horrific abandonment, betrayal, and denial of relation, as well as a rupture with the present order of the plantation and its inevitability as her future. Mabel's flight creates the conditions of possibility for Cora's own escape, all while being lived as a constraint on that possibility, a curse visited upon her, in that Mabel's disappearance spurs the frustrated Ridgeway to track her daughter, this aberrational and dangerous bloodline, with increased vengeance.

In fleeing generic conventions while rusing with them, *The Underground Railroad* also enacts *marronage* on the level of form, creating new relationships with readerly expectations, much like maroon communities enacted a form of sovereignty characterized by interdependence or relational autonomy, by breaking with yet remaining parasitic on and disruptive to the plantations alongside which maroon communities formed.[57] The novel becomes dreamlike, or nightmarish, because it functions to compress bits of historical experience together into a surreal, episodic, yet unfortunately plausible coherence for readers with some familiarity with historical events and contemporary racism. Whitehead makes use of anachronism to decontextualize and represent as contemporaneous a series of different forms of oppression unfolding in these states, some dating back to slavery, others, like the Tuskegee syphilis experiments, occurring more recently. In so doing he centers the narrative on a "falsehood" to reinvigorate the historicist-contextualist paradigm, to "offer [. . .] a new literary vision of historicist-activism" for the age of fake news, one that insists on the inseparability of political action and ideology critique.[58] In achieving this critico-dreamlike tone, the novel seems to take on the status of an origin story, or a counter-Genesis—it is mythlike in its statement about America's cruel foundations and original sin, yet it remains daunting in its literalness, in its depiction of racial nightmare as reality rather than allegory. In this, it could be said to operate a reverse alchemy—turning the more comforting gold of abstraction into the affective equivalent of lead in its ironic insistence on historical fact.

If the train, the major conceit of the novel, provides an ironic *mise en abyme* of this process, another striking moment of alchemy in the novel involves a different kind of rusing with allegory: the penultimate chapter of the book, which reveals the fate of Mabel, Cora's mother. Running through swampland to hide her tracks, Mabel stops to rest and ponders both her first taste of freedom and the daughter she has left behind. She decides she cannot proceed without Cora and that this moment of temporary escape will have to sustain her for now. But as she turns to head back to the plantation, she is bitten by a cottonmouth snake and dies swallowed up by the swamp, erased from view and from the historical record. This episode evokes of course the serpent of Genesis and invites allegorical interpretation, but it also insists on the concrete hazards of snakebite for captives at work or on the run, the flesh and blood bodies behind the fiction, and the role of contingency in a story in which Mabel's disappearance becomes a screen for projection, a founding myth and driving motivator, for Cora as well as for those who pursue her.

For the reader, Mabel also figures the utopian impulse at its purest. She knows that this white world is brutal and devoid of kindness, but she is still willing to care and love. This utopian urge manifests itself not only in her escape but even more intensely in her decision to share it. She turns back from her escape in order to turn Cora's life forward. As the narrator relates:

She was free.

This moment.

She had to go back. The girl was waiting on her. This would have to do for now. Her hopelessness had gotten the best of her, speaking under her thoughts like a demon. She would keep this moment close, her own treasure. When she found the words to share it with Cora, the girl would understand that there was something beyond the plantation, past all that she knew. That one day if she stayed strong, the girl could have it for herself.

The world may be mean, but people don't have to be, not if they refuse. (300)

Fugitivity's inventiveness takes shape in and through the refusal of reality, the refusal to settle in and for what is. In this, Mabel's flight echoes Lander's speech extolling Valentine farm, the Indiana cooperative run by the freeborn, emancipated, and fugitive Black folks who find refuge and community there: "We can't save everyone. But that doesn't mean we can't try. Sometimes a useful delusion is better than a useless truth. Nothing's going to grow in this mean cold, but we can still have flowers" (290). This embrace of the delusional, this refusal of reality, does not take the form of "fetishist disavowal" but rather displays a determination to refuse determination,[59] to ignore the weight of the anti-Black world and the cynicism and despair that its inertia should provoke.

For the reader attuned by the novel to the limitations of history as a genre, to the gaps overlooked by histories invested in dominant ideologies, Mabel's chapter surprises by filling in that gap, providing a form of closure that is unavailable to the characters. Of all the episodes in the novel, this one inhabits the tensions of utopian striving most painfully. Mabel dies; her freedom is so short-lived as to seem foreclosed as a future possibility for others. But what follows this episode is a new chapter, one introduced, significantly, by a runaway slave advertisement that both writes and rewrites the terms of the social order, tracking and also anticipating what has or might be transmuted: "RAN AWAY from her legal but not rightful master [. . .] a slave girl called CORA [. . .]. She has stopped running. Reward remains unclaimed. SHE WAS NEVER PROPERTY" (304). Mabel's submergence in the swamp figures the material and ideological erasure of the millions of enslaved exiled from life and unaccounted for in the historical record; the fiction of her story's recovery, in its very status as impossible fiction, ironically highlights that obliteration, but also the ineradicable rupture she (and others like her) brought about, her role in building the railroad at the center of the novel. Mabel's flight, along with the acts of others, becomes the origin of those rails "springing from some inconceivable source and shooting toward a miraculous terminus" (68), the rails that Cora herself forges at the end of the book, when, on a handcar in an unfinished branch of the line, she pumps her way through "the tunnel that no one had made, that led nowhere" (309), the miracle that only many could make, that no one actor could construct, and no one journey could complete.

Cora enters the underground railroad as property—property by law, property within a white order literally clad with iron—yet emerges never having been so. "Each time she brought her arms down on the lever, she drove a pickax into the rock, swung a sledge onto a railroad spike [. . .]," comments the narrator. "Who you are after you finish something this magnificent—in constructing it you have also journeyed through it, to the other side. On the one end there was who you were before you went underground, and on the other end a new person steps out into the light" (310). Cora's fugitivity, the act of refusal, of running, forges historicity itself, a pastness and open future unavailable to property, stripped from thingly possessions. In this respect, we can say with Moten that *The Underground Railroad* conducts an "experiment in anti-metaphysics."[60] Cora incompletes Ridgeway's closed metaphysics, the white order of things, refusing docility and casting her past as beyond or before being—the "other side" of being's reifications, the negativity and movement that both feeds and springs from the passage through the underground. The "North" in which she finds herself in the novel's final pages—as she heads west, toward California—is not a place but rather a movement. It is the motion of evading capture, the incompletion wrought by an inconceivable alchemy.

Unbecoming Belongings

The Underground Railroad and *The Wondrous and Tragic Life of Ivan and Ivana* probe the very possibility of alchemy in a leaden world of anti-Blackness. Revolving around the continuity between slavery and its afterlife, these novels point up first the oppressive heft of such a world, whose libidinal and material economies are fused together in an embrace immovable as iron. The clarity of Cora's unbelonging, her status as "an object among other objects" cast into a seemingly unending "zone of nonbeing," to recall Fanon's words, may dim as post-abolition models of state belonging, such as France's republican universalism, offer a lure of assimilation, yet objecthood is not easily shed, and the national body politic continues to build its coherence on whiteness, on the abjection of those who threaten the white analytic's hegemony, who reveal its worlding, its ontology, to be incomplete, to be shot through with cracks. For Ivan and Ivana, national belonging means giving oneself over to another form of capture, to the status of not-quite-human embodied in Ivana's not-so-joking nickname of "Snow White." On the threshold of the republic, Black bodies must "turn white or disappear" (*se blanchir ou disparaître*),[61] or, in other words, consent to be a single being. Accepted as docile partners to the nation-prince, they must maintain their innocence and unobtrusiveness. Yet as their difference is continually claimed not to exist, it is ceaselessly marked and remarked upon through the very denial that color matters, through the anxious naming that purports to erase race, to make it unseen, colorless as snow. The universalism that promises to be blank is in fact colored white and defined by a constitutive outside. "Belonging relies on nonbelonging":[62] Ivana's ability to assimilate requires Ivan's abjection. She must cut off a part of herself in order to be taken into the nation. To refuse to be dismembered in the name of belonging is a fugitive act.

Fanon underlined the bodily experience of this mutilating immersion in whiteness in his striking observation, "I am overdetermined from the outside. I am a slave not to the 'idea' others have of me, but to my appearance."[63] The body becomes the instrument of capture, turned against the self that is then plunged into a prison of whiteness: "The white man is all around me; up above the sky is tearing at its navel; the earth crunches under my feet and sings white, white. All this whiteness burns me to a cinder."[64] Reduced to an object among other objects, he is *in* this world but not *of* it. And yet he "refuse[s] to accept this amputation"; his body itself rebels against its own reduction to inert matter, becoming the source of questioning that he famously beseeches in the concluding lines to *Black Skin, White Masks*. Such an unruliness also spurs Cora's refusal to act as befits an object of property, an inert possession counted among another's belongings. It is the realization that her body is her master's possession—as he fondles her and asserts that he will mate her as he chooses—that splits her consciousness and impels her to run, and it is also through her body that she asserts her determination *not* to be a single being, to open a pathway to unbecoming, to reanimating that which had been fixed and thingified. When she escapes Ridgeway a first time, strangling his neck with her own chains, her scream is described as "a train whistle echoing in a tunnel," a vehicle of liberation (231); she delivers Ridgeway a final blow by using her arms as shackles, gripping him in a tight embrace and tumbling down a stairway to the underground. Fugitivity, in *The Underground Railroad*, springs from and fosters the incompleteness of a worlding that renders bodies, objects, and matter itself inert materials to be used as determined by the masters. Precisely because she is not *of* this world, Cora's very existence represents disorder *in* it, a disorder that cannot be fully contained; though Ridgeway and his kind may blunt it, Cora, and all those inhabiting its interstices, can feed its force of incompletion.

Against passions for the real that invest the white subject with the right to uplift, subjugate, or exterminate Blackness, that frame whiteness as all, identical to the universal and measure of all things desirable, *The Underground Railroad* and *The Wondrous and Tragic Life of Ivan and Ivana* cast Blackness as a compromising and defiant force. Disidentifying with the proper, with sanctioned modes of living and worlding, these novels advance an alchemy of unbecoming and a poiesis of reworlding, a fugitivity that takes shape as relation in motion.

Conclusion

Alchemy's Reason

A fugitive alchemy sows ontological disorder, enacting experiments in anti-metaphysics. If the alchemy underpinning an anti-Black world works to fix being, locking us into lines of descent and color, this other alchemy, or alchemy of the other, tarries with the paraontological and thrives on undoing beings, decompleting settled ontologies. In her fantastical vision of "guerrilla insemination" as a rebel intervention into the fertility industry's commodification and reproduction of whiteness, Patricia J. Williams takes us to the heart of alchemy's appealing fusion of techne and social magic, its tantalizing promise of altering ontology itself. "In a technological age, guerrilla warfare must be redefined," she writes.

> I dream of a New Age manifesto: We must all unite, perhaps with the help of white male college graduates who are willing to smuggle small hermetically sealed vials of black sperm into the vaulted banks of unborn golden people; we must integrate this world from the inside out. [. . .] We must shake up biological normativity [. . .]. We must be able to assert the battle from within, and in the most intimate terms conceivable.[1]

Guerrilla insemination attacks the very facticity on which phantasms of whiteness rest, mingling bloodlines and forcing an intimacy with the racialized other heretofore resisted. Yet in reaffirming the body's place as the foundation of communal identity, this rebellion falters, neutralized by an ontology of being inscribed in the law, upheld by the state, and energized by a passion for the real, for categorical stasis, that permeates the cultural imaginary and libidinal economy. As Williams quickly notes, drawing evidence from existing wrongful birth lawsuits filed by white parents after giving birth to babies they deem nonwhite, this surreptitious warfare is unlikely to succeed in countering dominant notions of property, rights, and contract, in reshaping the will to possess and dispossess: "Of course this won't work," she concludes. "We will end up with yet another generation of abandoned children, damaged in the manufacture, returned to the supplier, and sued for in the effort to undo their existence by the translation of the disaster of them into compensatory dollars and cents."[2]

Countering this pervasive alchemy of order, and its passion for being, the works studied in this book act to shift affect itself, to foster a passion for becoming, a passion for an open ontology aligned with Blackness itself, a passion for what blocks political ontology and its horizon of anti-Blackness. These interventions work to inseminate the cultural imaginary, expose alchemy's traces, and transform civil society's "economy of racial production" by exerting critical pressure on "the exclusion constitutive of the norm."[3] If guerilla insemination meets its match in the Law, alchemies of becoming dig deeper; they intervene in civil society's libidinal economy, exposing and confronting the appeal of whiteness and the ravenous enjoyment of anti-Blackness. They carry out anti-metaphysical experiments in undoing an anti-Black order and open novel ways of relating to being as becoming. Taking material conditions and embodiment seriously as conditions of possibility and constraint, what these works demonstrate, I argue, is that combatting the remarkable persistence of biological normativity, and the violence that springs from it, requires keeping playful, ironic, fanciful, speculative, and skeptical modes of storytelling alive, within the creative arts and also without, planting them like seeds in all those discursive wombs—literary, legal, historical, scientific—where distinctions between kin and stranger are both produced *and* interrogated. Only in so doing might we hope to maintain the interpretive dynamism needed to forestall the reification of categories, practices, and their meanings.

Slavery, as Saidiya Hartman puts it, "annulled lives, transforming men and women into dead matter, and then resuscitated them for servitude."[4] Slavery's alchemy sought to end alchemy itself, to erect an unyielding order founded on an irreversible conversion of humans to fungible tools of flesh. In its contemporary forms, white supremacy similarly yearns to permanently fix and possess Blackness, to ontologize Blackness as property for the consumption and enjoyment of white folks. The resistant alchemies that aim to reverse this transformation may yet follow a similar carceral logic in attempting to restore identity and inaugurate a new, golden order. Such alchemies dream of a techne that would deliver us into a secure, unshakeable, and unalienated/unalienable reality. A genomic logic that hungers passionately for a key to the world as code, a key that unlocks history and provides a map to the future, hinges on such a passion for being as rooted identity; so too do efforts to restore forgotten filiations and ancestral traditions, to make violated identities whole again through the recovery of bloodlines with which to anchor one's sense of self and guide the kinship bonds one forms. Such alchemies hold out so much appeal because they speak the grammar of phallic order, the grammar of humanism, the grammar of the current regime; they promise an alchemical change founded on recognition and inclusion in the language of the dominant ideology—

CONCLUSION

recognition of a "real" proven truer, more genuine, more solid than the world mistaken for our given reality. In this vision of the world, alchemy's power is taken to operate through the revelation of being itself; the work of the alchemist becomes covered over, reduced to discovery, void of invention. Driven by a passion for the real, alchemies of being can only engage in an identitarian battle of dueling touchstones, a struggle to replace one order with another that fails to exit the grammar of fixity, the grammar of whiteness.

Under such a horizon, marked by and mired in identitarian ambitions, an alchemy of becoming must first recall to memory, as Simone de Beauvoir did, that "*to be* is to have become,"[5] that alchemy's labor is precisely that—a labor of poiesis, a passionate labor of undoing and blurring, made possible by the malleability and entanglement of words and things, ideas, and beings. To recall Hortense Spillers's keen remark, "Sticks and bricks *might* break our bones, but words will most certainly *kill* us."[6] Words touch being. In an anti-Black world, language destroys. It spills blood, but it can also re-create and imagine otherwise. Though they disorient and foment dissatisfaction with what is, risking the void of disorder and the unsettling uncertainty of shifting foundations, alchemies of becoming do more than disabuse. Their discursive acts intervene on an ontological level, challenging modes of enclosure and shaping cultural imaginaries and affects. "There is cause for optimism," Fred Moten says, "as long as there is a need for optimism."[7] Born of the need for transformative invention, alchemies of becoming generate attachments to "being otherwise."[8] They foster fugitive forays, introducing negativity into the racial order of things; in their rusing, they queer, upend, or frustrate the instrumentalization of being and awaken a yearning for poiesis, for inventive modes of creation and unexpected relationships with co-creators foreclosed by static futurologies and foreordained lines of communal belonging. Alchemies of becoming trouble oppressive orders and identitarian solutions. They take hold by stirring a passion for creative possibility itself, an insurgent intuition that what is may not have to be, that the seemingly immovable is not immune to mutation. They offer neither the iron facts of being nor the gold of nostalgic return but the very possibility of wielding fire, of forging destruction and vital reimaginings alike.

NOTES

Introduction

1. "The Human Genome Project," National Human Genome Research Institute, last updated October 7, 2019, https://www.genome.gov/human-genome-project.
2. "The Human Genome Project."
3. Keith Wailoo, Alondra Nelson, and Catherine Lee. "Introduction: Genetic Claims and the Unsettled Past," in *Genetics and the Unsettled Past: The Collision of DNA, Race, and History*, ed. Keith Wailoo, Alondra Nelson, and Catherine Lee (New Brunswick: Rutgers University Press, 2012), 1.
4. Karl Marx, *Capital: A Critique of Political Economy*, vol. 1, trans. Ben Fowkes (New York: Penguin Books, 1982), 229.
5. Pierre Bourdieu, *Outline of a Theory of Practice*, trans. Richard Nice (Cambridge: Cambridge University Press, 1977), 195.
6. Stephanie E. Smallwood, *Saltwater Slavery: A Middle Passage from Africa to American Diaspora* (Cambridge, MA: Harvard University Press, 2007), 63.
7. Achille Mbembe, *Critique of Black Reason*, trans. Laurent Dubois (Durham: Duke University Press, 2017), 6.
8. Patricia J. Williams, *The Alchemy of Race and Rights* (Cambridge, MA: Harvard University Press, 1991), 163.
9. Quentin Meillassoux, *After Finitude: An Essay on the Necessity of Contingency*, trans. Ray Brassier (New York: Continuum, 2008), 5.
10. Meillassoux, *Time without Becoming*, ed. Anna Longo (Haverton: Mimesis International, 2014), 23, emphasis added.
11. Peter Gratton, *Speculative Realism: Problems and Prospects* (New York: Bloomsbury, 2014), 5.
12. Slavoj Žižek, *Welcome to the Desert of the Real! Five Essays on September 11 and Related Dates* (New York: Verso, 2002), 5–6. See Alain Badiou, *The Century*, trans. Alberto Toscano (Cambridge: Polity Press, 2007).
13. Badiou, *The Century*, 58.
14. Suspicion and paranoia characterize late capitalist consumer society, Žižek argues. Everything around us appears hollow, surrounded by an aura of fakeness and emptied of substance—whence the passion for the real,

the hunger for authenticity and re-enchantment, evident, for example, in enthusiasm for "reality TV and amateur pornography, up to snuff films" (Žižek, *Welcome to the Desert of the Real*, 12).

15 Meillassoux, "Interview with Quentin Meillassoux (August 2010)," trans. Graham Harman, in Graham Harman, *Quentin Meillassoux: Philosophy in the Making* (Edinburgh: Edinburgh University Press, 2011), 166.

16 François Laruelle, *Intellectuals and Power: The Insurrection of the Victim*, trans. Anthony Paul Smith (Cambridge: Polity Press, 2015), 9.

17 Bruce Robbins, "Fashion Conscious Phenomenon," *American Book Review* 38, no. 5 (2017): 5.

18 Stephen Best and Sharon Marcus, "Surface Reading: An Introduction," *Representations* 108, no. 1 (2009): 2.

19 The *Oxford English Dictionary* declared "post-truth" the word of year for 2016. Their definition of the term reads: "relating to or denoting circumstances in which objective facts are less influential in shaping public opinion than appeals to emotion and personal belief." See Michael P. Lynch, "Fake News and the Internet Shell Game," *The New York Times*, November 28, 2016, https://www.nytimes.com/2016/11/28/opinion/fake-news-and-the-internet-shell-game.html.

20 Bruno Latour, "Why Has Critique Run Out of Steam? From Matters of Fact to Matters of Concern," *Critical Inquiry* 30, no. 2 (2004): 227.

21 Latour, "Why Has Critique Run Out of Steam?" 231.

22 Latour, "Why Has Critique Run Out of Steam?" 248.

23 Latour, "Why Has Critique Run Out of Steam?" 240.

24 Latour, "Why Has Critique Run Out of Steam?" 232. With a focus on literary studies, Rita Felski expresses her own post-critical vision in terms of "dialogue" rather than "diagnosis." The drive for meaning has reached its limit, on this view; what we need now is more description and less explanation: "The role of the term 'postcritical' . . . is neither to prescribe the forms that reading should take nor dictate the attitudes critics must adopt; it is to steer us away from the kinds of arguments we know how to conduct in our sleep. These are some of the things postcritical reading will decline to do: subject a text to interrogation; diagnose hidden anxieties; demote recognition to yet another form of misrecognition; lament our incarceration in the prison-house of language; demonstrate that resistance is just another form of containment; read a text as a metacommentary on the undecidability of meaning; score points by showing that its categories are socially constructed; brood over the gap that separates word from world" (Rita Felski, *The Limits of Critique* [Chicago: University of Chicago Press, 2015], 173).

25 Karen Barad, "Interview with Karen Barad," in *New Materialism: Interviews and Cartographies*, ed. Rick Dophijn and Iris van der Tuin (Ann Arbor: Open Humanities Press, 2012), 49.

26 Barad, "Interview with Karen Barad," 59.

27 Jane Bennett, *Vibrant Matter: A Political Ecology of Things* (Durham: Duke University Press, 2010), ix.
28 Bennett, *Vibrant Matter*, xvi, xv.
29 Bennett, *Vibrant Matter*, 15.
30 Bennett, *Vibrant Matter*, xvi.
31 Bennett, *Vibrant Matter*, xvi, 97.
32 Bennett, *Vibrant Matter*, 3.
33 Bennett, "In Parliament with Things," in *Radical Democracy: Politics Between Abundance and Lack*, ed. Lars Tønder and Lasse Thomassen (Manchester: Manchester University Press, 2005), 135.
34 Bennett, *Vibrant Matter*, 122.
35 Bennett, *Vibrant Matter*, viii.
36 Bennett, *Vibrant Matter*, 117.
37 Bennett, "Systems and Things: On Vital Materialism and Object-Oriented Philosophy," in *The Nonhuman Turn*, ed. Richard Grusin (Minneapolis: University of Minnesota Press, 2015), 232.
38 Bennett, "Systems and Things," 232.
39 Bennett, *Vibrant Matter*, 30.
40 Bennett, *Vibrant Matter*, viii.
41 Che Gosset, "Blackness, Animality, and the Unsovereign," September 8, 2015, https://www.versobooks.com/blogs/2228-che-gossett-blackness-animality-and-the-unsovereign.
42 Zakiyyah Iman Jackson, *Becoming Human: Matter and Meaning in an Antiblack World* (New York: New York University Press, 2020), 1.
43 Graham Harman, *Object-Oriented Ontology: A New Theory of Everything* (New York: Pelican, 2017), 54.
44 Jeffrey Jerome Cohen, "The Ontological Turn," in *Posthuman Glossary*, ed. Rosi Braidotti and Maria Hlavajova (New York: Bloomsbury, 2018), 305.
45 Alexander Weheliye, *Habeas Viscus: Racializing Assemblages, Biopolitics, and Black Feminist Theories of the Human* (Durham: Duke University Press, 2014), 4.
46 Nahum Dimitri Chandler, *X—The Problem of the Negro as a Problem for Thought* (New York: Fordham University Press, 2014), 23.
47 Chandler, *X—The Problem of the Negro*, 21.
48 Zakiyyah Iman Jackson, "Outer Worlds: The Persistence of Race in Movement 'Beyond the Human,'" *GLQ* 21, no. 2–3 (2015): 216.
49 Hortense J. Spillers, "Mama's Baby, Papa's Maybe: An American Grammar Book," *Diacritics* 17, no. 2 (1987): 67.
50 Spillers, "Mama's Baby, Papa's Maybe," 67.
51 Wilderson, *Red, White & Black: Cinema and the Structure of U.S. Antagonisms* (Durham: Duke University Press, 2010), 38.

52 Wilderson, *Red, White & Black*, 18.

53 Mbembe, "Conversation: Achille Mbembe and David Theo Goldberg on *Critique of Black Reason*," *Theory, Culture, and Society*, July 3, 2018, https://www.theoryculturesociety.org/conversation-achille-mbembe-and-david-theo-goldberg-on-critique-of-black-reason/.

54 Saidiya V. Hartman, *Scenes of Subjection: Terror, Slavery, and Self-Making in Nineteenth-Century America* (Oxford: Oxford University Press, 1997), 62.

55 Wilderson, "Gramsci's Black Marx: Whither the Slave in Civil Society," *Social Identities* 9, no. 3 (2003): 230.

56 "If slavery persists as an issue in the political life of black America, it is not because of an antiquarian obsession with bygone days or the burden of a too-long memory, but because black lives are still imperiled and devalued by a racial calculus and a political arithmetic that were entrenched centuries ago. This is the afterlife of slavery—skewed life chances, limited access to health and education, premature death, incarceration, and impoverishment" (Hartman, *Lose Your Mother: A Journey Along the Atlantic Slave Route* [New York: Farrar, Straus and Giroux, 2007], 6).

57 Hartman, *Scenes of Subjection*, 234, n. 8.

58 Spillers, "Mama's Baby, Papa's Maybe," 68.

59 Spillers, "Difference," in *The Bloomsbury Handbook of 21st-Century Feminist Theory*, ed. Robin Truth Goodman (New York: Bloomsbury, 2019), 56.

60 Jared Sexton and Huey Copeland, "Raw Life: An Introduction," *Qui Parle* 13, no. 2 (Spring/Summer 2003): 53.

61 Frank B. Wilderson III, Saidya Hartman, Steve Martinot, Jared Sexton, and Hortense J. Spillers, "Editors' Introduction," in *Afro-Pessimism: An Introduction*, ed. Frank B. Wilderson III, Saidya Hartman, Steve Martinot, Jared Sexton, and Hortense J. Spillers (Minneapolis: Racked & Dispatched, 2017), 7, n. 1.

62 The magnitude of the transformation at issue is difficult to overstate, argues Wilderson: "The liberation of Black people is tantamount to moving into an epistemology that we cannot imagine. Once Blacks become incorporated and recognized I don't think we have the language or the concepts to think of what that is. It's not like moving from Capitalism to Communism, it's like the end of the world" (Wilderson, "Wallowing in the Contradictions, Part 2 with Percy Howard," July 14, 2010, https://percy3.wordpress.com/2010/07/14/frank-wilderson-wallowing-in-the-contradictions-part-2/).

63 Wilderson, *Red, White & Black*, 28.

64 George Yancy, "Afropessimism Forces Us to Rethink Our Most Basic Assumptions About Society," *Truthout*, September 14, 2022, https://truthout.org/articles/afropessimism-forces-us-to-rethink-our-most-basic-assumptions-about-society/.

65 Afropessimists draw heavily on the work of Orlando Patterson: "Slavery . . . is a highly symbolized domain of human experience. While all aspects of

the relationship are symbolized, there is an overwhelming concentration of the profound natal alienation of the slave. The reason for this is not hard to discern: it was the slave's isolation, his strangeness that made him most valuable to the master, but it was his very strangeness that most threatened the community... On the cognitive and mythic level, one dominant theme emerges, which lends an unusually loaded meaning to the act of natal alienation: this is the social death of the slave" (Patterson, *Slavery and Social Death: A Comparative Study* [Cambridge, MA: Harvard University Press, 1982], 38).

66 On the rise in genetic genealogy's global popularity, see Jerome de Groot, "The Genealogy Boom: Inheritance, Family History, and the Popular Historical Imagination," in *The Impact of History? Histories at the Beginning of the 21st Century*, ed. Bertrand Taithe and Pedro Ramos Pinto (London: Routledge, 2015), 21–34.

67 Ta-Nehisi Coates, *Between the World and Me* (New York: Spiegel and Grau, 2015), 7.

68 Dave Davies, "Historian Henry Louis Gates Jr. On DNA Testing and Finding His Own Roots," *NPR*, January 21, 2019, https://www.npr.org/2019/01/21/686531998/historian-henry-louis-gates-jr-on-dna-testing-and-finding-his-own-roots.

69 For Afropessimists the ontological neglect of Black people is irremediable from within the existing order, an order that genomics does not disrupt. The very being of Black folks is out of joint with white civil society. As constitutive outsiders, the diasporic Black population simply does not belong: "Blackness is a positionality of 'absolute dereliction' (Fanon), abandonment, in the face of civil society, and therefore cannot establish itself, or be established, through hegemonic interventions" (Wilderson, "The Prison Slave as Hegemony's (Silent) Scandal," *Social Justice* 30, no. 2 [2003]: 18). On this view the pervasiveness of anti-Blackness renders Black integration impossible: "Blackness cannot become one of civil society's many junior partners: Black citizenship, or Black civic obligation, are oxymorons" (Wilderson, "The Prison Slave," 18).

70 Nadia Abu El-Haj, *The Genealogical Science: Genetics, The Origins of the Jews, and The Politics of Epistemology* (Chicago: The University of Chicago Press, 2012), 159.

71 Alondra Nelson, *The Social Life of DNA: Race, Reparations, and Reconciliation After the Genome* (Boston: Beacon Press, 2015), xi.

72 Gil Anidjar, *Blood: A Critique of Christianity* (New York: Columbia University Press, 2014), 130. "Beginning with the conception of humans as 'flesh and blood,'" Anidjar writes, "Christianity was the first community to understand and conceive of itself as a community of blood" (Anidjar, *Blood*, 38). In tracing the secular life of blood in Western modernity, Anidjar adopts Carl Schmitt's view that "all significant concepts of the history of the modern world are liquidated theological concepts" (Anidjar, *Blood*, 85).

73 Anidjar, *Blood*, 89.

74 Anidjar, *Blood*, 106, 48.

75 Mbembe, "Decolonizing the University: New Directions," *Arts and Humanities in Higher Education* 15, no. 1 (2016): 43.

76 "We can no longer assume," Mbembe explains, "that there are incommensurable differences between us, tool makers, sign makers, language speakers and other animals, or between social history and natural history" (Mbembe, "Decolonizing the University," 44). Genomics creates an opportunity for a posthuman vision that, if informed by the legacy of racism, can lead to "a new understanding of ontology, epistemology, ethics and politics," which, he specifies, "can only be achieved by *overcoming anthropocentrism and humanism*, the split between nature and culture" (Mbembe, "Decolonizing the University," 42).

77 Mbembe, "Decolonizing the University," 43.

78 Mbembe, "Decolonizing the University," 44.

79 Mbembe, "Decolonizing the University," 44.

80 Abram Gabriel, "A Biologist's Perspective on DNA and Race in the Genomics Era," in *Genetics and the Unsettled Past: The Collision of DNA, Race, and History*, ed. Keith Wailoo, Alondra Nelson, and Catherine Lee (New Brunswick: Rutgers University Press, 2012), 54.

81 On this topic, see also Troy Duster, "Race and Reification in Science," *Science* 307, no. 5712 (2005): 1050–1.

82 Gabriel, "A Biologist's Perspective," 61. Gabriel discusses the case of sickle-cell anemia, which provides an informative example of the ways in which race (defined phenotypically) can serve as a "red herring" in disease studies. The beta globin mutation involved in sickle-cell anemia "arose independently in different populations at least five times in human evolution" (60), becoming more common in populations exposed to malaria, because it increased chances of survival in people with a single copy of the mutant allele. Though associated in American popular culture with darker skin, "from a genetic perspective, the disease is associated with individuals whose ancestors originated in specific parts of West Africa, central Africa, and central India," explains Gabriel (61). "An Ethiopian from East Africa or a Namibian from South Africa is no more likely to have sickle cell anemia than a person from Iceland or North Korea" (61). Likelihood is determined by genetic descent, not by phenotypical traits. To assume otherwise would be to misunderstand the etiology and also to risk misdiagnosis in individuals with the trait who do not fit social preconceptions of at-risk populations.

83 Abu El-Haj, *The Genealogical Science*, 5.

84 Abu El-Haj, *The Genealogical Science*, 2–3.

85 Abu El-Haj, *The Genealogical Science*, 141.

86 "Why DNA Tests." Orig3n.com, orig3n.com/why-dna-tests. Accessed June 28, 2020. An investigation in 2018 by the Centers for Medicare & Medicaid Services found major quality control deficiencies in Orig3n labs (following complaints that the company failed to detect nonhuman DNA in customer

samples). Following a new investigation by the Massachusetts Department of Health in 2020, the Centers for Medicare & Medicaid Services suspended the company's clinical lab certification. Its DTC website has since ceased functioning; archived copies of Orig3n.com pages can be browsed on the Internet Archive Wayback Machine at https://archive.org/web/. See Jeannette Hinkle and Trevor Ballantyne, "Orig3n Analysis ID'd Dog and Tap Water DNA as Human. Then the Company Produced Hundreds of False Positive COVID-19 Test Results," *Worcester Telegram*, October 15, 2020, https://www.telegram.com/story/lifestyle/health-fitness/2020/10/15/orig3n-analysis-idd-dog-and-tap-water-dna-as-human-then-company-produced-hundreds-of-false-positive-/114372264/.

87 "Shop." Orig3n.com, shop.orig3n.com. Accessed June 28, 2020.

88 "Behavior." Orig3n.com, shop.orig3n.com/collections/featured-products/products/behavior. Accessed June 28, 2020.

89 "Child development." Orig3n.com, shop.orig3n.com/collections/featured-products/products/child-development. Accessed June 28, 2020.

90 "What Your Results Will Include." Ancestry.com, www.ancestry.com/dna/#dnaLohpProof. Accessed June 28, 2020.

91 "AncestryDNA® Ethnicity." Ancestry.com, https://support.ancestry.com/s/article/AncestryDNA-Ethnicity. Accessed November 9, 2022.

92 AncestryDNA's region list is, however, constantly expanding, and numerous American regional-settler groups, defined in increasingly narrow geographical terms, have been added to it in recent years. Thus, a 2020 list included regions such as "Maine Settlers," "Middle Tennessee Settlers," and "Mid-Atlantic Coast African Americans," while in 2022 we find regions as fine-tuned as "Marshall County Settlers" or "Bibb, Shelby & Chilton County Settlers," to take just two examples classified under "Alabama Settlers." That these populations are found in the "Additional European Communities" section suggests that "Europeanness" remains salient to understandings of ethnicity, all while American regions and subregions are increasingly read as meaningfully distinct markers of origin ("List of AncestryDNA® Regions." Ancestry.com, https://support.ancestry.com/s/article/List-of-AncestryDNA-Regions?o_iid=108659&o_lid=108659&o_sch=Web+Property#America. Accessed June 28, 2020 and November 9, 2022).

93 Catherine A. Ball et al., "Ethnicity Estimate White Paper," AncestryDNA, October 30, 2013. www.ancestry.com/dna/resource/whitePaper/AncestryDNA-Ethnicity-White-Paper.pdf.

94 Ball et al., "Ethnicity Estimate White Paper." Subsequent versions of this paper nuance this description slightly: the specific example of the Angles and Saxons is removed, and the term "ancient" is replaced with "samples from people who lived hundreds of years ago" as a descriptor for the ideal reference population. The premises underlying the methodology—including the assumption that reference panels of living individuals with known roots in a single location can be used as representative proxies for populations living in that location "hundreds of years ago"—remain unchanged. Jeffrey

Adrion et al., "Ethnicity Estimate 2022 White Paper," AncestryDNA, https://www.ancestrycdn.com/support/us/2022/08/ethnicity2022whitepaper.pdf. Accessed November 12, 2022.

95 Ball et al., "Ethnicity Estimate White Paper."
96 Troy Duster, "Buried Alive: The Concept of Race in Science," in *Genetic Nature/Culture: Anthropology and Science beyond the Two-Culture Divide*, ed. Alan H. Goodman, Deborah Heath, and M. Susan Lindee (Berkeley: University of California Press, 2003), 265. Stephan Palmié draws on this quotation as well in "Genomics, Divination, Racecraft," *American Ethnologist* 34, no. 2 (2007): 210.
97 Paul Gilroy, "Never Again: Refusing Race and Salvaging the Human," 2019 Holberg Lecture, June 20, 2019, https://www.newframe.com/long-read-refusing-race-and-salvaging-the-human/.
98 Williams, "Emotional Truth," *The Nation*, February 16, 2006, https://www.thenation.com/article/archive/emotional-truth/.
99 Kim TallBear, "Genomic Articulations of Identity," *Social Studies of Science* 43, no. 4 (2013): 516.
100 Kim TallBear, *Native American DNA: Tribal Belonging and the False Promise of Genetic Science* (Minneapolis: University of Minnesota Press, 2013), 10.
101 TallBear, *Native American DNA*, 178.
102 Nelson, *The Social Life of DNA*, 17.
103 Nelson, *The Social Life of DNA*, 165.
104 Nelson, *The Social Life of DNA*, 17.
105 For an overview of this trend and geneticists' response to it, see Amy Harmon, "Why White Supremacists Are Chugging Milk (and Why Geneticists Are Alarmed)," *New York Times*, October 17, 2018, https://nyti.ms/2AeE3Xg.
106 As Nelson notes, these efforts include, for example, the African Burial Ground Initiative (an archaeological study of a New York cemetery for Africans and African Americans), the Innocence Project (focused on exonerating the wrongly convicted), the reparations litigation movement in the United States, and various philanthropic projects encouraging engagement between diaspora members and their African DNA kin communities.
107 Gilroy, "Never Again."
108 Gilroy, "Never Again."
109 Mbembe, "Conversation."
110 Gilroy, "Never Again." Other critics of Afropessimism have raised similar questions about centrality of the US context to Afropessimism's understanding of Black lived experience. For instance, Annie Olaloku-Teriba objects to the exceptionalism of the Afro-American experience, scrutinizing "the subsumption of 'Africanness' by an Americanised conception of

Blackness" as well as the suspicion that Afropessimism casts on non-Black people of color ("Afro-Pessimism and the (un)Logic of Anti-Blackness," *Historical Materialism* 26, no. 2 [2018]: 99). See also Kevin Ochieng Okoth, "The Flatness of Blackness: Afro-Pessimism and the Erasure of Anti-Colonial Thought," *Salvage*, January 16, 2020, https://salvage.zone/the-flatness-of-blackness-afro-pessimism-and-the-erasure-of-anti-colonial-thought/.

111 Gilroy, "Never Again."

112 Gilroy, "Never Again."

113 Frantz Fanon, *Black Skin, White Masks*, trans. Richard Philcox (New York: Grove Press, 2008), 89.

114 Žižek, *Violence: Six Sideways Reflections* (New York: Picador, 2008), 72. "The 'being' of blacks (as of whites or anyone else)," Žižek reiterates, echoing Simone de Beauvoir's earlier insight, "is socio-symbolic. When they are treated as inferior by whites, this does indeed make them inferior at the level of their socio-symbolic identity. In other words, white racist ideology exerts a performative efficiency: it doesn't merely interpret what blacks are, it determines their very being and social existence" (Žižek, *Like a Thief in Broad Daylight: Power in the Era of Post-Humanity* [New York: Allen Lane, 2018], 206).

115 Spillers, "Mama's Baby, Papa's Maybe," 68.

116 As Spillers puts it in the conclusion to "Mama's Baby, Papa's Maybe," the "problematizing of gender places her [the African-American female, 'both mother and mother-dispossessed'], in my view, out of the traditional symbolics of female gender, and it is our task to make a place for this different social subject. In doing so, we are less interested in joining the ranks of gendered femaleness than gaining the insurgent ground as female social subject. Actually claiming the monstrosity (of a female with the potential to 'name'), which her culture imposes in blindness, 'Sapphire' might rewrite after all a radically different text for a female empowerment" (80).

117 Fanon, *Black Skin*, 1–2.

118 Fanon, *Alienation and Freedom*, trans. Steven Corcoran (New York: Bloomsbury, 2018), 315 (*Our Journal*, 24 December 1953, no. 1, "Memory and Journal"). Fanon explains the mission of the journal (which was addressed to both patients and staff, and to which patients also contributed pieces) through the example of a ship: "On a ship, it is commonplace to say that one is between sky and water; that one is cut off from the world; that one is alone. This journal, precisely, is to fight against the possibility of letting oneself go, against that solitude. Every day a news-sheet comes out, often poorly printed, without photos and bland. But every day, that news-sheet works to liven up the boat. In it, you are informed about the 'on-board' news: recreation, cinema, concerts, the next ports of call. You also learn, of course, about the news on land. The boat, though isolated, keeps contact with the outside, that is to say, with the world. Why? Because in two or three days, the passengers will meet up again with their parents and friends, and return to their homes" (315).

119 Francis Jeanson, "Préface à *Peau noire, masques blancs*," in Frantz Fanon, *Peau noire, masques blancs* (Paris: Seuil, 1952), reprint, *Sud/Nord* 14 (2001): 179, https://www.cairn.info/revue-sud-nord-2001-1-page-175.htm. Translations from this piece are my own.

120 Donna V. Jones, *The Racial Discourses of Life Philosophy: Negritude, Vitalism and Modernity* (New York: Columbia University Press, 2010), 177.

121 Fanon, *Black Skin*, 112.

122 Robert Bernasconi, "The European Knows and Does Not Know: Fanon's Response to Sartre," in *Frantz Fanon's "Black Skin, White Masks": New Interdisciplinary Essays*, ed. Max Silverman (Manchester: Manchester University Press, 2005), 108.

123 Fanon, *Black Skin*, 117, 112.

124 Bernasconi, "The European Knows," 107.

125 Bernasconi, "The European Knows," 100.

126 Bernasconi argues cogently that Fanon's approach to knowledge is one that "today might be understood as a version of standpoint theory or the epistemology of provenance, but which was in its own time developed by him in terms of existential phenomenology" ("The European Knows," 101).

127 As he comments in *The Wretched of the Earth*, "a memorable example" of colonialist resistance to disalienation "was the reaction of white jazz fans when after the Second World War new styles such as bebop established themselves. For them jazz could only be the broken, desperate yearning of an old 'Negro,' five whiskeys under his belt, bemoaning his own misfortune and the racism of whites. As soon as he understands himself and apprehends the world differently, as soon as he elicits a glimmer of hope and forces the racist world to retreat, it is obvious he will blow his horn to his heart's content and his husky voice will ring out loud and clear" (Fanon, *The Wretched of the Earth*, trans. Richard Philcox [New York: Grove Press, 2004], 175–6).

128 Jeanson, "Préface," 179.

129 "This book is a clinical study," Fanon asserts in the introduction to *Black Skin*. "The attitudes I propose describing are true. I have found them any number of times" (xvi).

130 Fred Moten, *The Universal Machine* (Durham: Duke University Press, 2018), 150.

131 Moten, *Stolen Life* (Durham: Duke University Press, 2018), 131.

132 Patrick Chamoiseau, "Les Secrets de Chamoiseau," *Antilla Special* 11 (December 1988–January 1989): 25; see also Lucien Taylor, "Créolité Bites: A Conversation with Patrick Chamoiseau. Raphaël Confiant, and Jean Bernabé," *Transition* 74 (1997): 138–9.

133 Moten, "Black Optimism/Black Operation," unpublished paper, 2007, https://lucian.uchicago.edu/blogs/politicalfeeling/files/2007/12/moten-black-optimism.doc.

134 Moten, *In the Break: The Aesthetics of the Black Radical Tradition* (Minneapolis: University of Minnesota Press, 2003), 1.

135 Neil Roberts, *Freedom as Marronage* (Chicago: The University of Chicago Press, 2015), 27. Similarly, Cedric J. Robinson locates slave agency in the possibility of hybridity. Robinson characterizes the racialization of Africans as alchemically tumultuous: "the production of race is chaotic. It is an alchemy of the intentional and the unintended, of known and unimagined fractures of cultural forms, of relations of power and the power of social and cultural relations" (Cedric J. Robinson, *Forgeries of Memory and Meaning: Blacks and the Regimes of Race in American Theater and Film before World War II* [Chapel Hill: University of North Carolina Press, 2007], xii). But this alchemy, the alchemy produced by the Middle Passage and the slave trade, was countered by another alchemy—the counter-alchemy of creolization. On the slave ships, "African labor brought the past with it"; what gets smuggled back into white culture is a set of practices and beliefs, a trace of other languages, that indexes a rebellious will, "the embryo of the demon that would be visited on the whole enterprise of primitive accumulation" (Robinson, *Black Marxism: The Making of the Black Radical Tradition* [Chapel Hill: University of North Carolina Press, 2000], 122).

136 Moten, "Black Optimism/Black Operation."

137 Édouard Glissant famously insists on the demand for "the right to opacity for everyone" (Glissant, *Poetics of Relation*, trans. Betsy Wing [Ann Arbor: University of Michigan Press, 1997], 194). This assertion does not a priori bar this right to the nonhuman, however. On this point, see Mbembe, "Decolonizing the University," 35, 43.

138 Moten, "Black Optimism/Black Operation." Glissant's phrase is "consentir à ne pas être un seul"; Moten credits Christopher Winks for the English translation here and also adopts this phrase as a title for the trilogy of works including *Black and Blur*, *Stolen Life*, and *The Universal Machine*.

139 Manthia Diawara, "One World in Relation: Édouard Glissant in Conversation with Manthia Diawara," *Journal of Contemporary African Art* 28 (Spring 2011): 5.

140 Diawara, "One World in Relation," 5.

141 Diawara, "One World in Relation," 5.

142 Diawara, "One World in Relation," 19.

143 Diawara, "One World in Relation," 19.

144 David Theo Goldberg, *Are We All Postracial Yet?* (Cambridge: Polity Press, 2015), 94.

145 Gilroy, *Darker than Blue: On the Moral Economies of Black Atlantic Culture* (Cambridge, MA: Harvard University Press, 2010), 157.

146 Goldberg, *Are We All Postracial Yet?*, 170.

147 James Baldwin, "A Report from Occupied Territory," *The Nation* 300, 14/17 (March 23, 2015), reprinted from July 11, 1966, https://www.thenation.com/article/archive/report-occupied-territory-2/.

148 Ruha Benjamin, "Black AfterLives Matter: Cultivating Kinfulness as Reproductive Justice," in *Making Kin Not Population*, ed. Adele E. Clarke and Donna Haraway (Chicago: Prickly Paradigm Press, 2018), 61.

149 Édouard Glissant, *Caribbean Discourse: Selected Essays*, trans. Michael Dash (Charlottesville: University of Virginia Press, 1989), 64.

150 Fanon, *Black Skin*, xii.

Chapter 1

1 Benjamin, "Black AfterLives Matter," 61.
2 Benjamin, "Black AfterLives Matter," 61, 65.
3 Hartman, *Lose Your Mother*, 155.
4 Hartman, *Lose Your Mother*, 155.
5 Hartman, *Lose Your Mother*, 155, 157.
6 Hartman, *Lose Your Mother*, 155.
7 Abu El-Haj, *The Genealogical Science*, 158.
8 Henry Louis Gates, Jr., *In Search of Our Roots: How 19 Extraordinary African Americans Reclaimed Their Past* [2009] (New York: Skyhorse Publishing, 2017), 7, 10.
9 Gates, *In Search of Our Roots*, 10.
10 Gates, *Finding Your Roots, season 2: The Official Companion to the PBS Series* (Chapel Hill: The University of North Carolina Press, 2016), 9–10.
11 "Slavery [. . .] is a highly symbolized domain of human experience. While all aspects of the relationship are symbolized, there is an overwhelming concentration of the profound natal alienation of the slave. The reason for this is not hard to discern: it was the slave's isolation, his strangeness that made him most valuable to the master, but it was his very strangeness that most threatened the community [. . .] On the cognitive and mythic level, one dominant theme emerges, which lends an unusually loaded meaning to the act of natal alienation: this is the social death of the slave" (Patterson, *Slavery and Social Death*, 38).
12 Hartman, *Scenes of Subjection*, 19.
13 Hartman, *Scenes of Subjection*, 6. As Hartman shows in her close study of instructional manuals for freedmen, which emphasized the blood and treasure spilt by others to secure the liberation of the enslaved—effectively ignoring the blood, labor, and military service given by the enslaved themselves over hundreds of years—"indebtedness was central to the creation of a memory of the past in which white benefactors, courageous soldiers, and virtuous mothers sacrificed themselves for the enslaved. This memory was to be seared into the minds of the freed. Debt was at the center of a moral economy of submission and servitude and was instrumental in the production of peonage. Above all, it operated to bind the subject by compounding the service owed, augmenting

the deficit through interest accrued, and advancing credit that extended interminably the obligation of service" (*Scenes of Subjection*, 131).

14 This viewership figure was provided by PBS in its outreach to potential corporate sponsors, based on a study of Season 4's audience (https://www.pbs.org/sponsorship/programs/finding-your-roots/).

15 Henry Louis Gates, Jr., *Finding Your Roots, season 1: The Official Companion to the PBS Series* (Chapel Hill: The University of North Carolina Press, 2014), 33.

16 Gates, *Finding Your Roots, season 1: The Official Companion*. Season 1 episodes are named after their guests (in this case, jazz musicians Branford Marsalis and Harry Connick, Jr.), while the companion book gives each pairing a thematic title ("Genetic Gumbo"); beginning with Season 2, episodes bear the name of the organizing theme, such as "The Irish Factor" (Season 3, Episode 2), "Black Like Me" (Season 4, Episode 6), or "Laughing on the Inside" (Season 7, Episode 8).

17 Gates, *Finding Your Roots, season 1: The Official Companion*, 93.

18 Gates, *Finding Your Roots, season 1: The Official Companion*, 155.

19 Gates, *Finding Your Roots, season 1: The Official Companion*, 70–1.

20 Gates, *Finding Your Roots, season 2: The Official Companion*, 352.

21 Gates, *Finding Your Roots, season 2: The Official Companion*, 365–6.

22 Gates, *Finding Your Roots, season 1: The Official Companion*, 107.

23 "Finding Your Roots General Curriculum 5.18.18," PDF download, 17. Curricular materials are available for download by request at https://fyrclassroom.org/curriculum/index.html.

24 Episode 4.

25 Episode 3.

26 Episode 3.

27 Funding for *Finding Your Roots: The Seedlings* was provided by private foundations (such as the Benkovic Family Foundation and the Rockefeller Foundation), educational centers (including the Hutchins Center for African & African American Research at Harvard and Penn State College of the Liberal Arts), public television (WETA Public Television for Greater Washington), and private donors; the initiative also received assistance from institutions such as the New England Historic Genealogical Society and the State Library of Pennsylvania (credits, Episode 1, "Overview," https://fyrclassroom.org/episodes/episode-1-overview.html). PBS's *Finding Your Roots* sponsorship disclosure for Season 7 (which ran January 19–May 4, 2021) acknowledges a similar range of sources (nonprofit foundations, philanthropical donations, and government-funded entities), with additional support from for-profit companies: "Corporate support for FINDING YOUR ROOTS WITH HENRY LOUIS GATES, JR., Season Seven is provided by Ancestry and Johnson & Johnson. Support is also provided by Gordon and Betty Moore Foundation, The Carnegie Corporation of New York, Candace King Weir, The Zegar Family Foundation, Lloyd Carney Foundation, and by The Inkwell Society

and its members Felicia A. and Benjamin A. Horowitz Fund; Demond Martin; Sheryl Sandberg and Tom Bernthal; Jim and Susan Swartz; Anne Wojcicki; John H. N. Fisher and Jennifer Caldwell; Fletcher and Benaree Wiley; Gwen and Peter Norton; and Darnell Armstrong and Nicole Commissiong. Major support is provided by the Corporation for Public Broadcasting and PBS" (https://www.pbs.org/weta/finding-your-roots/about/about-series). The Corporation for Public Broadcasting is a federally funded private nonprofit corporation; PBS is funded by local public television stations and donations from private sponsors. See the CPB website for more detailed information about the relationship between the CPB and PBS: https://www.cpb.org/faq.

28 Nelson, *The Social Life of DNA*, 165. See my introduction for more discussion of this term.

29 Julie Taboh, "First African American to Head Smithsonian Shares Highlights, Challenges," *Voice of America News*, February 27, 2021, https://www.voanews.com/usa/first-african-american-head-smithsonian-shares-highlights-challenges.

30 Anthony Bogues and Lonnie Bunch, "'This Museum Is about American Identity as Much as It Is about African American History': An Interview with Lonnie Bunch," *Callaloo* 38, no. 4 (2015): 706.

31 In June 2021, the Florida State Board of Education unanimously approved amendments to Rule 6A-1.094124, "Required Instruction Planning and Reporting," forbidding the instruction of Critical Race Theory (as defined in the guidance) in public schools. Effective July 26, 2021, section 3b of the rule reads in full: "Instruction on the required topics must be factual and objective, and may not suppress or distort significant historical events, such as the Holocaust, slavery, the Civil War and Reconstruction, the civil rights movement and the contributions of women, African American and Hispanic people to our country, as already provided in Section 1003.42(2), F.S. Examples of theories that distort historical events and are inconsistent with State Board approved standards include the denial or minimization of the Holocaust, and the teaching of Critical Race Theory, meaning the theory that racism is not merely the product of prejudice, but that racism is embedded in American society and its legal systems in order to uphold the supremacy of white persons. Instruction may not utilize material from the 1619 Project and may not define American history as something other than the creation of a new nation based largely on universal principles stated in the Declaration of Independence. Instruction must include the U.S. Constitution, the Bill of Rights and subsequent amendments" (Florida Administrative Code & Florida Administrative Register, Florida Department of State, https://www.flrules.org/gateway/ruleNo.asp?id=6A-1.094124).

32 Paul Williams, *Memorial Museums: The Global Rush to Commemorate Atrocities* (Oxford: Berg, 2007), 25.

33 "Smithsonian Secretary Lonnie Bunch III: Full Face the Nation Interview," *Face the Nation*, CBS News, June 20, 2021, https://www.cbsnews.com/video/smithsonian-secretary-lonnie-bunch-iii-full-face-the-nation-interview/?intcid=CNM-00-10abd1h#x.

34 "Smithsonian Secretary Lonnie Bunch III: Full Face the Nation interview."

35 The phrase is Lonnie Bunch's. Lonnie G. Bunch III, *A Fool's Errand: Creating the National Museum of African American History and Culture in the Age of Bush, Obama, and Trump* (Washington, D.C.: Smithsonian Books, 2019), 87.

36 Frank James, "Emmett Till's Casket Discarded By Chicago-Area Grave Workers," NPR, July 10, 2009, https://www.npr.org/sections/thetwo-way/2009/07/emmitt_tills_casket_discarded.html; Abby Callard, "Emmett Till's Casket Goes to the Smithsonian," *Smithsonian Magazine*, November 2009, https://www.smithsonianmag.com/arts-culture/emmett-tills-casket-goes-to-the-smithsonian-144696940/.

37 Callard, "Emmett Till's Casket."

38 Sam Roberts, "Simeon Wright, Witness to Abduction of Emmett Till, Dies at 74," *New York Times*, September 6, 2017, https://www.nytimes.com/2017/09/06/obituaries/simeon-wright-witness-to-abduction-of-emmett-till-dies-at-74.html.

39 Cheryl Corley, "Body of Emmett Till to Be Exhumed," *NPR*, May 5, 2005, https://www.npr.org/templates/story/story.php?storyId=4631506.

40 Monica Davey and Gretchen Ruethling, "After 50 Years, Emmett Till's Body Is Exhumed," *New York Times*, June 2, 2005, https://www.nytimes.com/2005/06/02/us/after-50-years-emmett-tills-body-is-exhumed.html.

41 Bradley stated in her testimony, "I looked at the face very carefully. I looked at the ears, and the forehead, and the hairline, and also the hair; and I looked at the nose and the lips, and the chin. I just looked at it all over very thoroughly. And I was able to find out that it was my boy. And I knew definitely that it was my boy beyond a shadow of a doubt." She also confirmed that the ring found on the body, engraved with the initials L.T., was Louis Till's, Emmett's late father's, and that the child had been wearing it when he left for Mississippi. Mississippi, "J.W. Milam and Roy Bryant Trial Transcript," Special Collections & Archives, Florida State University Libraries, Tallahassee, Florida, http://purl.flvc.org/fsu/fd/FSU_MSS_2015-007_S03_SS04_I003.

42 Mississippi, "J.W. Milam and Roy Bryant Trial Transcript."

43 Radiclani Clytus, "Freedom Comes in a Box: Reflections on the National Museum of African American History and Culture," *Callaloo* 38, no. 4 (2015): 747.

44 Bogues and Bunch, "'This Museum Is about American Identity,'" 707.

45 Bogues and Bunch, "'This Museum Is about American Identity,'" 707–8.

46 Bunch, *A Fool's Errand*, 92.

47 Bunch, *A Fool's Errand*, 90.

48 Williams, *Memorial Museums*, 25.

49 Bunch, *A Fool's Errand*, 114.

50 Bunch, *A Fool's Errand*, 92.

51 Bunch, *A Fool's Errand*, 96.

52 For the NMAAHC's description of the program (and its newer iterations, District Treasures and Hometown Treasures), see https://nmaahc.si.edu/explore/initiatives/african-american-treasures.

53 Deputy director, Kinshasha Holman Conwill, quoted in Krissah Thompson, "Painful but Crucial: Why You'll See Emmett Till's Casket at the African American Museum," *Washington Post*, August 18, 2016, https://www.washingtonpost.com/lifestyle/style/painful-but-crucial-why-youll-see-emmett-tills-casket-at-the-african-american-museum/2016/08/18/66d1dc2e-484b-11e6-acbc-4d4870a079da_story.html; Lonnie Bunch has similarly described the casket as "one of the most sacred artifacts in the museum's collections" (Bunch, *A Fool's Errand*, 112).

54 As Lonnie Bunch explains, "Equally important for me was to use this donation to honor Mamie Till Mobley. She always reminded me that someone else had to carry the burden of ensuring Emmett was remembered. By accepting the casket into the collections of the museum, Emmett Till and Mamie Till Mobley would always be associated with Chicago and Mississippi, but now that they were part of the Smithsonian, they belonged to the nation" (Bunch, *A Fool's Errand*, 113).

55 Benjamin, "Black AfterLives Matter," 46.

56 Benjamin, "Black AfterLives Matter," 47.

57 Bunch, *A Fool's Errand*, 34.

58 Édouard Glissant, *Mémoires des esclavages: Pour la fondation d'un Centre national pour la mémoire des esclavages et de leurs abolitions* (Paris: Gallimard, 2007), 138. All translations from this work are my own. Glissant uses the plural for both "memories" and "slaveries" in his title (a fairly literal English rendering would thus read "Remembrances of Slaveries: Founding a National Center for the Remembrance of Slaveries and Their Abolition") stressing slavery's multiple historical forms as well as the plurality of personal and collective memories that have arisen in their wake.

59 Glissant, *Mémoires des esclavages*, 172.

60 Fanon, *Black Skin*, xiii–iv.

61 Fanon, *Black Skin*, xii.

62 Fanon, *Black Skin*, 202, 204–6.

63 Fanon, *Black Skin*, xiv.

64 Glissant, *Mémoires des esclavages*, 37.

65 Glissant, *Mémoires des esclavages*, 139.

66 Glissant, *Mémoires des esclavages*, 124.

67 Glissant, *Caribbean Discourse*; *Le Discours antillais* (Paris: Éditions du Seuil, 1981). On Glissant's contributions to memory studies from *Caribbean Discourse* to his later writings, see Bonnie Thomas, "Édouard Glissant and the Art of Memory," *Small Axe* 30 (2009): 25–36.

68 Glissant, *Mémoires des esclavages*, 36.

69 Renée Gosson, "Breaking Museal Tradition: Guadeloupe's 'Mémorial ACTe' and the Scenography of Slavery," *Histoire Sociale/Social History* 53, no. 107

(May 2020): 182. Yvan Amar, writing for Radio France Internationale, hears in the unusual capitalization and word order of Mémorial ACTe (the French word for "act," spelled "acte," ends in a silent 'e') a "distinct American accent" that perhaps recalls the Caribbean's geographic proximity to America, but also recalls that an "acte," in the sense of a certificate or a title, signifies "a material object that is there to attest to a particular meaning" ("un objet matériel qui est là pour témoigner d'un certain sens"). The name Mémorial ACTe thus calls attention to the center's function as a material document, an attestation ("Acte—04/06/2015," RFI.fr, 4 June, 2015, https://www.rfi.fr/fr/emission/20150604-acte-04062015). Both the French and English-language versions of the MACTe's catalogue cite the "many movements in the English-speaking world that associated resistance with acts" as inspiration for the name (Thierry L'Étang, Jean-Loup Pivin, Laetitia Réal-Moretto, and Farid Abdelouahab, eds., *Memorial ACTe: Exploring Slavery and the African Slave Trade in the Caribbean and Around the World*, trans. Simon Beaver [Pointe-à-Pitre, Guadeloupe: Memorial ACTe Éditions, 2015], 145–6; see also Thierry L'Étang, Jean-Loup Pivin, Farid Abdelouahab, and Mntchini Traoré, eds., *Mémorial ACTe: L'esclavage et la traite négrière dans la Caraïbe et le monde* [Pointe-à-Pitre, Guadeloupe: Memorial ACTe Éditions, 2015], 379).

70 Quoted in Mémorial ACTe, Centre Caribéen d'expressions et de mémoire de la Traite et de l'Esclavage, "La Mémoire Inspire L'avenir," brochure, https://www.regionguadeloupe.fr/fileadmin/Site_Region_Guadeloupe/Mediatheque/Brochures_et_publications/MacteBrochure_La_M__R_moire_Inspire_l_avenir_VF.pdf, my translation.

71 Known in the Anglophone Caribbean as the bearded fig-tree, the *figuier maudit*, or "cursed fig tree" (*ficus citrifolia*), grows epiphytically on trees and other structures and often overtakes its host. The MACTe's use of this imagery is inspired in part by the large *figuier maudit* growing through the ruins of the Darboussier sugar factory, the site in Pointe-à-Pitre on which the center was constructed.

72 Glissant, *Mémoires des esclavages*, 153–4.

73 Glissant, *Mémoires des esclavages*, 155.

74 The full passage cited here reads, "Les décors et installations éviteront le style de reconstitution réaliste, qui ne rend compte de rien du tout, car il n'approchera jamais la cruauté des ventres des bateaux et des antres des Plantations. L'essentiel sera d'inventer chaque fois, en ce qui se rapporte à une pédagogie dans ce domaine, des modes de relation et d'interaction avec les établissements scolaires et les groupes de jeunes qui visiteront le centre" (Glissant, *Mémoires des esclavages*, 153–4). For additional reflections on the notion of the deferred, see Glissant's chapters on "The Real—The Deferred" and "The Deferred—The Word," in *Faulkner, Mississippi*, trans. Barbara B. Lewis and Thomas Spear (Chicago: University of Chicago Press, 2000).

75 "Nous restons convaincus que les phénomènes de l'esclavage, de cet esclavage-ci, ne seront jamais vus, ni visibles ni perceptibles ni compréhensibles, par les seules méthodes de la pensée objective, qui est dégagée de toute implication,

mais à partir aussi de points d'exposition particuliers, où le *risque* de la compréhension (ne serait-ce que par les excès d'une subjectivité trop partisane) engage, et force à affronter l'obscur et le différé" (Glissant, *Mémoires des esclavages*, 41–2).

76 Reproductions of *Génération biométrique*, *The Palmetto Libretto*, and *Toussaint Louverture – Jean-Jacques Dessalines – Le roi Christophe* can be found in the MACTe's inauguration press kit (https://www.regionguadeloupe.fr/fileadmin/Site_Region_Guadeloupe/actus/agenda/Macte_DP_ENGLISH_WEB.pdf); see also Kara Walker's professional website (http://www.karawalkerstudio.com/55832413e4b02143d66e777d) and the Library of Congress entry for Currier & Ives's "Bombardment of Fort Sumter, Charleston Harbor: 12th & 13th of April, 1861," which Walker's piece visually recalls (https://www.loc.gov/pictures/item/90711987/).

77 Thierry Alet, "Manifeste pour un code couleur," https://www.thierryalet.com/manifeste, my translation. Alet describes this text as a work in progress not to be circulated as a final draft, but the ideas he expresses here are also taken up in the catalogue description of *La voleuse d'enfants* and in "Superpositions culturelles: parcours pédagogique," a guide prepared by the MACTe for middle school and high school instructors working with the piece among other objects in the Center's collections (this guide is made available for download by the Région Académique Guadeloupe, https://pedagogie.ac-guadeloupe.fr/histoire_arts/parcours_pedagogiques_memorial_acte).

78 Alet, "Manifeste." In English, the full prayer is as follows: "Hail, Mary, full of grace, the Lord is with thee. Blessed art thou amongst women and blessed is the fruit of thy womb, Jesus. Holy Mary, Mother of God, pray for us sinners, now and at the hour of our death. Amen."

79 Alet, "Manifeste."

80 Yarimar Bonilla, *Non-Sovereign Futures: French Caribbean Politics in the Wake of Disenchantment* (Chicago: University of Chicago Press, 2015), 43.

81 Fanon, *Black Skin*, 201.

82 Fanon, *Black Skin*, 204, translation modified.

Chapter 2

1 Patrick Chamoiseau, *L'empreinte à Crusoé* (Paris: Gallimard, 2012); Octavia Butler, *Fledgling* (New York: Grand Central Publishing, 2005). References to these texts will henceforth be given parenthetically. Translations from Chamoiseau's novel are my own.

2 Bernard Liger, "Chamoiseau: 'L'objet de la littérature n'est plus de raconter des histoires,'" *L'Express*, March 6, 2012, http://www.lexpress.fr/culture/livre/patrick-chamoiseau-l-objet-de-la-litterature-n-est-plus-de-raconter-des-histoires_1089728.html#pZsGBjlpGpPLxAOv.99 . My translation.

3 Liger, "Chamoiseau."

4 Liger, "Chamoiseau."
5 Liger, "Chamoiseau."
6 Pheng Cheah, *What Is a World? On Postcolonial Literature as World Literature* (Durham and London: Duke University Press, 2016), 5.
7 Marx, *Capital*, 170.
8 Bénédicte Boisseron, *Afro-Dog: Blackness and the Animal Question* (New York: Columbia University Press, 2018), 114.
9 Emmanuel Levinas, *Totality and Infinity: An Essay on Exteriority*, trans. Alphonso Lingis (Pittsburgh: Duquesne University Press, 1969), 40.
10 For new materialist Jane Bennett, the primacy attributed to the human Other makes a Levinasian orientation a priori problematic, running against her push "to elide the question of the human." Only by "postpon[ing] for a while the topics of subjectivity or the nature of human interiority, or the question of what really distinguishes the human from the animal, plant, and thing" can we fashion a more open and expansive ethics, one that does not "obstruct freethinking about what agency really entails" (Bennett, *Vibrant Matter*, 2). Speculative realist Steven Shaviro laments Levinas's anthropocentric prejudice, the exclusivity that he assigns to the human: "we cannot escape the pervasive sense, endemic to Western culture, that we are alone in our aliveness: trapped in a world of dead, or merely passive, matter" (Steven Shaviro, *The Universe of Things: On Speculative Realism* [Minneapolis: University of Minnesota Press, 2014], 46). Object-oriented ontologist Graham Harman also objects that "[Levinasian] ethics cannot be first philosophy, since ethics unjustly divides the world between full-fledged humans and robotic causal pawns, in a manner little different from Descartes" (Graham Harman, "Aesthetics as First Philosophy: Levinas and the Non-Human," *Naked Punch* [2012], http://www.nakedpunch.com/articles/147).
11 Liger, "Chamoiseau."
12 Jacques Derrida and Elisabeth Roudinesco, *For What Tomorrow . . . : A Dialogue*, trans. Jeff Fort (Stanford: Stanford University Press, 2004), 176.
13 Jacques Derrida and Maurizio Ferraris, *A Taste for the Secret*, trans. Giacomo Donis (Cambridge: Polity Press, 2001), 27.
14 Chamoiseau, *L'empreinte*, 215.
15 Kathleen Gyssels, "The *Département* Writes Back: On Chamoiseau's Rewrite of *Robinson Crusoe*," in *Postcoloniality-Decoloniality-Black Critique: Joints and Fissures*, ed. Sabine Broeck and Carsten Junker (Frankfurt: Campus Verlag, 2014), 295.
16 Gyssels, "The *Département* Writes Back," 303.
17 Alexandre Leupin, *Édouard Glissant, Philosopher: Heraclitus and Hegel in the Whole-World*, trans. Andrew Brown (Albany: Suny Press, 2021), 200.
18 Leupin, *Édouard Glissant*, 204.
19 Leupin, *Édouard Glissant*, 202.
20 Leupin, *Édouard Glissant*, 152.

21 Glissant, *Poetics of Relation*, 194.
22 The unhealed wound becomes an important figure as well in Maryse Condé's novel *The Wondrous and Tragic Life of Ivan and Ivana*, as I discuss in Chapter 4.
23 Moten, "Black Optimism/Black Operation." Glissant's phrase is "consentir à ne pas être un seul"; Moten credits Christopher Winks for the English translation here and also adopts this phrase as a title for the trilogy of works including *Black and Blur*, *Stolen Life*, and *The Universal Machine*.
24 Leupin, *Édouard Glissant*, 188.
25 Derrida, "Autoimmunity: Real and Symbolic Suicides—A Dialogue with Jacques Derrida," in *Philosophy in a Time of Terror: Dialogues with Jürgen Habermas and Jacques Derrida*, ed. Giovanna Borradori (Chicago: University of Chicago Press, 2004), 191n.14.
26 Derrida, *On Cosmopolitanism and Forgiveness*, trans. Mark Dooley and Michael Hughes (New York: Routledge, 2001), 57.
27 Moten, *Stolen Life*, 180. Moten draws on Gayatri Spivak's claim that "at the bottom, the first right is the right to refuse" (Steve Paulson, "Critical Intimacy: An Interview with Gayatri Chakravorty Spivak," *Los Angeles Review of Books* [July 29, 2016], https://lareviewofbooks.org/article/critical-intimacy-interview-gayatri-chakravorty-spivak/).
28 Sophie Fuggle, "Reimagining the Ruins of the Penalscape: Patrick Chamoiseau's Carceral Ruinology," *Social Identities* 26, no. 6 (2020): 824.
29 "Glissant returns to the origin to produce the future" (Leupin, *Édouard Glissant*, 207).
30 Chuck Robinson, "Minority and Becoming-Minor in Octavia Butler's *Fledgling*," *Science Fiction Studies* 42, no. 3 (2015): 494.
31 Anidjar, *Blood*, 87.
32 Robinson, "Minority and Becoming-Minor," 486.
33 Robinson, "Minority and Becoming-Minor," 486.
34 Robinson, "Minority and Becoming-Minor," 489. As Robinson explains, "by the end of the novel Shori has accrued a strange collection of symbionts: one met haphazardly, one who is introduced to her, two she adopts from deceased Ina (an extreme rarity, she is told), and one older woman who, for most Ina, would be considered beyond ideal age for a new symbiont. Partly through necessity (enemies keep burning down the homes where she lives or seeks refuge) and partly through the suspicion and self-reliance this necessity breeds, Shori resists conventional filiation even once the threats to her safety have been resolved. As an orphan Ina, she would typically be adopted into another family, yet the plan she espouses at the conclusion of the novel forecasts a more itinerant lifestyle, moving from homestead to homestead among the Ina, learning what she can and setting up her family on her own terms when she feels ready" (489).
35 Robinson, "Minority and Becoming-Minor," 484.

36 Jasbir Puar, "Bodies with New Organs: Becoming Trans, Becoming Disabled," *Social Text* 33, no. 3 (124) (2015): 63.
37 Jackson, *Becoming Human*, 129.
38 Jackson, *Becoming Human*, 129.
39 Jackson, *Becoming Human*, 129.
40 Robinson, "Minority and Becoming-Minor," 486.

Chapter 3

1 Shaviro, "Defining Speculation."
2 Shaviro, "Defining Speculation."
3 Shaviro, "Defining Speculation."
4 Marek Oziewicz, "Speculative Fiction," *Oxford Research Encyclopedias*, March 29, 2017, https://oxfordre.com/view/10.1093/acrefore/9780190201098.001.0001/acrefore-9780190201098-e-78.
5 Fanon, *Black Skin*, xiv.
6 Fanon, *Black Skin*, 201.
7 Žižek, *Incontinence of the Void: Economico-Philosophical Spandrels* (Cambridge, MA: MIT Press, 2017), 160.
8 Glissant, *Caribbean Discourse*, 64.
9 Hartman, *Lose Your Mother*, 6.
10 Donald Byrd, "What 'Black Panther' Means to a Black Baby Boomer," *Crosscut*, February 20, 2018, https://crosscut.com/2018/02/what-black-panther-means-black-baby-boomer. Lewis R. Gordon makes a similar observation, but argues that the film shows not simply what might have been, but rather the disregarded potential of current African reality: "Wakanda stands as a challenge to the racist 'not out of Africa' thesis (that is, nothing positive comes out of Africa), raising the question of what Africa could offer the world if it were seen with open eyes" (*Fear of Black Consciousness* [New York: Farrar, Straus and Giroux, 2022], 186).
11 Kodwo Eshun, "Further Considerations of Afrofuturism," *CR: The New Centennial Review* 3, no. 2 (2003): 288.
12 Steven W. Thrasher, "Afrofuturism: Reimagining Science and the Future from a Black Perspective," *The Guardian*, December 7, 2015, https://www.theguardian.com/culture/2015/dec/07/afrofuturism-black-identity-future-science-technology.
13 Fanon, *Black Skin*, 123, translation modified.
14 Jamil Smith, "The Revolutionary Power of *Black Panther*," *Time*, February 19, 2018, time.com/black-panther/.
15 Smith, "The Revolutionary Power of *Black Panther*." Released in November 2022, the film's sequel, *Black Panther: Wakanda Forever*, has produced similar

feelings of excitement and joy for its representation of Indigenous and Latinx identities through its new antihero, Namor (Tenoch Huerta Mejía), and his people, a Mayan civilization that has escaped European conquest through the discovery of vibranium and a vibranium-based plant that gives them the ability to breathe water and build a brilliant, flourishing, clandestine nation under the sea. As David Betancourt writes, "The true power of Namor is that he's played by a Latino man—and one with brown skin—taking center stage in a Black superhero universe. And that's not something that can be taken lightly. The movie depicts two nations bordering each other—one on land (Wakanda), the other below the sea (Talokan), both led by superheroes. One is Black, the other is Indigenous, both powerful and refusing to adhere to colonization by force. I can count on one finger the number of times I've seen that in a superhero movie. And as someone who walks in both of those worlds, I can honestly say I never expected to connect so closely to a superhero film unless it was one I made myself" ("Tenoch Huerta's Role in 'Wakanda Forever' Is a Huge Moment for Latinos," *The Washington Post*, November 12, 2022, https://www.washingtonpost.com/comics/2022/11/12/tenoch-huerta-namor-wakanda-forever/).

16 Carvell Wallace, "Why 'Black Panther' Is a Defining Moment for Black America," *New York Times Magazine*, February 12, 2018, www.nytimes.com/2018/02/12/magazine/why-black-panther-is-a-defining-moment-for-black-america.html?smid=url-share.

17 Wallace, "Why 'Black Panther.'"

18 Fanon, *Black Skin*, xiv–xv.

19 Qtd. in Hazel Rowley, *Richard Wright: The Life and Times* (New York: Henry Holt, 2001), 491.

20 Eve Kosofsky Sedgwick, "Paranoid Reading and Reparative Reading, or, You're So Paranoid, You Probably Think This Essay Is About You," in *Touching Feeling* (Durham: Duke University Press, 2003), 128, emphasis in the original.

21 Sedgwick, "Paranoid Reading," 130.

22 Sedgwick, "Paranoid Reading," 130.

23 Jacques Derrida, *Rogues: Two Essays on Reason*, trans. Pascale-Anne Brault and Michael Naas (Stanford: Stanford University Press, 2005), 152.

24 Wallace, "Why 'Black Panther.'"

25 Wallace, "Why 'Black Panther.'"

26 Wilderson, *Red, White & Black*, 18.

27 Sedgwick, "Paranoid Reading," 146.

28 Sedgwick, "Paranoid Reading," 146.

29 Chloe Hall and Mariel Tyler, "'I'm Rooting for Everybody Black': Black People on Black Panther," *ELLE*, March 19, 2018, www.elle.com/culture/movies-tv/a18242052/black-panther-audience-reactions/. Indeed, numerous critics of the film have stressed that seeing one's identities represented in popular culture is key to well-being: "Those of us who are not white have

considerably more trouble not only finding representation of ourselves in mass media and other arenas of public life, but also finding representation that indicates that our humanity is multifaceted. Relating to characters onscreen is necessary not merely for us to feel seen and understood, but also for others who need to see and understand us. When it doesn't happen, we are all the poorer for it," comments Jamil Smith, for example ("The Revolutionary Power of *Black Panther*"). "I haven't been this enthralled with the loving representation of black bodies since Julie Dash's Daughters of the Dust," wrote Kimberlé Crenshaw in a review critical of major elements of the film yet impressed with its success in this particular respect. "The sheer joy of drinking it all in made me realize just how thirsty I was for such visual treats. I savored every last drop, the fierce warrior sistas, the humor, the geniuses, Black love, all the things we just don't get to see. Joy. I can imagine now what it must be like to be part of a group that can expect to see a celebrated view of themselves in 99% of what gets produced. Now that we've got a taste, we will surely demand more. I hope" (reposted by Acra[dot]alt, February 19 2018, accradotalt.tumblr.com/post/171077996580/kimberle-crenshaws-take-on-bl ack-panther-rings). Issac Bailey emphasized similar points: "For a few hours, all shades of black people, African and African-American, will be able to see themselves become the center of the most influential image-making industry on the planet. Slavery and racism will be neither soft-pedaled nor portrayed as the totality of the black experience.... I'm not sure the rest of America understands the weight of that reality [Trump's election to the presidency] as experienced by black America. It feels like daily punishment for the sin of having felt overjoyed that black excellence was chosen in 2008, and again in 2012, to lead all Americans. That's where we are, and that's why seeing black excellence unapologetically take center stage again—if only for two hours and 15 minutes—on the big screen means so much" ("Black Panther Is for Film What Barack Obama Was for the Presidency," CNN.com, February 9, 2018, www.cnn.com/2018/02/09/opinions/black-panther-black-america-donald -trump-bailey-opinion).

30 Hartman, *Lose Your Mother*, 5.
31 Hartman, *Lose Your Mother*, 5.
32 Hartman, *Lose Your Mother*, 6.
33 Like his fellow Black Americans, Killmonger "suffers the status of being neither the native nor the foreigner, neither the colonizer nor the colonized" (Jared Sexton, "People-of-Color-Blindness: Notes on the Afterlife of Slavery," *Social Text* 28, no. 2 [2010]: 41).
34 Gordon, *Fear of Black Consciousness*, 180.
35 Racquel Gates and Kristen J. Warner, "Wakanda Forever: The Pleasures, the Politics, and the Problems," *Film Quarterly*, March 9, 2018, filmquarterly .org/2018/03/09/wakanda-forever-the-pleasures-the-politics-and-the-probl ems/. Christopher Lebron makes a similar point in his compelling analysis, observing that it is "a real shame that *Black Panther*, a movie unique for its black star power and its many thoughtful portrayals of strong black women, depends on a shocking devaluation of black American men. [...] Killmonger is

the revolutionary willing to take what he wants by any means necessary, but he lacks any coherent political philosophy. Rather than the enlightened radical, he comes across as the black thug from Oakland hell bent on killing for killing's sake—indeed, his body is marked with a scar for every kill he has made. The abundant evidence of his efficacy does not establish Killmonger as a hero or villain so much as a receptacle for tropes of inner-city gangsterism" (Christopher Lebron, "'Black Panther' Is Not the Movie We Deserve," *Boston Review*, February 17, 2018, bostonreview.net/race/christopher-lebron-black-panther).

36 The sequel, *Black Panther: Wakanda Forever*, gives more attention to the legitimacy of the colonized's grievances by explicitly engaging with the violence of Spanish settlement in the Americas from the perspective of Indigenous peoples. Yet the sequel pursues a very similar logic as the original, pitting Talokan against Wakanda in a struggle, once again, over the use of violence to repel colonialist incursions. Namor, like Killmonger, advocates war against the "surface" nations, the United States and France chief among them, who are attempting to extract vibranium from the ocean, threatening his people; unlike Killmonger, Namor yields to the new Black Panther, T'Challa's sister Shuri, who defeats him in battle but promises him an alliance with Wakanda in exchange for submitting. This ending is novel and refreshing in representing anticolonial solidarity in a positive light, yet this plot displaces a direct confrontation with the colonial forces who triggered the conflict in the first place. The major action of the film revolves instead around the anticipation and then spectacle of war between Black and Brown peoples. And while the film also breaks with convention by placing Wakandan women in a range of leadership roles, the shift away from patriarchal rule is brief, for not only does Shuri not fully assume the mantle of queen, but it is revealed in a mid-credits scene that the deceased T'Challa has left behind a son, setting up the promise of a return to male rule in some future film.

37 Gates and Warner, "Wakanda Forever."

38 Leslie Lee, "Fear of a Black Superhero," *In These Times*, May 12, 2021, https://inthesetimes.com/article/black-captain-america-the-falcon-and-the-winter-soldier.

39 Hartman, *Lose Your Mother*, 6.

40 Gates and Warner, "Wakanda Forever."

41 Lewis R. Gordon, Annie Menzel, George Shulman, and Jasmine Syedullah, "Afro Pessimism," *Contemporary Political Theory* 17, no. 1 (2018): 126.

42 As Asad Haider writes, "In *Black Panther*, we are presented with a mythology that makes anti-imperialist resistance unnecessary. In the Marvel myth [. . .] Third World poverty is not a result of the ravages of colonialism and the uneven exploitation of global capitalism. Rather, this poverty simply does not exist—it is an illusion intended to hide the wealth cultivated and protected by an African monarchy from time immemorial" (Asad Haider, "Black Atlantis," *Viewpoint Magazine*, March 5, 2018, https://viewpointmag.com/2018/03/05/black-atlantis/). For Žižek, "Killmonger's political vision" remains "radically open" despite the film's inner logic and promotion of its putative hero,

T'Challa. Killmonger's refusal to conform to the will of his victorious cousin registers a protest and obliquely gestures to "a really new world, a world which does not just reflect, invert, or supplement the existing one" (Žižek, "Quasi Duo Fantasias: A Straussian Reading of 'Black Panther,'" *Los Angeles Review of Books*, March 3, 2018, lareviewofbooks.org/article/quasi-duo-fantasias-straussian-reading-black-panther/).

43 Gates and Warner, "Wakanda Forever."
44 Žižek, "We Need a Socialist Reset, Not a Corporate 'Great Reset,'" *Jacobin*, December 31, 2020, jacobinmag.com/2020/12/slavoj-zizek-socialism-great-reset.
45 Fredric Jameson, *Archaeologies of the Future: The Desire Called Utopia and Other Science Fictions* (New York: Verso, 2005), xvi.
46 Lorna Piatti-Farnell, "'For God's Sake, Cover Yourself': Sexual Violence, Disrupted Histories, and the Gendered Politics of Patriotism in *Watchmen*," *Journal of Graphic Novels and Comics* 8, no. 3 (2017): 239.
47 On the collaborative dynamic established in the writers' room and the challenges of writing racism, intergenerational trauma, and police violence, see Craig Mazin, "Interview with Writers Lila Byock, Christal Henry, and Stacy Osei-Kuffour," *The Official* Watchmen *Podcast*, Apple Podcasts, August 26, 2020, https://podcasts.apple.com/us/podcast/interview-with-writers-lila-byock-christal-henry-and/id1485052917?i=1000492837048.
48 Michael Boyce Gillespie, "Thinking about Watchmen: A Roundtable," *Film Quarterly* 73, no. 4 (Summer 2020), https://filmquarterly.org/2020/06/26/thinking-about-watchmen-with-jonathan-w-gray-rebecca-a-wanzo-and-kristen-j-warner/.
49 Emily Nussbaum, "The Incendiary Aims of HBO's 'Watchmen,'" *The New Yorker*, December 2, 2019, https://www.newyorker.com/magazine/2019/12/09/the-incendiary-aims-of-hbos-watchmen.
50 Jeremy Egner, "Who Will Watch 'Watchmen'?" *The New York Times*, October 16, 2019, https://www.nytimes.com/2019/10/16/arts/television/watchmen-hbo-damon-lindelof-regina-king.html.
51 Lawrence Ware, "*Watchmen*'s Tulsa Massacre Is American History. It's Also Mine," *Slate*, October 25, 2019, https://slate.com/culture/2019/10/watchmen-tulsa-massacre-history-tv.html.
52 Nussbaum, "The Incendiary Aims."
53 Victor Luckerson, "The Great Achievement of 'Watchmen' Is in Showing How Black Americans Shape History," *The New Yorker*, December 23, 2019, https://www.newyorker.com/culture/cultural-comment/the-great-achievement-of-watchmen-is-in-showing-how-black-americans-shape-history.
54 Luckerson, "The Great Achievement."
55 Luckerson, "The Great Achievement."
56 Daniel Pollack-Pelzner, "The Hidden History of 'Oklahoma!'" *Oregon ArtsWatch*, November 19, 2018, https://www.orartswatch.org/the-hidden-history-of-oklahoma/. Accessed May 10, 2020.

57 See the Smithsonian American Art Museum's photograph of the work and a quotation from Catlin's journal describing the scene at https://americanart.si.edu/artwork/comanche-feats-horsemanship-4004.

58 See Kalen Goodluck, "Far-Right Extremists Appropriate Indigenous Struggles for Violent Ends," *High Country News*, August 27, 2019, https://www.hcn.org/issues/51.16/tribal-affairs-far-right-extremists-appropriate-indigenous-struggles-for-violent-ends. In Judd's universe, white resentment over "Redfordations" fuels an alchemical mutation, converting white suffering into an identity—white victimhood. Alchemy here takes the form of a counterinsurgency. If alchemy always risks unsettling ontological realities, this deployment of alchemy distorts the language of victimization in an effort to neutralize demands for racial justice and cast white folks as the injured party.

59 Anidjar, *Blood*, 87.

60 For an account of Bà Triệu or Triệu Thị Tr (renowned for rising up against Wu Chinese invaders in 248 CE), see, for example, Hữu Ngọc, *Viet Nam: Tradition and Change* (Athens: Ohio University Press, 2016) and Vu Hong Lien and Peter Sharrock, *Descending Dragon, Rising Tiger: A History of Vietnam* (London: Reaktion Books, 2014).

61 This center is inspired by the actual Greenwood Cultural Center in Tulsa, which works to preserve the memory of the 1921 events. See the organization's website at https://greenwoodculturalcenter.com/.

62 Regina King and Damen Lindelof also made a cross-promotional appearance as guests on *Finding Your Roots*, Season 8, Episode 9 ("Watchmen"), an episode that focuses, interestingly, almost entirely on genealogy, relegating genetics to a brief glimpse of King's and Lindelof's genetic ethnicity test result pie charts in a closing shot.

63 The exact form these reparations take is left unspecified in the show, but both the white backlash against any material compensation for the destruction of life and wealth and the liberal restriction of reparations to survivors and their "direct" descendants rely, in different ways, on bloodline as a criterion discriminating between groups. The protestors' use of the term "abomination" revives old, anti-integration discourse and the conceptions of sexual sin and racial impurity that it purveyed. The Redford administration's reliance on descent is more complicated, in part because we know little about it. This restriction plausibly represents a political compromise and pragmatic judicial maneuver, particularly when read against the actual fate of *Alexander v. Oklahoma*, the case for reparations brought against the State of Oklahoma, the City of Tulsa, and the Tulsa Police Department by Greenwood survivors, which was dismissed in 2004 (for a record of the decision and the text of the dissent, see *Alexander v. Oklahoma*, 391 F.3d 1155, 2004 U.S. App. LEXIS 25755 [United States Court of Appeals for the Tenth Circuit December 13, 2004, Filed], Nexis Uni. Accessed May 16, 2020). Considering what we know of the fictional law, however, we can see that it has at least two major effects. First, it recognizes the multigenerational impact of trauma on every, interconnected level of well-being, emotional and economic, and it repairs some measure of the damage

done to wealth and security. Second, it draws a necessary line between victims and non-victims (necessary, in that inequities involve distinct parties), but in grounding this distinction in descent, it suggests that inheritance is the primary vector by which equity—in both senses—should be maintained. Direct descent becomes the burden one must prove to be awarded redress. In other words, the reparations we see here do not extend to those whose family histories or family genetic information has been destroyed, nor, significantly, to victims of systemic racialized inequities less easily identified as "violence."

64 Alan Moore and Dave Gibbons, *Watchmen: The Deluxe Edition* (DC Comics, 2013), I:21. References to the Deluxe Edition cited here list the original chapter and page numbers reproduced internally in the collected volume.

65 Moore and Gibbons, *Watchmen*, IV:16.

66 Luckerson, "The Great Achievement."

67 Fabienne Kanor, *Humus*, trans. Lynn E. Palermo (Charlottesville: University of Virginia Press, 2020). Henceforth, references to this work will be cited parenthetically in the text.

68 Doyle Calhoun, "A Fugue for the Middle Passage? Suicidal Resistance Takes Flight in Fabienne Kanor's *Humus* (2006)," *The French Review* 95, no. 2 (2021): 133.

69 The term "spirit murder" is Patricia J. Williams's, who describes it as "disregard for others whose lives qualitatively depend on our regard," a disregard that generates "a system of formalized distortions of thought" and "social structures centered on fear and hate" (*The Alchemy of Race and Rights*, 73).

70 For a sensitive study of this figure in Chamoiseau's work, see Wendy Knepper, *Patrick Chamoiseau: A Critical Introduction* (Jackson: University Press of Mississippi, 2012).

71 Žižek, *Less Than Nothing: Hegel and the Shadow of Dialectical Materialism* (New York: Verso, 2012), 859.

72 Gladys M. Francis, "Afterword," in Fabienne Kanor, *Humus*, trans. Lynn E. Palermo (Charlottesville: University of Virginia Press, 2020), 194.

73 Francis, "Afterword," 194.

74 Ann Laura Stoler, "Colonial Aphasia: Race and Disabled Histories in France," *Public Culture* 23, no. 1 (2011): 122.

75 Stoler, "Colonial Aphasia," 125.

76 Stoler, "Colonial Aphasia," 133.

77 "I could say after a famous philosopher that what we know of Venus in her many guises amounts to 'little more than a register of her encounter with power' and that it provides 'a meager sketch of her existence'" (Hartman, "Venus in Two Acts," *Small Axe* 12, no. 2 [2008]: 11, 2). Hartman is quoting Michel Foucault's essay "Lives of Infamous Men").

78 Hartman, "Venus in Two Acts," 12.

79 Lauren Berlant, *On the Inconvenience of Other People* (Durham: Duke University Press, 2022), 99.
80 Jason Herbeck, "Entretien avec Fabienne Kanor," *The French Review* 86, no. 5 (2013): 971. My translation.
81 Saidiya V. Hartman and Frank B. Wilderson III, "The Position of the Unthought," *Qui Parle* 13, no. 2 (2003): 185.
82 Robinson, *Black Marxism*, 121–2.
83 Robinson, *Black Marxism*, 122.
84 Robinson, *Black Marxism*, 125.
85 Stefano Harney and Fred Moten, *All Incomplete* (New York: Minor Compositions, 2021), 140.
86 Harney and Moten, *All Incomplete*, 140–1.
87 Cedric J. Robinson and Elizabeth P. Robinson, "Preface," in *Futures of Black Radicalism*, ed. Gaye Theresa Johnson and Alex Lubin (New York: Verso, 2017), 7. Published after Cedric Robinson's death, this cowritten piece draws on a 2012 address he gave at UC Irvine, passages from which are signaled as his words through italics.
88 Robinson and Robinson, "Preface," 7.
89 Herbeck, "Entretien," 970.
90 Herbeck, "Entretien," 970.
91 Saidiya Hartman, *Wayward Lives, Beautiful Experiments: Intimate Histories of Social Upheaval* (New York: W.W. Norton & Company, 2019), xv.
92 Stoler, "Colonial Aphasia," 144.
93 Herbeck, "Entretien," 967.
94 Herbeck, "Entretien," 967–8.
95 Kennan Ferguson, "No Politics," in *The Big No*, ed. Kennan Ferguson (Minneapolis: University of Minnesota Press, 2021), x.
96 Ferguson, "No Politics," x.
97 Herbeck, "Entretien," 970.

Chapter 4

1 Glissant, *Caribbean Discourse*, 64.
2 Jean-Luc de Laguarigue, "Un autre monde," *Gens de pays*, blog, http://gensdepays.blogspot.com/search/label/Bio, my translation.
3 Moten, *Stolen Life*, 131.
4 Wicky Mochama, "'If You Don't Have Hope, Then Why Go On?': An Interview with Colson Whitehead," *Hazlitt*, September 15, 2016, https://hazlitt.net/feature/if-you-dont-have-hope-then-why-go-interview-colson-whitehead. While Ridgeway stresses what he deems unique about the

"American" capacity to carry out this imperative, it is in fact just one instantiation of "an imperial philosophy that plays out around the world and in different phases of history even today" (Mochama, "If You Don't Have Hope").

5   Colson Whitehead, *The Underground Railroad* (New York: Doubleday, 2016), 238. Henceforth, references to this work will be cited parenthetically in the text.

6   Wilderson, Hartman, Martinot, Sexton, and Spillers, "Editors' Introduction," 7, n. 1.

7   Jared Sexton, "Affirmations in the Dark: Racial Slavery and Philosophical Pessimism," *The Comparatist* 43 (2019): 102.

8   "'Every state is different,' Lumbly was saying. 'Each one a state of possibility, with its own customs and way of doing things. Moving through them, you'll see the breadth of the country before you reach your final stop'" (70).

9   Spillers, "Mama's Baby, Papa's Maybe," 67.

10 David S. Marriott, *Lacan Noir: Lacan and Afro-pessimism* (New York: Palgrave, 2021), 126.

11 I am borrowing this formulation—"in you more than you"—from Lacan. See Lacan, *The Four Fundamental Concepts of Psycho-analysis*, trans. Alan Sheridan (New York: Routledge, 2018), 263–76.

12 Likewise, we could say that there is slavecatcher in every white subject. From the antebellum period to the present, anti-Blackness persists and thrives. As Wilderson observes, "White people are not simply 'protected' by the police, they are the police" (Wilderson, *Red, White & Black*, 82).

13 Maya Jaggi, "The Wondrous and Tragic Life of Ivan and Ivana by Maryse Condé Review—A Scurrilous Picaresque," *The Guardian*, 16 July 2020, https://www.theguardian.com/books/2020/jul/16/the-wondrous-and-tragic-life-of-ivan-and-ivana-by-maryse-conde-review-a-scurrilous-picaresque.

14 Alana Lentin, "Charlie Hebdo: White Context and Black Analytics," *Public Culture* 31, no. 1 (2019): 51.

15 Lentin, "Charlie Hebdo," 48.

16 See Lentin, "Charlie Hebdo"; Barnor Hesse, "Racism's Alterity: The After-life of Black Sociology," in *Racism and Sociology*, ed. Wulf D. Hund and Alana Lentin (Berlin: Lit Verlag 2014), 141–74.

17 Condé, "Maryse Condé: 'La négritude est morte à Montrouge le 8 janvier 2015,'" interview by Tirthankar Chanda, *RFI*, July 28 2017, my translation. http://www.rfi.fr/hebdo/20170728-maryse-conde-negritude-antilles-guadeloupe-ivan-ivana-creolite-aime-cesaire. The full section reads, "In Utero or Bounded in a Nutshell (*Hamlet*—William Shakespeare)," referring to Act II, Scene 2, where Hamlet famously dodges Rosencrantz and Guildenstern's prying questions about his ambitions to the throne with an equivocal rejoinder evoking the power of thought to turn a vast space into a prison or a constrained one into a joy: "Oh God, I could be bounded in a nut shell and count myself a king of infinite space, were it not that I have bad dreams"

(William Shakespeare et al., *Hamlet* [Yale University Press, 2003], JSTOR, www.jstor.org/stable/j.ctt1njkw8, II.2.250).

18 Condé, "Maryse Condé,'" my translation.
19 Condé, "Entretien avec Maryse Condé: Quelques acquis et manques de la littérature francophone des Antilles," interview by Roger Célestin, *Contemporary French and Francophone Studies* 22, no. 2 (2018): 155, my translation.
20 Condé, "Maryse Condé."
21 Condé, "Entretien," 155.
22 Condé, *The Wondrous and Tragic Life of Ivan and Ivana*, trans. Richard Philcox (New York: World Editions, 2020), 15, 16. Henceforth, references to this work will be cited parenthetically in the text.
23 Spillers, "Mama's Baby, Papa's Maybe," 67.
24 Lisa Guenther, "The Most Dangerous Place: Pro-Life Politics and the Rhetoric of Slavery," *Postmodern Culture* 22, no. 2 (2012), http://www.pomoculture.org/2013/04/07/the-most-dangerous-place-pro-life-politics-and-the-rhetoric-of-slavery/.
25 Spillers, "Mama's Baby, Papa's Maybe," 67.
26 Sylvia Wynter, "Unsettling the Coloniality of Being/Power/Truth/Freedom: Toward the Human, after Man, Its Overrepresentation—An Argument," *New Centennial Review* 3, no. 3 (2003): 269, 260.
27 Weheliye, *Habeas Viscus*, 4.
28 Weheliye, *Habeas Viscus*, 3.
29 Weheliye, *Habeas Viscus*, 22.
30 Cheah, *What Is a World*, 116.
31 The narrator uses but also questions the term "radicalization," suggesting that Ivan's case exceeds existing models while also having something in common with them. "It was from this moment on that his radicalization began, a word that is bandied about today, rightly or wrongly" the narrator states of a humiliating episode in Ivan's adolescence (37), later identifying other "beginnings" or turning points in this process: "If you ask my opinion," the narrator declares after the murder of Ivan's close friends and lovers, Alex and Cristina, "I would say that it was at this precise moment that Ivan became radicalized, as they say" (164), but revises this opinion some pages later, commenting, "it was at that very moment [a sexual proposition that offends Ivan], that Ivan's radicalization came to completion. Up till then certain events, such as the deaths of his beloved Alix and Cristina, had not radically changed him" (199).
32 Žižek, *Violence*, 46.
33 Gayatri Chakravorty Spivak, *An Aesthetic Education in the Era of Globalization* (Cambridge, MA: Harvard University Press, 2012), 297.
34 This applies, moreover, to the stories we tell of ourselves: "The experience that we have of our lives from within, the story we tell ourselves about ourselves in

order to account for what we are doing, is fundamentally a lie—the truth lies outside, in what we do" (Žižek, *Violence*, 47). Žižek returns to the example of *Frankenstein* and the limits of humanization in his discussion of the *Charlie Hebdo* attacks. See Žižek, "In the Grey Zone: Slavoj Žižek on Responses to the Paris killings," *London Review of Books*, February 5, 2015, https://www.lrb.co.uk/2015/02/05/slavoj-zizek/in-the-grey-zone.

35 The television series dangerously flirts with this question through its elevation of the father/son dynamics. We follow a young Rigdeway struggling to find his calling, anxious about his own masculinity (he can't match his father's physical strength—whence the appeal of the slavecatcher as an alternative model of strength), looking for his father's admiration, which he sees as extended to his rival, a Black child, the son of his enslaved worker. The series suggests that Ridgeway's alienation from his father contributed a great deal to the forging of his anti-Blackness. Moreover, the series creates a stark contrast between Ridgeway and his father (who, on many occasions, demonstrates kindness toward his enslaved) whereas the novel underscores the ways they are two sides of the same coin.

36 Sigmund Freud, *Beyond the Pleasure Principle*. Standard Edition, vol. 18 (London: Hogarth, 1920), 36.

37 Elizabeth Freeman, *Time Binds: Queer Temporalities, Queer Histories* (Durham: Duke University Press, 2010), 3. I thank Zahi Zalloua for this reference.

38 Dana Luciano, *Arranging Grief: Sacred Time and the Body in Nineteenth-Century America* (New York: New York University Press, 2007), 9.

39 Freeman, *Time Binds*, 4.

40 Žižek, *The Parallax View* (Cambridge, MA: MIT Press, 2006), 61.

41 Žižek, *The Parallax View*, 62.

42 "The true evil, which is the death drive, involves self-sabotage. It makes us act against our own interests" (Žižek, *Violence*, 87).

43 Žižek, "Unbehagen and the Subject: An Interview with Slavoj Žižek," *Psychoanalysis, Culture & Society* 15 (2010): 422.

44 Adrian Johnson, *Žižek's Ontology* (Evanston: Northwestern University Press, 2008), 185.

45 Stephanie Li, "Genre Trouble and History's Miseries in Colson Whitehead's *The Underground Railroad*," *Melus* 44, no. 2 (2019): 2.

46 Matthew Dischinger, "States of Possibility in Colson Whitehead's *The Underground Railroad*," *The Global South* 11, no. 1 (2017): 90.

47 Grace Heneks, "'What Race Problem?': The Satirical Gaze of (White) History in *The Underground Railroad*," *MELUS* 45, no. 4 (2020): 145.

48 Moten, *The Universal Machine*, 204.

49 Nihad M. Farooq, "'A Useful Delusion': Valentine Farm and the Flight for Freedom Utopian Studies," *Utopian Studies* 30, no. 1 (2019): 100.

50 Farooq, "'A Useful Delusion,'" 105.

51 "There is cause for optimism as long as there is a need for optimism. Cause and need converge in the bent school or marginal church in which we gather together to be in the name of being otherwise" (Moten, "Black Optimism/Black Operation," 1747).

52 Farooq, "'A Useful Delusion,'" 105. For Jameson, "the Utopian form itself is the answer to the universal ideological conviction that no alternative is possible, that there is no alternative to the system. But it asserts this by forcing us to think the break itself, and not by offering a more traditional picture of what things would be like after the break" (Jameson, *Archaeologies of the Future*, 232). Cora and all the enslaved who contest their enslavement embody this break, the belief that one can *be otherwise*. Might does not make right. The American imperative is not (manifest) destiny. Under the horizon of slavery's afterlife, there is an "increasing inability to imagine a different future" (Jameson, *Archaeologies of the Future*, 232). Returning to Cora's world, infusing it with a utopian impulse, constitutes an intervention, "a meditation on the impossible, on the unrealizable in its own right" (Jameson, *Archaeologies of the Future*, 232).

53 Farooq, "'A Useful Delusion,'" 99.

54 Farooq, "'A Useful Delusion,'" 100.

55 Martha Feldman, "Fugitive Voice," *Representations* 154, no. 1 (2021): 10.

56 Jack Halberstam, "Go Gaga: Anarchy, Chaos, and the Wild," *Social Text* 31, no. 3(116) (2013): 130, emphasis added.

57 Bonilla, *Non-Sovereign Futures*, 41–3.

58 Lee Konstantinou, "Critique Has Its Uses," *American Book Review* 38, no. 5 (2017): 18.

59 Žižek, *Surplus Enjoyment* (New York: Bloomsbury, 2022), 212.

60 Fred Moten, Stefano Harney, and Stevphen Shukaitis, "Refusing Completion: A Conversation," *e-flux* 116 (2021): 9.

61 Frantz Fanon, *Peau noire, masques blancs*, Collection Points (Paris: Seuil, 1952), 80.

62 Todd McGowan, *Universality and Identity Politics* (New York: Columbia University Press, 2020), 183.

63 Fanon, *Black Skin*, 95.

64 Fanon, *Black Skin*, 94.

Conclusion

1 Williams, *Alchemy of Race*, 188.

2 Williams, *Alchemy of Race*, 188.

3 Hartman, *Scenes of Subjection*, 234, n. 8.

4 Hartman, *Lose Your Mother*, 68.

5 Beauvoir, *The Second Sex*, trans. Constance Borde and Sheila Malovany-Chevallier (New York: Alfred Knopf, 2010), 12.
6 Spillers, "Mama's Baby, Papa's Maybe," 68.
7 Moten, "Black Optimism/Black Operation," 1747.
8 Moten, "Black Optimism/Black Operation," 1747.

WORKS CITED

Abu El-Haj, Nadia. *The Genealogical Science: Genetics, The Origins of the Jews, and the Politics of Epistemology*. Chicago: The University of Chicago Press, 2012.

Adrion, Jeffrey, Keith Noto, Alisa Sedghifar, Barry Starr, David Turissini, Yong Wang, and Aaron Wolf . "Ethnicity Estimate 2022 White Paper." AncestryDNA. https://www.ancestrycdn.com/support/us/2022/08/ethnicity2022whitepaper.pdf.

Alet, Thierry. "Manifeste pour un code couleur." https://www.thierryalet.com/manifeste.

Amar, Yvan. "Acte—04/06/2015." RFI.fr, June 4, 2015. https://www.rfi.fr/fr/emission/20150604-acte-04062015.

Ancestry.com. www.ancestry.com.

"AncestryDNA® Ethnicity." Ancestry.com. https://support.ancestry.com/s/article/AncestryDNA-Ethnicity.

Anidjar, Gil. *Blood: A Critique of Christianity*. New York: Columbia University Press, 2014.

Badiou, Alain. *The Century*. Trans. Alberto Toscano. Cambridge: Polity Press, 2007.

Bailey, Issac. "Black Panther Is for Film What Barack Obama Was for the Presidency." CNN.com, February 9, 2018. www.cnn.com/2018/02/09/opinions/black-panther-black-america-donald-trump-bailey-opinion.

Baldwin, James. "A Report from Occupied Territory." *The Nation* 300, no. 14, March 23, 2015. Reprinted from July 11, 1966. https://www.thenation.com/article/archive/report-occupied-territory-2/.

Ball, Catherine A., Mathew J. Barber, Jake K. Byrnes, Josh Callaway, Kenneth G. Chahine, Ross E. Curtis, Kenneth Freestone, Julie M. Granka, Natalie M. Myres, Keith Noto, Yong Wang, and Scott R. Woodward. "Ethnicity Estimate White Paper." AncestryDNA, October 30, 2013. www.ancestry.com/dna/resource/whitePaper/AncestryDNA-Ethnicity-White-Paper.pdf.

Barad, Karen. "Interview with Karen Barad." In *New Materialism: Interviews and Cartographies*. Ed. Rick Dophijn and Iris van der Tuin. Ann Arbor: Open Humanities Press, 2012. 48–70.

"Behavior." Orig3n.com. shop.orig3n.com/collections/featured-products/products/behavior.

Benjamin, Ruha. "Black AfterLives Matter: Cultivating Kinfulness as Reproductive Justice." In *Making Kin Not Population*. Ed. Adele E. Clarke and Donna Haraway. Chicago: Prickly Paradigm Press, 2018. 41–66.

Bennett, Jane. "In Parliament with Things." In *Radical Democracy: Politics Between Abundance and Lack*. Ed. Lars Tønder and Lasse Thomassen. Manchester: Manchester University Press, 2005. 133–48.

Bennett, Jane. "Systems and Things: On Vital Materialism and Object-Oriented Philosophy." In *The Nonhuman Turn*. Ed. Richard Grusin. Minneapolis: University of Minnesota Press, 2015. 223–39.

Bennett, Jane. *Vibrant Matter: A Political Ecology of Things*. Durham: Duke University Press, 2010.

Berlant, Lauren. *On the Inconvenience of Other People*. Durham: Duke University Press, 2022.

Bernasconi, Robert. "The European Knows and Does Not Know: Fanon's Response to Sartre." In *Frantz Fanon's "Black Skin, White Masks": New Interdisciplinary Essays*. Ed. Max Silverman. Manchester: Manchester University Press, 2005. 100–11.

Best, Stephen and Sharon Marcus. "Surface Reading: An Introduction." *Representations* 108, no. 1 (2009): 1–21.

Bogues, Anthony and Lonnie Bunch. "This Museum Is About American Identity as Much as It Is About African American History: An Interview with Lonnie Bunch." *Callaloo* 38, no. 4 (2015): 703–9.

Boisseron, Bénédicte. *Afro-Dog: Blackness and the Animal Question*. New York: Columbia University Press, 2018.

Bonilla, Yarimar. *Non-Sovereign Futures: French Caribbean Politics in the Wake of Disenchantment*. Chicago: University of Chicago Press, 2015.

Bourdieu, Pierre. *Outline of a Theory of Practice*. Trans. Richard Nice. Cambridge: Cambridge University Press, 1977.

Bunch, Lonnie G. III. *A Fool's Errand: Creating the National Museum of African American History and Culture in the Age of Bush, Obama, and Trump*. Washington, D.C.: Smithsonian Books, 2019.

Butler, Octavia. *Fledgling*. New York: Grand Central Publishing, 2005.

Byrd, Donald. "What 'Black Panther' Means to a Black Baby Boomer." *Crosscut*, February 20, 2018. https://crosscut.com/2018/02/what-black-panther-means-black-baby-boomer.

Calhoun, Doyle. "A Fugue for the Middle Passage? Suicidal Resistance Takes Flight in Fabienne Kanor's *Humus* (2006)." *The French Review* 95, no. 2 (2021): 127–44.

Callard, Abby. "Emmett Till's Casket Goes to the Smithsonian." *Smithsonian Magazine*, November 2009. https://www.smithsonianmag.com/arts-culture/emmett-tills-casket-goes-to-the-smithsonian-144696940.

Chamoiseau, Patrick. *L'empreinte à Crusoé*. Paris: Gallimard, 2012.

Chamoiseau, Patrick. "Les Secrets de Chamoiseau." *Antilla Special* 11 (December 1988–January 1989): 23–6.

Chandler, Nahum Dimitri. *X—The Problem of the Negro as a Problem for Thought*. New York: Fordham University Press, 2014.

Cheah, Pheng. *What Is a World? On Postcolonial Literature as World Literature*. Durham: Duke University Press, 2016.

"Child Development." Orig3n.com. shop.orig3n.com/collections/featured-products/products/child-development.

Clytus, Radiclani. "Freedom Comes in a Box: Reflections on the National Museum of African American History and Culture." *Callaloo* 38, no. 4 (2015): 742–51.

Coates, Ta-Nehisi. *Between the World and Me*. New York: Spiegel and Grau, 2015.

Cohen, Jeffrey Jerome. "The Ontological Turn." In *Posthuman Glossary*. Ed. Rosi Braidotti and Maria Hlavajova. New York: Bloomsbury, 2018. 304–6.

Condé, Maryse. "Entretien avec Maryse Condé: Quelques acquis et manques de la littérature francophone des Antilles." Interview by Roger Célestin, *Contemporary French and Francophone Studies* 22, no. 2 (2018): 152–5.

Condé, Maryse. "La négritude est morte à Montrouge le 8 janvier 2015." Interview by Tirthankar Chanda, *RFI*, July 28, 2017. http://www.rfi.fr/hebdo/20170728-maryse-conde-negritude-antilles-guadeloupe-ivan-ivana-creolite-aime-cesaire. Accessed January 16, 2021.

Condé, Maryse. *Le fabuleux et triste destin d'Ivan et Ivana*. Paris: JC Lattès, 2017.

Condé, Maryse. *The Wondrous and Tragic Life of Ivan and Ivana*. Trans. Richard Philcox. New York: World Editions, 2020.

Corley, Cheryl. "Body of Emmett Till to Be Exhumed." *NPR*, May 5, 2005. https://www.npr.org/templates/story/story.php?storyId=4631506.

Crenshaw, Kimberlé. "Reposted by Acra[dot]alt." February 19, 2018. accradotalt.tumblr.com/post/171077996580/kimberle-crenshaws-take-on-black-panther-rings.

Davey, Monica and Gretchen Ruethling. "After 50 Years, Emmett Till's Body Is Exhumed." *New York Times*, June 2, 2005. https://www.nytimes.com/2005/06/02/us/after-50-years-emmett-tills-body-is-exhumed.html.

Davies, Dave. "Historian Henry Louis Gates Jr. On DNA Testing and Finding His Own Roots." *NPR*, January 21, 2019. https://www.npr.org/2019/01/21/686531998/historian-henry-louis-gates-jr-on-dna-testing-and-finding-his-own-roots.

de Groot, Jerome. "The Genealogy Boom: Inheritance, Family History, and the Popular Historical Imagination." In *The Impact of History? Histories at the Beginning of the 21st Century*. Ed. Bertrand Taithe and Pedro Ramos Pinto. London: Routledge, 2015. 21–34.

Derrida, Jacques. "Autoimmunity: Real and Symbolic Suicides—A Dialogue with Jacques Derrida." In *Philosophy in a Time of Terror: Dialogues with Jürgen Habermas and Jacques Derrida*. Ed. Giovanna Borradori. Chicago: University of Chicago Press, 2004. 85–136.

Derrida, Jacques. *On Cosmopolitanism and Forgiveness*. Trans. Mark Dooley and Michael Hughes. New York: Routledge, 2001.

Derrida, Jacques. *Rogues: Two Essays on Reason*. Trans. Pascale-Anne Brault and Michael Naas. Stanford: Stanford University Press, 2005.

Derrida, Jacques and Elisabeth Roudinesco. *For What Tomorrow . . .: A Dialogue*. Trans. Jeff Fort. Stanford: Stanford University Press, 2004.

Derrida, Jacques and Maurizio Ferraris. *A Taste for the Secret*. Trans. Giacomo Donis. Cambridge: Polity Press, 2001.

Diawara, Manthia. "One World in Relation: Édouard Glissant in Conversation with Manthia Diawara." *Journal of Contemporary African Art* 28 (Spring 2011): 4–19.

Dischinger, Matthew. "States of Possibility in Colson Whitehead's *The Underground Railroad*." *The Global South* 11, no. 1 (2017): 82–99.

Duster, Troy. "Buried Alive: The Concept of Race in Science." In *Genetic Nature/Culture: Anthropology and Science beyond the Two-Culture Divide*. Ed. Alan H. Goodman, Deborah Heath and M. Susan Lindee. Berkeley: University of California Press, 2003. 258–77.

Duster, Troy. "Race and Reification in Science." *Science* 307, no. 5712 (2005): 1050–1.

Egner, Jeremy. "Who Will Watch 'Watchmen'?" *The New York Times*, October 16, 2019. https://www.nytimes.com/2019/10/16/arts/television/watchmen-hbo-damon-lindelof-regina-king.html.

Eshun, Kodwo. "Further Considerations of Afrofuturism." *CR: The New Centennial Review* 3, no. 2 (2003): 287–302.

Fanon, Frantz. *Alienation and Freedom*. Trans. Steven Corcoran. New York: Bloomsbury, 2018.

Fanon, Frantz. *Black Skin, White Masks*. Trans. Richard Philcox. New York: Grove Press, 2008.

Fanon, Frantz. *Peau noire, masques blancs*. Collection Points. Paris: Seuil, 1952.

Fanon, Frantz. *The Wretched of the Earth*. Trans. Richard Philcox. New York: Grove Press, 2004.

Farooq, Nihad M. "'A Useful Delusion': Valentine Farm and the Flight for Freedom Utopian Studies." *Utopian Studies* 30, no. 1 (2019): 87–110.

Feldman, Martha. "Fugitive Voice." *Representations* 154, no. 1 (2021): 10–22.

Felski, Rita. *The Limits of Critique*. Chicago: University of Chicago Press, 2015.

Ferguson, Kennan. "No Politics." In *The Big No*. Ed. Kennan Ferguson. Minneapolis: University of Minnesota Press, 2021. ix–xxi.

Florida Administrative Code & Florida Administrative Register, Florida Department of State. https://www.flrules.org/gateway/ruleNo.asp?id=6A-1.094124.

Francis, Gladys M. "Afterword." In Fabienne Kanor's *Humus*. Trans. Lynn E. Palermo. Charlottesville: University of Virginia Press, 2020. 191–202.

Freeman, Elizabeth. *Time Binds: Queer Temporalities, Queer Histories*. Durham: Duke University Press, 2010.

Freud, Sigmund. *Beyond the Pleasure Principle*, standard edition, vol. 18. London: Hogarth, 1920. 1–64.

Fuggle, Sophie. "Reimagining the Ruins of the Penalscape: Patrick Chamoiseau's Carceral Ruinology." *Social Identities* 26, no. 6 (2020): 811–28.

Gabriel, Abram. "A Biologist's Perspective on DNA and Race in the Genomics Era." In *Genetics and the Unsettled Past: The Collision of DNA, Race, and History*. Ed. Keith Wailoo, Alondra Nelson, and Catherine Lee. New Brunswick: Rutgers University Press, 2012. 43–66.

Gates, Henry Louis, Jr. *Finding Your Roots, Season 1: The Official Companion to the PBS Series*. Chapel Hill: The University of North Carolina Press, 2014.

Gates, Henry Louis, Jr. *Finding Your Roots, Season 2: The Official Companion to the PBS Series*. Chapel Hill: The University of North Carolina Press, 2016.

Gates, Henry Louis, Jr. *In Search of Our Roots: How 19 Extraordinary African Americans Reclaimed Their Past* [2009]. New York: Skyhorse Publishing, 2017.

Gates, Henry Louis, Jr., Sabin Streeter, Natalia Warchol, Regina King, and Damon Lindelof. *Finding Your Roots. Season 8, Episode 9, Watchmen*. Arlington: Public Broadcasting Service, 2022.

Gates, Racquel and Kristen J. Warner. "Wakanda Forever: The Pleasures, the Politics, and the Problems." *Film Quarterly*, March 9, 2018. filmquarterly.org/2018/03/09/wakanda-forever-the-pleasures-the-politics-and-the-problems/.

Gillespie, Michael Boyce. "Thinking about Watchmen: A Roundtable." *Film Quarterly* 73, no. 4 (Summer 2020). https://filmquarterly.org/2020/06/26/

thinking-about-watchmen-with-jonathan-w-gray-rebecca-a-wanzo-and-kristen-j-warner/.

Gilroy, Paul. *Darker than Blue: On the Moral Economies of Black Atlantic Culture*. Cambridge, MA: Harvard University Press, 2010.

Gilroy, Paul. "Never Again: Refusing Race and Salvaging the Human." 2019 Holberg Lecture, June 20, 2019. https://www.newframe.com/long-read-refusing-race-and-salvaging-the-human/.

Glissant, Édouard. *Caribbean Discourse: Selected Essays*. Trans. Michael Dash. Charlottesville: University of Virginia Press, 1989.

Glissant, Édouard. *Faulkner, Mississippi*. Trans. Barbara B. Lewis and Thomas Spear. Chicago: University of Chicago Press, 2000.

Glissant, Édouard. *Le Discours antillais*. Paris: Éditions du Seuil, 1981.

Glissant, Édouard. *Mémoires des esclavages: Pour la fondation d'un Centre national pour la mémoire des esclavages et de leurs abolitions*. Paris: Gallimard, 2007.

Glissant, Édouard. *Poetics of Relation*. Trans. Betsy Wing. Ann Arbor: University of Michigan Press, 1997.

Goldberg, David Theo. *Are We All Postracial Yet?*. Cambridge: Polity Press, 2015.

Goodluck, Kalen. "Far-Right Extremists Appropriate Indigenous Struggles for Violent Ends." *High Country News*, August 27, 2019. https://www.hcn.org/issues/51.16/tribal-affairs-far-right-extremists-appropriate-indigenous-struggles-for-violent-ends.

Gordon, Lewis R. *Fear of Black Consciousness*. New York: Farrar, Straus and Giroux, 2022.

Gordon, Lewis R., Annie Menzel, George Shulman, and Jasmine Syedullah. "Afropessimism." *Contemporary Political Theory* 17, no. 1 (2018): 105–37.

Gosset, Che. "Blackness, Animality, and the Unsovereign." September 8, 2015. https://www.versobooks.com/blogs/2228-che-gossett-blackness-animality-and-the-unsovereign.

Gosson, Renée. "Breaking Museal Tradition: Guadeloupe's 'Mémorial ACTe' and the Scenography of Slavery." *Histoire Sociale/Social History* 53, no. 107 (May 2020): 179–94.

Gratton, Peter. *Speculative Realism: Problems and Prospects*. New York: Bloomsbury, 2014.

Guenther, Lisa. "The Most Dangerous Place: Pro-Life Politics and the Rhetoric of Slavery." *Postmodern Culture* 22, no. 2 (2012). http://www.pomoculture.org/2013/04/07/the-most-dangerous-place-pro-life-politics-and-the-rhetoric-of-slavery/.

Gyssels, Kathleen. "The *Département* Writes Back: On Chamoiseau's Rewrite of *Robinson Crusoe*." In *Postcoloniality-Decoloniality-Black Critique: Joints and Fissures*. Ed. Sabine Broeck and Carsten Junker. Frankfurt: Campus Verlag, 2014. 287–309.

Haider, Asad. "Black Atlantis." *Viewpoint Magazine*, March 5, 2018. www.viewpointmag.com/2018/03/05/black-atlantis/.

Halberstam, Jack. "Go Gaga: Anarchy, Chaos, and the Wild." *Social Text* 31, no. 3(116) (2013): 123–34.

Hall, Chloe and Mariel Tyler. "'I'm Rooting for Everybody Black': Black People on Black Panther." *ELLE*, March 19, 2018. www.elle.com/culture/movies-tv/a18242052/black-panther-audience-reactions/.

Harman, Graham. "Aesthetics as First Philosophy: Levinas and the Non-Human." *Naked Punch*, 2012. http://www.nakedpunch.com/articles/147.

Harman, Graham. *Object-Oriented Ontology: A New Theory of Everything*. New York: Pelican, 2017.

Harmon, Amy. "Why White Supremacists Are Chugging Milk (and Why Geneticists Are Alarmed)." *New York Times*, October 17, 2018. https://nyti.ms/2AeE3Xg.

Harney, Stefano and Fred Moten. *All Incomplete*. New York: Minor Compositions, 2021.

Hartman, Saidiya. *Scenes of Subjection: Terror, Slavery, and Self-Making in Nineteenth-Century America*. Oxford: Oxford University Press, 1997.

Hartman, Saidiya. "Venus in Two Acts." *Small Axe* 12, no. 2 (2008): 1–14.

Hartman, Saidiya. *Wayward Lives, Beautiful Experiments: Intimate Histories of Social Upheaval*. New York: W.W. Norton & Company, 2019.

Hartman, Saidiya V. *Lose Your Mother: A Journey Along the Atlantic Slave Route*. New York: Farrar, Straus and Giroux, 2007.

Hartman, Saidiya V. and Frank B. Wilderson III. "The Position of the Unthought." *Qui Parle* 13, no. 2 (2003): 183–201.

Herbeck, Jason. "Entretien avec Fabienne Kanor." *The French Review* 86, no. 5 (2013): 964–76.

Hesse, Barnor. "Racism's Alterity: The After-life of Black Sociology." In *Racism and Sociology*. Ed. Wulf D. Hund and Alana Lentin. Berlin: Lit Verlag 2014. 141–74.

Hinkle, Jeannette and Trevor Ballantyne. "Orig3n Analysis ID'd Dog and Tap Water DNA as Human. Then the Company Produced Hundreds of False Positive COVID-19 Test Results." *Worcester Telegram*, October 15, 2020. https://www.telegram.com/story/lifestyle/health-fitness/2020/10/15/orig3n-analysis-idd-dog-and-tap-water-dna-as-human-then-company-produced-hundreds-of-false-positive-/114372264/.

"The Human Genome Project." National Human Genome Research Institute, last updated October 7, 2019. https://www.genome.gov/human-genome-project.

Jackson, Zakiyyah Iman. *Becoming Human: Matter and Meaning in an Antiblack World*. New York: New York University Press, 2020.

Jackson, Zakiyyah Iman. "Outer Worlds: The Persistence of Race in Movement 'Beyond the Human'." *GLQ* 21, no. 2–3 (2015): 215–18.

James, Frank. "Emmett Till's Casket Discarded by Chicago-Area Grave Workers." *NPR*, July 10, 2009. https://www.npr.org/sections/thetwo-way/2009/07/emmitt_tills_casket_discarded.html

Jameson, Fredric. *Archaeologies of the Future: The Desire Called Utopia and Other Science Fictions*. New York: Verso, 2005.

Jeanson, Francis. "Préface à *Peau noire, masques blancs*." In Frantz Fanon, *Peau noire, masques blancs*. Paris: Seuil, 1952. Reprint, *Sud/Nord* 14 (2001): 175–88. https://www.cairn.info/revue-sud-nord-2001-1-page-175.htm.

Johnson, Adrian. *Žižek's Ontology*. Evanston: Northwestern University Press, 2008.

Jones, Donna V. *The Racial Discourses of Life Philosophy: Negritude, Vitalism and Modernity*. New York: Columbia University Press, 2010.

Kanor, Fabienne. *Humus*. Trans. Lynn E. Palermo. Charlottesville: University of Virginia Press, 2020.

Knepper, Wendy. *Patrick Chamoiseau: A Critical Introduction*. Jackson: University Press of Mississippi, 2012.

Konstantinou, Lee. "Critique Has Its Uses." *American Book Review* 38, no. 5 (2017): 15–18.

Lacan, Jacques. *The Four Fundamental Concepts of Psycho-analysis*. Trans. Alan Sheridan. New York: Routledge, 2018.

Laguarigue, Jean-Luc de. "Un autre monde." *Gens de pays*. Blog. http://gensdepays.blogspot.com/search/label/Bio.

Laruelle, François. *Intellectuals and Power: The Insurrection of the Victim*. Trans. Anthony Paul Smith. Cambridge: Polity Press, 2015.

Latour, Bruno. "Why Has Critique Run Out of Steam? From Matters of Fact to Matters of Concern." *Critical Inquiry* 30, no. 2 (2004): 225–48.

Lebron, Christopher. "'Black Panther' Is Not the Movie We Deserve." *Boston Review*, February 17, 2018. bostonreview.net/race/christopher-lebron-black-panther.

Lee, Leslie. "Fear of a Black Superhero." *In These Times*, May 12, 2021. https://inthesetimes.com/article/black-captain-america-the-falcon-and-the-winter-soldier.

Lentin, Alana. "Charlie Hebdo: White Context and Black Analytics." *Public Culture* 31, no. 1 (2019): 45–67.

L'Étang, Thierry, Jean-Loup Pivin, Farid Abdelouahab, and Mntchini Traoré, eds. *Mémorial ACTe: L'esclavage et la traite négrière dans la Caraïbe et le monde*. Pointe-à-Pitre, Guadeloupe: Memorial ACTe Éditions, 2015.

L'Étang, Thierry, Jean-Loup Pivin, Laetitia Réal-Moretto, and Farid Abdelouahab, eds. *Memorial ACTe: Exploring Slavery and the African Slave Trade in the Caribbean and Around the World*. Trans. Simon Beaver. Pointe-à-Pitre, Guadeloupe: Memorial ACTe Éditions, 2015.

Leupin, Alexandre. *Édouard Glissant, Philosopher: Heraclitus and Hegel in the Whole-World*. Trans. Andrew Brown. Albany: Suny Press, 2021.

Levinas, Emmanuel. *Totality and Infinity: An Essay on Exteriority*. Trans. Alphonso Lingis. Pittsburgh: Duquesne University Press, 1969.

Li, Stephanie. "Genre Trouble and History's Miseries in Colson Whitehead's *The Underground Railroad*." *Melus* 44, no. 2 (2019): 1–23.

Lien, Vu Hong and Peter Sharrock. *Descending Dragon, Rising Tiger: A History of Vietnam*. London: Reaktion Books, 2014.

Liger, Bernard. "Chamoiseau: 'L'objet de la littérature n'est plus de raconter des histoires'." *L'Express*, March 6, 2012. http://www.lexpress.fr/culture/livre/patrick-chamoiseau-l-objet-de-la-litterature-n-est-plus-de-raconter-des-histoires_1089728.html#pZsGBjlpGpPLxAOv.99.

"List of AncestryDNA® Regions." Ancestry.com. https://support.ancestry.com/s/article/List-of AncestryDNA-Regions?o_iid=108659&o_lid=108659&o_sch=Web+Property#America.

Luciano, Dana. *Arranging Grief: Sacred Time and the Body in Nineteenth-Century America*. New York: New York University Press, 2007.

Luckerson, Victor. "The Great Achievement of 'Watchmen' Is in Showing How Black Americans Shape History." *The New Yorker*, December 23, 2019. https://www.newyorker.com/culture/cultural-comment/the-great-achievement-of-watchmen-is-in-showing-how-black-americans-shape-history.

Lynch, Michael P. "Fake News and the Internet Shell Game." *The New York Times*, November 28, 2016. https://www.nytimes.com/2016/11/28/opinion/fake-news-and-the-internet-shell-game.html.

Marriott, David S. *Lacan Noir: Lacan and Afro-pessimism*. New York: Palgrave, 2021.

Marx, Karl. *Capital: A Critique of Political Economy*. Vol. 1. Trans. Ben Fowkes. New York: Penguin Books, 1976.

Mazin, Craig. "Interview with Writers Lila Byock, Christal Henry, and Stacy Osei-Kuffour." *The Official* Watchmen *Podcast*. Apple Podcasts, August 26, 2020. https://podcasts.apple.com/us/podcast/interview-with-writers-lila-byock-christal-henry-and/id1485052917?i=1000492837048.

Mbembe, Achille. "Conversation: Achille Mbembe and David Theo Goldberg on *Critique of Black Reason*." *Theory, Culture, and Society*, July 3, 2018. https://www.theoryculturesociety.org/conversation-achille-mbembe-and-david-theo-goldberg-on-critique-of-black-reason/.

Mbembe, Achille. *Critique of Black Reason*. Trans. Laurent Dubois. Durham: Duke University Press, 2017.

Mbembe, Achille. "Decolonizing the University: New Directions." *Arts and Humanities in Higher Education* 15, no. 1 (2016): 29–45.

McGowan, Todd. *Universality and Identity Politics*. New York: Columbia University Press, 2020.

Meillassoux, Quentin. *After Finitude: An Essay on the Necessity of Contingency*. Trans. Ray Brassier. New York: Continuum, 2008.

Meillassoux, Quentin. "Interview with Quentin Meillassoux (August 2010)." Trans. Graham Harman. In Graham Harman, *Quentin Meillassoux: Philosophy in the Making*. Edinburgh: Edinburgh University Press, 2011. 159–74.

Meillassoux, Quentin. *Time without Becoming*. Ed. Anna Longo. Haverton: Mimesis International, 2014.

Mémorial ACTe, Centre Caribéen d'expressions et de mémoire de la Traite et de l'Esclavage. "La Mémoire Inspire L'avenir." https://www.regionguadeloupe.fr/fileadmin/Site_Region_Guadeloupe/Mediatheque/Brochures_et_publications/MacteBrochure_La_M__R_moire_Inspire_l_avenir_VF.pdf.

Mémorial ACTe, Centre Caribéen d'expressions et de mémoire de la Traite et de l'Esclavage. "Superpositions culturelles: parcours pédagogique." Région Académique Guadeloupe. https://pedagogie.ac-guadeloupe.fr/histoire_arts/parcours_pedagogiques_memorial_acte.

Mississippi. "J.W. Milam and Roy Bryant Trial Transcript." Special Collections & Archives, Florida State University Libraries, Tallahassee, Florida. http://purl.flvc.org/fsu/fd/FSU_MSS_2015-007_S03_SS04_I003.

Mochama, Wicky. "'If You Don't Have Hope, Then Why Go On?': An Interview with Colson Whitehead." *Hazlitt*, September 15, 2016. https://hazlitt.net/feature/if-you-dont-have-hope-then-why-go-interview-colson-whitehead.

Moore, Alan and Dave Gibbons. *Watchmen: The Deluxe Edition*. DC Comics, 2013.

Moten, Fred. *Black and Blur*. Durham: Duke University Press, 2017.

Moten, Fred. "Black Optimism/Black Operation." Unpublished paper, 2007. https://lucian.uchicago.edu/blogs/politicalfeeling/files/2007/12/moten-black-optimism.doc.

Moten, Fred. *In the Break: The Aesthetics of the Black Radical Tradition.* Minneapolis: University of Minnesota Press, 2003.
Moten, Fred. *Stolen Life.* Durham: Duke University Press, 2018.
Moten, Fred. *The Universal Machine.* Durham: Duke University Press, 2018.
Moten, Fred, Stefano Harney, and Stevphen Shukaitis. "Refusing Completion: A Conversation." *e-flux* 116 (2021): 1–14.
Nelson, Alondra. *The Social Life of DNA: Race, Reparations, and Reconciliation After the Genome.* Boston: Beacon Press, 2015.
Ngọc, Hữu. *Viet Nam: Tradition and Change.* Athens: Ohio University Press, 2016.
Nussbaum, Emily. "The Incendiary Aims of HBO's 'Watchmen'." *The New Yorker*, December 2, 2019. https://www.newyorker.com/magazine/2019/12/09/the-incendiary-aims-of-hbos-watchmen.
Okoth, Kevin Ochieng. "The Flatness of Blackness: Afro-Pessimism and the Erasure of Anti-Colonial Thought." *Salvage*, January 16, 2020. https://salvage.zone/the-flatness-of-blackness-afro-pessimism-and-the-erasure-of-anti-colonial-thought/.
Olaloku-Teriba, Annie. "Afro-Pessimism and the (un)Logic of Anti-Blackness." *Historical Materialism* 26, no. 2 (2018): 96–122.
Oziewicz, Marek. "Speculative Fiction." *Oxford Research Encyclopedias*, March 29, 2017. https://oxfordre.com/view/10.1093/acrefore/9780190201098.001.0001/acrefore-9780190201098-e-78.
Palmié, Stephan. "Genomics, Divination, Racecraft." *American Ethnologist* 34, no. 2 (2007): 205–22.
Patterson, Orlando. *Slavery and Social Death: A Comparative Study.* Cambridge, MA: Harvard University Press, 1982.
Paulson, Steve. "Critical Intimacy: An Interview with Gayatri Chakravorty Spivak." *Los Angeles Review of Books*, July 29, 2016. https://lareviewofbooks.org/article/critical-intimacy-interview-gayatri-chakravorty-spivak/.
Piatti-Farnell, Lorna. "'For God's Sake, Cover Yourself': Sexual Violence, Disrupted Histories, and the Gendered Politics of Patriotism in *Watchmen.*" *Journal of Graphic Novels and Comics* 8, no. 3 (2017): 238–51.
Pollack-Pelzner, Daniel. "The Hidden History of 'Oklahoma!'" *Oregon ArtsWatch*, November 19, 2018. https://www.orartswatch.org/the-hidden-history-of-oklahoma/. Accessed May 10, 2020.
Puar, Jasbir. "Bodies with New Organs: Becoming Trans, Becoming Disabled." *Social Text* 33, no. 3(124) (2015): 45–73.
Robbins, Bruce. "Fashion Conscious Phenomenon." *American Book Review* 38, no. 5 (2017): 5–6.
Roberts, Neil. *Freedom as Marronage.* Chicago: The University of Chicago Press, 2015.
Roberts, Sam. "Simeon Wright, Witness to Abduction of Emmett Till, Dies at 74." *New York Times*, September 6, 2017. https://www.nytimes.com/2017/09/06/obituaries/simeon-wright-witness-to-abduction-of-emmett-till-dies-at-74.html.
Robinson, Cedric J. *Black Marxism: The Making of the Black Radical Tradition.* Chapel Hill: University of North Carolina Press, 2000.
Robinson, Cedric J. *Forgeries of Memory and Meaning: Blacks and the Regimes of Race in American Theater and Film before World War II.* Chapel Hill: University of North Carolina Press, 2007.

Robinson, Cedric J. and Elizabeth P. Robinson. "Preface." In *Futures of Black Radicalism*. Ed. Gaye Theresa Johnson and Alex Lubin. New York: Verso, 2017. 1–8.

Robinson, Chuck. "Minority and Becoming-Minor in Octavia Butler's *Fledgling*." *Science Fiction Studies* 42, no. 3 (2015): 483–99.

Rowley, Hazel. *Richard Wright: The Life and Times*. New York: Henry Holt, 2001.

Sedgwick, Eve Kosofsky. "Paranoid Reading and Reparative Reading, or, You're So Paranoid, You Probably Think This Essay Is About You." In *Touching Feeling*. Durham: Duke University Press, 2003. 123–51.

Sexton, Jared. "Affirmations in the Dark: Racial Slavery and Philosophical Pessimism." *The Comparatist* 43 (2019): 90–111.

Sexton, Jared. "People-of-Color-Blindness: Notes on the Afterlife of Slavery." *Social Text* 28, no. 2(103) (2010): 31–56.

Sexton, Jared and Huey Copeland. "Raw Life: An Introduction." *Qui Parle* 13, no. 2 (Spring/Summer 2003): 53–62.

Shaviro, Steven. "Defining Speculation: Speculative Fiction, Speculative Philosophy, and Speculative Finance." *Alienocene: Journal of the First Outernational*, December 23, 2019. https://alienocene.files.wordpress.com/2019/12/sts-speculation.pdf.

Shaviro, Steven. *The Universe of Things: On Speculative Realism*. Minneapolis: University of Minnesota Press, 2014.

"Shop." Orig3n.com. shop.orig3n.com.

Smallwood, Stephanie E. *Saltwater Slavery: A Middle Passage from Africa to American Diaspora*. Cambridge, MA: Harvard University Press, 2007.

Smith, Jamil. "The Revolutionary Power of *Black Panther*." *Time*, February 19, 2018. time.com/black-panther/.

"Smithsonian Secretary Lonnie Bunch III: Full Face the Nation Interview." *Face the Nation*. CBS News, June 20, 2021. https://www.cbsnews.com/video/smithsonian-secretary-lonnie-bunch-iii-full-face-the-nation-interview/?intcid=CNM-00-10abd1h#x.

Spillers, Hortense J. "Difference." In *The Bloomsbury Handbook of 21st-Century Feminist Theory*. Ed. Robin Truth Goodman. New York: Bloomsbury, 2019. 45–58.

Spillers, Hortense J. "Mama's Baby, Papa's Maybe: An American Grammar Book." *Diacritics* 17, no. 2 (1987): 64–81.

Stoler, Ann Laura. "Colonial Aphasia: Race and Disabled Histories in France." *Public Culture* 23, no. 1 (2011): 121–56.

Taboh, Julie. "First African American to Head Smithsonian Shares Highlights, Challenges." *Voice of America News*, February 27, 2021. https://www.voanews.com/usa/first-african-american-head-smithsonian-shares-highlights-challenges.

TallBear, Kim. "Genomic Articulations of Identity." *Social Studies of Science* 43, no. 4 (2013): 509–33.

TallBear, Kim. *Native American DNA: Tribal Belonging and the False Promise of Genetic Science*. Minneapolis: University of Minnesota Press, 2013.

Taylor, Lucien. "Créolité Bites: A Conversation with Patrick Chamoiseau. Raphaël Confiant, and Jean Bernabé." *Transition* 74 (1997): 124–61.

Thomas, Bonnie. "Édouard Glissant and the Art of Memory." *Small Axe* 30 (2009): 25–36.

Thompson, Krissah. "Painful but Crucial: Why You'll See Emmett Till's Casket at the African American Museum." *Washington Post*, August 18, 2016. https://www.washingtonpost.com/lifestyle/style/painful-but-crucial-why-youll-see-emmett-tills-casket-at-the-african-american-museum/2016/08/18/66d1dc2e-484b-11e6-acbc-4d4870a079da_story.html.

Thrasher, Steven W. "Afrofuturism: Reimagining Science and the Future from a Black Perspective." *The Guardian*, December 7, 2015. https://www.theguardian.com/culture/2015/dec/07/afrofuturism-black-identity-future-science-technology.

Wailoo, Keith, Alondra Nelson, and Catherine Lee. "Introduction: Genetic Claims and the Unsettled Past." In *Genetics and the Unsettled Past: The Collision of DNA, Race, and History*. Ed. Keith Wailoo, Alondra Nelson, and Catherine Lee. New Brunswick: Rutgers University Press, 2012. 1–10.

Wallace, Carvell. "Why 'Black Panther' Is a Defining Moment for Black America." *New York Times Magazine*, February 12, 2018. www.nytimes.com/2018/02/12/magazine/why-black-panther-is-a-defining-moment-for-black-america.html?smid=url-share.

Ware, Lawrence. "*Watchmen*'s Tulsa Massacre Is American History. It's Also Mine." *Slate*, October 25, 2019. https://slate.com/culture/2019/10/watchmen-tulsa-massacre-history-tv.html.

Weheliye, Alexander. *Habeas Viscus: Racializing Assemblages, Biopolitics, and Black Feminist Theories of the Human*. Durham: Duke University Press, 2014.

"What your results will include." Ancestry.com. www.ancestry.com/dna/#dnaLohpProof.

Whitehead, Colson. *The Underground Railroad*. New York: Doubleday, 2016.

"Why DNA Tests." Orig3n.com. orig3n.com/why-dna-tests.

Wilderson, Frank B. III. "Gramsci's Black Marx: Whither the Slave in Civil Society." *Social Identities* 9, no. 3 (2003): 225–40.

Wilderson, Frank B. III. "The Prison Slave as Hegemony's (Silent) Scandal." *Social Justice* 30, no. 2 (2003): 18–27.

Wilderson, Frank B. III. *Red, White & Black: Cinema and the Structure of U.S. Antagonisms*. Durham: Duke University Press, 2010.

Wilderson, Frank B. III. "Wallowing in the Contradictions, Part 2 with Percy Howard." July 14, 2010. https://percy3.wordpress.com/2010/07/14/frank-wilderson-wallowing-in-the-contradictions-part-2/).

Wilderson, Frank B. III, Saidya Hartman, Steve Martinot, Jared Sexton, and Hortense J. Spillers. "Editors' Introduction." In *Afro-Pessimism: An Introduction*. Ed. Frank B. Wilderson III, Saidya Hartman, Steve Martinot, Jared Sexton, and Hortense J. Spillers. Minneapolis: Racked & Dispatched, 2017. 7–13.

Williams, Patricia J. *The Alchemy of Race and Rights*. Cambridge, MA: Harvard University Press, 1991.

Williams, Patricia J. "Emotional Truth." *The Nation*, February 16, 2006. https://www.thenation.com/article/archive/emotional-truth/.

Williams, Paul. *Memorial Museums: The Global Rush to Commemorate Atrocities*. Oxford: Berg, 2007.

Wynter, Sylvia. "Unsettling the Coloniality of Being/Power/Truth/Freedom: Toward the Human, after Man, Its Overrepresentation—An Argument." *New Centennial Review* 3, no. 3 (2003): 257–337.

Yancy, George. "Afropessimism Forces Us to Rethink Our Most Basic Assumptions About Society." *Truthout*, September 14, 2022. https://truthout.org/articles/afropessimism-forces-us-to-rethink-our-most-basic-assumptions-about-society/.

Žižek, Slavoj. "In the Grey Zone: Slavoj Žižek on Responses to the Paris Killings." *London Review of Books*, February 5, 2015. https://www.lrb.co.uk/2015/02/05/slavoj-zizek/in-the-grey-zone.

Žižek, Slavoj. *Incontinence of the Void: Economico-Philosophical Spandrels.* Cambridge, MA: MIT Press, 2017.

Žižek, Slavoj. *Less Than Nothing: Hegel and the Shadow of Dialectical Materialism.* New York: Verso, 2012.

Žižek, Slavoj. *Like a Thief in Broad Daylight: Power in the Era of Post-Humanity.* New York: Allen Lane, 2018.

Žižek, Slavoj. *The Parallax View.* Cambridge, MA: MIT Press, 2006.

Žižek, Slavoj. "Quasi Duo Fantasias: A Straussian Reading of 'Black Panther'." *Los Angeles Review of Books*, March 3, 2018. lareviewofbooks.org/article/quasi-duofantasias-straussian-reading-black-panther/).

Žižek, Slavoj. *Surplus Enjoyment.* New York: Bloomsbury, 2022.

Žižek, Slavoj. "Unbehagen and the Subject: An Interview with Slavoj Žižek." *Psychoanalysis, Culture & Society* 15 (2010): 418–28.

Žižek, Slavoj. *Violence: Six Sideways Reflections.* New York: Picador, 2008.

Žižek, Slavoj. "We Need a Socialist Reset, Not a Corporate 'Great Reset'." *Jacobin*, December 31, 2020. jacobinmag.com/2020/12/slavoj-zizek-socialism-great-reset.

Žižek, Slavoj. *Welcome to the Desert of the Real! Five Essays on September 11 and Related Dates.* New York: Verso, 2002.

INDEX

Note: Page numbers followed by "n" refer to notes.

actor-network theory 4, 5
Adorno, Theodor 6
affect theory 4
African American Lives (Gates) 34
African Burial Ground
    Initiative 162 n.106
Afrofuturism 86–7
Afropessimism 10, 11, 12, 24, 158–9 n.65, 159 n.69 162–3 n.110
    ontology 20
alchemy, *see also individual entries*
    alchemies of becoming 27, 29, 152, 153
    alchemies of being 27, 153
    counter-alchemy 26, 27, 165 n.135
    definition of 3
    fugitive 19–29, 127–50
    historical understandings of 61–82
    marooning 24, 72, 145, 146
    reason 151–3
    social 2, 49
Alchemy of Race and Rights, The (Williams) 3, 151, 181 n.69
Alet, Thierry 56, 57, 172 n.177
alienation 62–5
    Black 53
    natal 12, 33, 57, 62, 94, 159 n.65, 166 n.11
    worker's, under capitalism 10
amnesia 28, 32–3, 51, 61–83, 116
Anidjar, Gil 13, 159 n.72
animalization 8
anthropocentrism 7, 8, 160 n.76
anthropomorphism 7

anti-Blackness 9–11, 73, 86, 93, 113, *see also* blackness
    naturalization of 72
    states of 128–35
aphasia 116
authoritarianism 6
autoimmunity 92

Bacon, Kevin 36
Badiou, Alain 4
Baldwin, James 27
Barad, Karen 5–7
Beauvoir, Simone de 153
Benjamin, Mario
    Toussaint Louverture – Jean-acques Dessalines – Le roi Christophe 56
Benjamin, Ruha 28, 50
Bennett, Jane 6–7, 173 n.10
Berlant, Lauren 117
Bernasconi, Robert 23, 164 n.126
Best, Sharon 5–6
Betancourt, David 176 n.15
biological determinism 13, 34, 37
biological racism 2
Biometric Generation (Konaté) 55
Black feminism 138
Black Lives Matter movement 87
blackness 8–11, 22, 24, 52, 94, 159 n.69, *see also* anti-Blackness
    absolutization of 20
    history of 24
    worlding 135–44
Black Panther (Ryan Coogler) 29, 85–99, 119, 124, 177 n.35
Black Panther: Wakanda Forever (Ryan Coogler) 178 n.36

Black Skin, White Masks (Fanon) 21–3, 52, 150, 164 n.129
Bland, Sandra 50
Bochte, Frank 45
Bogues, Anthony 42, 46
Boisseron, Bénédicte 67
Bourdieu, Pierre 2
Boyd, Zhaleh 50
Brown, Michael 50
Bryant, Roy 45
Bunch III, Lonnie G. 41–2, 47, 170 n.54
Butler, Octavia 63, 80, 83, 138
  Fledgling 28, 62, 73–81
  Kindred 84
Byrd, Donald 86

Calhoun, Doyle 114
Canada, Geoffrey 37
capital
  economic 2, 42
  political 42
  social 42
  symbolic 2
Capital (Marx) 2
capitalism 2
  worker's alienation under 10
captivity 10, 34, 36, 114, 117, 121, 131
Caribbean Center for the Expression and Memory of the Slave Trade and Slavery, *see* Mémorial ACTe
Caribbean Discourse (Glissant) 55
Carlton, C. Sidney 45
Catlin, George
  Comanche Feats of Horsemanship 106
causality and correlation, distinction between 37
Césaire, Aimé 11, 22
Chamoiseau, Patrick 24, 63, 83
  L'empreinte à Crusoé 28, 62, 65–82
  Old Man Slave 84
Chandler, Nahum 9, 24
Charlie Hebdo 133
chattel slavery 9, 86, 128
Cheah, Pheng 66

Chiles, Joyce 45
Chirac, Jacques 51
Christianity 13, 159 n.72
chronobiopolitics 142
chrononormativity 142
CIPN, *see* Comité International des Peuples Noirs (CIPN)
civil rights movement 43
Clytus, Radiclani 46
Coates, Ta-Nehisi 12
Code Noir 57, 58
Cohen, Jeffrey Jerome 8
Cole, Joe Robert 89
color-blind republican universalism 27, 115–16, 128, 129, 133–4, 137
Comité International des Peuples Noirs (CIPN) 55
Condé, Maryse 142
  Wondrous and Tragic Life of Ivan and Ivana, The 29, 127–9, 133–5, 144, 149, 150
Coogler, Ryan
  Black Panther 29, 85–99, 119, 124, 177 n.35
Copeland, Huey 11
correlationism 4–5
counter-alchemy 26, 27, 165 n.135
counter-history 122
creolization 3
Critical Black Studies 8, 9
Critical Race Theory 168 n.31

Dash, Julie
  Daughters of the Dust 121
Daughters of the Dust 121
deconstruction 6
Defoe, Daniel 28, 62
  Life and Strange Surprising Adventures of Robinson Crusoe, The 65
Delany, Samuel R. 84
demystification 6
demythification 6
Derrida, Jacques 69, 72–3
  on autoimmunity 92
direct-to-consumer (DTC) genomic testing 15
disalienation 84

disavowal 24, 115
discrimination 36, 180 n.63
DNA 33–6, 38, 39, 42
    analysis 19, 31
    ancestry testing 16, 17
    historic 42
    swabbing 18
    transforming 42
DTC, *see* direct-to-consumer (DTC) genomic testing
Duster, Troy 17–18

ecocriticism 4
economic capital 2, 42
El-Haj, Nadia Abu 12, 33
embodiment 26, 34, 36, 80, 152
Emmett Till Memorial 47, 48
Eshun, Kodwo 86–7
"Essay on Exteriority, An" (Levinas) 68
ethnicity 3
    as biological and cultural identity 17
    genetic 16, 17, 39, 180 n.62
    testing 16–18
ethnic traits 37
ethno-racial identity 15
European imperialism 16

Faces of America (Gates) 34–5
Fanon, Frantz 11, 20, 25, 29, 54, 84, 87, 149, 163 n.118, 164 n.126
    Black Skin, White Masks 21–3, 52, 150, 164 n.129
    Wretched of the Earth, The 164 n.127
Felski, Rita 155 n.24
feminism
    Black 138
feminization 57
Fey, Tina 38
Finding Your Roots (Gates) 12, 34, 35, 37, 40, 108
Finding Your Roots: The Seedlings (Gates) 38
Fledgling (Butler) 28, 62, 77, 81
flesh 9–10
    hieroglyphics of 137

France
    color-blind republican universalism 27, 115–16, 128, 129, 133–4, 137
Francis, Gladys M. 115–16
Frankenstein (Shelley) 141
freedom 43, 69, 72, 75
Freeman, Elizabeth 142
Fruitvale Station (Ryan Coogler) 87
fugitive alchemies 19–29, 127–50
future ancestors 83–125
    origins and reckonings 99–113
    rebellious foresisters 113–23
    violent inheritances and reparative promise 86–99

Gabriel, Abram 14
Gates, Henry Louis, Jr. 27, 31, 33–8, 108–9
    African American Lives 34
    Faces of America 34–5
    Finding Your Roots 12, 34, 35, 37, 40, 108
    Finding Your Roots: The Seedlings 38, 40–1
Gates, Racquel 95–8
gender 138
    equality 134
    gendered femaleness 163 n.116
    gendered positioning 140
    and slavery 9, 21, 56
genealogy 31–59
    entanglements 58–9
    objects of meaning 41–51
    rhizomes and refusals 51–8
    roots, reclaiming 32–41
genetic
    ancestry testing 13, 14, 34
    causality 36–7
    determinism 14
    ethnicity 16, 17, 39, 180 n.62
    genealogy 12, 13, 27, 28, 31, 33, 41, 43, 58, 59, 159 n.66
    kinship 36
    predisposition 14
genomic hopes 11–19
genomic thinking 13, 15, 18, 26
Gibbons, Dave
    Watchmen 28, 85, 99–113, 124

INDEX

Gillespie, Michael Boyce   100
Gilroy, Paul   18–20
Glissant, Édouard   24–6, 29, 51, 54, 55, 61, 70–2, 85, 127, 165 n.137, 170 n.158
  Caribbean Discourse   55
Goldberg, David Theo   26
Gordon, Lewis R.   95
Gossett, Che   8
grammar
  of anti-Blackness   130
  of humanism   24, 152
  phallic   119, 152
  of whiteness   153
Green Grow the Lilacs (Lynn Riggs)   105
Griffin, Bird   38
Grigg, Nanny   120
Guenther, Lisa   137
guerrilla insemination   151
Gyssels, Kathleen   70–1

Haider, Asad   178 n.42
Haraway, Donna   80
Harman, Graham   8
Harney, Stefano   120
Hartman, Saidiya V.   10, 34, 94–6, 116, 119, 122, 152
  Lose Your Mother: A Journey Along the Atlantic Slave Route   32
  Scenes of Subjection   166–7 n.13
Heraclitus   70, 71
Hesse, Barnor   133
HGP, *see* Human Genome Project (HGP)
historical memory   61, 94, 114, 127
historiography   42
human exceptionalism
  critiques of   5, 8, 13
Human Genome Project (HGP)   1
humanism   66–7
  grammar of   24, 152
  violence of   11
Humus (Kanor)   29, 85, 86, 113–23, 125

immunity   92
information wars   6

institutionalized kinlessness   28, 31
institutionalized violence   41

Jablonski, Nina   38
Jackson, Zakiyyah Iman   8, 9, 80
Jeanson, Francis   22
Johnson, Adrian   143
Jones, Ayana   50
Jones, Donna V.   22

Kanor, Fabienne
  Humus   29, 85, 86, 113–23, 125
Kindred (Butler)   84
kinfulness   31, 43, 44, 58, 59
King Louis XIV   55
kin-keeping   31, 46, 48, 50, 96
kinship, *see* institutionalized kindlessness; kin-keeping
Klein, Melanie   88
Konaté, Abdoulaye
  Biometric Generation   55

Laguarigue, Jean-Luc de   127
language   4, 7, 21–3, 42, 57–8, 71, 74, 84, 117, 153, 156 n.24, 158 n.62
Laruelle, François   5
Latour, Bruno   6, 7
La voleuse d'enfants (The Thief of Children) (Alet)   56–8
Lee, Catherine   1
Lee, Leslie   96
L'empreinte à Crusoé (Chamoiseau)   28, 62, 65–82
Leupin, Alexandre   72, 73
Levinas, Emmanuel
  "Essay on Exteriority, An"   68
Life and Strange Surprising Adventures of Robinson Crusoe, The (Defoe)   65
Lindelof, Damon
  Watchmen   28, 85, 86, 99–113, 124
Lose Your Mother: A Journey Along the Atlantic Slave Route (Hartman)   32
Luciano, Dana   142
Luckerson, Victor   102

Lurel, Victorin   55
Lynch, John   15
lynching   45, 100, 102, 103, 131

MACTe, *see* Mémorial ACTe (MACTe)
Marcus, Stephen   5–6
Marriott, David   131
marronage   24, 56, 58, 72, 127, 131, 145, 146
Marvel Studios
  Black Panther   29, 85–99, 119, 124
Marx, Karl
  Capital   2
materialism   5, 22
  enchanted   7
  new   3, 4, 6, 8
materiality   3, 6–7, 28, 31, 78, 80, 113
Mbembe, Achille   2, 13, 20, 160 n.76
Meillassoux, Quentin   4, 5
Mémorial ACTe (MACTe)   31, 54, 55, 57–9
metaphysical holocaust   9
metaphysical infrastructure   10
Milam, J. W.   45
Mobley, Mamie Till   45, 49–50
modernity   7, 11
  "diseased" modes of individuation   28
  European   138
  racialized   20
  secular   13
  Western   2, 93, 130, 159 n.72
monarchy   58, 178 n.42
Moore, Alan
  Watchmen   28, 85, 99–113, 124
Moten, Fred   24, 25, 72, 120, 145, 153

NAACP   44
natal alienation   12, 33, 57, 62, 94, 159 n.65, 166 n.11
National Museum of African American History and Culture (NMAAHC)   31, 43, 44, 46–51, 58
nature–nurture relationship   36
Négritude movement   22, 23, 87
Nelson, Alondra   1, 12, 19, 41
neoliberalism   2, 3
new materialism   3, 4, 6, 8

NMAAHC, *see* National Museum of African American History and Culture (NMAAHC)
nobility   13
Notre Journal (*Our Journal*)   21

object-oriented ontology (OOO)   4, 5, 8, 9
Ogbunu, Brandon   38, 39
Old Man Slave (Chamoiseau)   84
ontology/ontological   2–11, 19–29, 49, 65, 68–71, 80, 140, 149, 151, 153, 180 n.58
  Afropessimist   20
  of dehiscence   24
  devastation   9, 144
  of disorder   24
  flat   5, 8
  political   9, 18, 24, 93
  relational   5
  risks   20
  security   129
  slavery and   9–10, 21, 24, 33–4, 54, 62, 77, 120, 121, 144, 152, 159 n.69
  totality   120, 121
  transmutation   9
OOO, *see* object-oriented ontology (OOO)
Orig3n Inc.   15, 160–1 n.86
Other, the   67–8

Palmetto Libretto (*Sketch for an American Comic Opera with Fort Sumter*), *The* (Walker)   56
paranoia   88–92, 155 n.14
paraontology   24, 29, 72, 127, 128, 151
Parmenides   70, 71
patriarchy   94, 99, 106, 139, 178 n.36, *see also* phallic grammar
Patterson, Orlando   158–9 n.65
PBS, *see* Public Broadcasting Service (PBS)
Perse, Saint-John   65
personality traits   13, 36
phallic grammar, *see* grammar, phallic
phylogenetic turn   15
plastic harmony   71

plenitude 72
political capital 42
political ontology 9, 24, 93
political solidarity 34, 41, 134
postcritical 155 n.24
posthumanism 4, 8, 11
posthumanist politics 7
post-truth, definition of 156 n.19
property 2, 24, 55, 57, 77, 127, 129–31, 144, 148, 150
Puar, Jasbir 79
Public Broadcasting Service (PBS) 31, 38

queering 24, 28, 79–81, 84, 85, 112, 119, 120, 143

race 3, 9, 12–14, 40, 75, 77, 138, *see also* racial; racism
  politics 14, 20
racial, *see also* race; racism
  difference 14, 19
  diversity 14
  hierarchy 8, 14
  identity 13, 15, 52, 53, 134
  injustice 14
  postracial 26
  racial-species superiority 63
  slavery 9, 11, 66, 125
  solidarity 95, 96
  stratification 14
  traits 37
  violence 39, 99, 108
racialization 8
racialized capitalist order 3
racism 7–9, 27, 36, 75, 134, *see also* race
  anti-Black 11
  biological 2
racist
  ideology 21, 26, 130, 163 n.114
  violence 21, 104
radical
  exteriority 68
radicalization 184 n.31
realism 3
rebirth 62–5
relationality 21, 72, 77, 84, 145
relational ontology 5

rhizomatic identity 55
rhizomes 51–8
Rice, Tamir 50
Riggs, Lynn 105
Robbins, Bruce 5
Robert Frederick Smith Explore Your Family History Center 43
Robinson, Cedric 120, 121
Robinson, Chuck 76, 79, 174 n.34
roundabout resistance [*résistance détournée*] 24

Sartre, Jean-Paul 23, 67
Save Our African American Treasures program 48
Scenes of Subjection (Hartman) 166–7 n.13
secular modernity 13
Sedaris, David 38
Sedgwick, Eve Kosofsky 88–9, 91, 93
segregation 43
sexism 36
Sexton, Jared 11, 130
sexual behavior 74
sexual violence 36, 39, 56, 117
Shaviro, Steven 83
Shelley, Mary
  Frankenstein 141
Shulman, George 97
sickle-cell anemia 160 n.82
Sinatra, Frank 111
slavery 166 n.11
  afterlife of 10, 24, 29, 85, 86, 127, 149, 158 n.56, 186 n.52
  chattel 9, 86, 128
  and disruption of kinship ties 96
  and gender 9, 21, 56
  and modernity 2
  and ontology 9–10, 21, 24, 33–4, 54, 62, 77, 120, 121, 144, 152, 159 n.69
  racial 9, 11, 66, 125
slave trade 2
  Atlantic 94
  transatlantic 9
Smallwood, Stephanie 2
Smith, Jamil 87
social alchemy 2, 49
social capital 42

social death   12, 31, 42, 58, 72, 145, 159 n.65, 166 n.11
solidarity
  Black   94
  political   34, 41, 134
  racial   95, 96
  symbiotic   62
solitude   65–73
  and isolation, distinction between   68
Southern Poverty Law Center   44
speculation   83
  philosophical   84
speculative fiction   84–125
speculative historytelling   85
speculative realism   4, 5
Spillers, Hortense   9, 10, 21, 131, 137, 153, 163 n.116
Stoler, Ann Laura   116
symbiotic solidarity   62
symbolic capital   2
systemic violence   41

TallBear, Kim   18–19
Thrasher, Steven W.   87
Till, Emmett   44–50
Till, Mamie, *see* Mobley, Mamie Till
Tournier, Michel
  Vendredi ou les limbes du Pacifique   65, 69
Toussaint Louverture – Jean-acques Dessalines – Le roi Christophe (Benjamin)   56
transatlantic slave trade   9
transhumanist utopia   75
Turner, Nat   120

Underground Railroad, The (Whitehead)   29, 127, 128, 144–50
United States (US)
  decentralized identity politics   27
  Statue of Liberty   55

Vendredi ou les limbes du Pacifique (Tournier)   65, 69
violence   6, 18, 20, 27, 36, 40, 63, 71, 72, 75–7, 80, 86, 89, 91–5, 97, 105, 108, 114, 142, 144, 152, 178 n.36, 181 n.63

anti-Black   31, 88, 113, 124
  of humanism   11
  institutionalized   10, 41
  lynching   45, 100, 102, 103, 131
  police   32
  racial   39, 84, 87, 99, 108
  racist   21, 44–51, 75, 77, 87, 103, 104, 169 n.41, 170 n.54
  retributive   131
  sexual   36, 39, 56, 117
  systemic   32, 41, 48, 181 n.63
  terrorist   129, 134

Wailoo, Keith   1
Walker, C. J.   47
Walker, Kara
  Palmetto Libretto (Sketch for an American Comic Opera with Fort Sumter), The   56
Wallace, Carvell   87–8, 92
Warner, Kristen J.   97
Warren, Rick   38
Watchmen (Lindelof, Damon)   28, 85, 86, 99–113, 124
  Oklahoma!   104–6, 110–12
Weheliye, Alexander   8, 137, 138
Whitehead, Alfred   83–4
Whitehead, Colson
  Underground Railroad, The   29, 127, 128, 144–50
whiteness   8, 19, 29, 36, 52, 53, 94, 96, 106, 129, 131, 134, 140, 143, 149–53
Wilderson III, Frank B.   9, 11, 158 n.62
Williams, Patricia J.   18, 151
  Alchemy of Race and Rights, The   3, 151, 181 n.69
Williams, Paul   42–3, 47–8
women of color   138
Wondrous and Tragic Life of Ivan and Ivana, The (Condé)   29, 127–9, 133–5, 144, 149, 150
Wretched of the Earth, The (Fanon)   164 n.127
Wright, Simeon   44
Wynter, Sylvia   137, 138
Zeitgeist   4
Žižek, Slavoj   4, 20, 85, 141, 143, 155–6 n.14

www.ingramcontent.com/pod-product-compliance
Lightning Source LLC
Chambersburg PA
CBHW052042300426
44117CB00012B/1933